MW00903214

The Marketing Manager – Journey to the Summit

http://www.flawlessinbound.ca/

Cover image by:
Flawless Inbound Team

The Marketing Manager - Journey to the Summit

Why are only a few Marketers, CEOs and VPs of Sales successful and the rest are struggling, especially when it comes to Marketing for B2B organizations?
This is a business fictional book about a 'day in the life' of a marketing manager and how she is challenged, either by external or internal corporate beliefs that limit her in achieving her target as a successful marketing manager.
We go inside the boardroom and listen to boardroom meetings; we learn how she overcomes obstacles and how she builds a very successful marketing framework. In each chapter, we share a marketing playbook that can be applied to your organization. We show you the trials and challenges she faces, and how she figures out her model and begins to rise above the noise to prove herself as a successful marketing manager.

The Acknowledgments
Thank you!

First, I want to thank the hundreds of B2B Organizations in Technology, BioTech, Clean Energy, Construction, and the Medical space who have worked with Flawless Inbound and given us the opportunity to build frameworks and Playbooks.

Inspired
I want to personally thank my father, who was always my role model and my mentor throughout my life. I lost him to cancer on May 2017. He always coached me to understand that we're all a work in progress in this journey called life. Discipline, focus, positivity, continued learning and personal improvement are the keys to enable us to grow and mature. And another very special thank you to my mother, who taught me to always follow my gut feeling, and to look around and understand why sometimes things work and other times not. To learn from my mistakes and never let them break me, and most importantly to always bounce back faster, stronger and higher. And to learn to turn the next page in life without looking back.

I owe a deep and special thank you to my wife Liliane, for always keeping me honest to my vision, and making me strong on my journey. I could not have done it without her true love and support each and every step of the way.

And, to my two amazing supporters, my children; Jonathan and Nathalie. I want to thank you for believing in me and accepting me for who I am and always encouraging and guiding me throughout the journey. I could not have done it without your support.

Thought Leaders

I want to thank the Flawless Inbound Team for giving me the time to reflect on the book, for coaching me, sharing your expertise and giving feedback, while working with hundreds for B2B organizations in Canada & the US.

A very special thank you to Mandy Eve-Barnett, my amazing ghostwriter, who has been so patient with me during the process, for her ability to create the book's characters and framework along the way.

Partners and Vendors

Special thank you to the HUBSPOT Leadership team for coaching me and the Flawless Inbound team each and every day, while working with complex Marketing Campaigns. I have learned a lot from your framework and process.

Dedication

Why we wrote this book.

This book is dedicated to marketing managers, and CMOs of B2B organizations around the world, who are tasked with bringing transformation to their organizations by creating a functional Marketing Department that is 100% Revenue Driven, while being challenged with the ultimate 'mission impossible' on the planet - Sales and Marketing Alignment. This book is also dedicated to CEOs, who know that marketing is critical in bringing them 10X or more exponential growth for their B2B organization, and to VPs of Sales, who are 100% frustrated by the marketing effort. They are praying, each day that their team can help them by bringing them closer to their Annual Revenue numbers.

Also, to the Entrepreneurs, CEOs and Business Owners, who are working hard every day to build an organization, who are tasked with exponential growth and who believe that marketing should be doing more than just branding and storytelling. You are not alone, and this book is also for you.

Index	Pages	Lessons Learned
Chapter One – Call to Adventure	6-35	Lessons learned 36
Chapter Two – Meeting the Mentors	38-62	Lessons learned 63
Chapter Three – Crossing the Threshold	65-111	Lessons learned 112
Chapter Four – Road of Trials	115-157	Lessons learned 158
Chapter Five – Confronting the Shadow	159-183	Lessons learned 184
Chapter Six – Into the Darkness	186-225	Lessons learned 226
Chapter Seven – Re-birth of the B2B Buyer's Journey	228-249	Lessons learned 250
Chapter Eight – Return with the Elixir	251-281	Lessons learned 282
Chapter Nine – Preparing for the Future	283-298	Lessons learned 299
Chapter Ten – The Summit, Are You Ready?	301-334	
Saher Ghattas	335	
Flawless Inbound	337	
Links	338	

Chapter One – Call to Adventure

Connie took a couple deep calming breaths, her pen tapping through her fingers on the desk showed her anxiety. Another sales meeting, Gibbons-style was due tomorrow, she had revised multiple methods to convey the need for social media management as a necessary tool for marketing, especially for the role of marketing manager, whose job, as far as Connie was concerned, was to adapt, adopt and improve marketing methods. In preparation for these meetings she employed Bruce, her husband, as a sounding board over several nights. He took on the role of Mr. Gibbons' dismissive attitude to all things 'new', maybe a bit too far at times but at least he'd made her laugh and released some of the tension in the process. Now she read through her notes and despaired that no matter how she explained it, old Gibbons would reject her ideas. He could not understand that although social media is basic promotion on many levels, it is also a necessary evil. One she knew they could utilize for all departments, from sales to production to marketing.

"Are you ready for the onslaught of tomorrow's sales meeting, Connie?"

She turned to give a weak smile to Derek, one of four sales representatives tasked with selling the Gibbons way. His mantra and usual statement to the sales team, 'ABC – always be closing' that is your job and only job – to sell. I expect you to meet or indeed surpass your targets every month.'

"You are right, Connie he's like a broken record on a continuous loop."

Old ABC – always be closing versus New ABC – always be consulting.

"It's a mantra that needs to change, we should be using ABC – always be consulting. And again, I'm sure I will bear the brunt of his negative attitude, Derek. No matter how I try to 'package' how companies are developing and utilizing technology, he always goes back to the old traditional methods. He lists them as if they're the Holy Grail to me, like reiterating them will make me comply. It is so annoying."

Direct Mail

"He'll say we can utilize direct-mail through postcards, brochures, letters and fliers sent through the mail, Connie."

"When I told him direct-mail marketing is expensive as the business incurs design and printing costs as well as postage expenses to reach its target, he said, 'well it's worked for us for a long time!'

"I don't think you will ever achieve any change with him, Connie."

Print

"I know, Derek. He said using print marketing and advertising products and services through newspapers and magazines, enables us to reach a wider audience."

"And my answer was print marketing is both a mass-marketing and niche-marketing strategy. As a mass-marketing strategy, printed advertisements reach different classes of people, who may or may not have an interest in our products. In magazines, print marketing reaches out to the niche market that reads the magazine, such as women, fathers, teens or car lovers. His replied, 'we only advertise in industry specific magazines, Connie so we do have a niche as you call it.'

Broadcast

"I also told him broadcast marketing reaches a large audience within a limited period, and that television advertisements can bring authenticity and realism to a product as people can see how the product works. However, I did say broadcast messages have a shorter lifespan compared with printed messages and additionally, marketing through television and radio is costlier, compared with other forms of traditional marketing. Gibbons of course wanted a low budget option, which was impossible to get with the funds he was prepared to give me."

Referral

"Referrals are one of Gibbons favourite methods."

"Word of mouth, Connie is a true reflection of our company's expertise. Our customers spread information about our products or services thus giving us 'free' advertising - it's a win-win."

"I said that referrals are not a strategic or planned marketing activity, although it can help a business build a loyal client base. It's certainly not able to reach a wider target market. He told me not to be so unwilling to use the methods he knows work. It is so frustrating. I understand Gibbons own experience has always been the traditional sales team hustling any and all prospects, trying every trick in the book to get the deal signed. It was driven by numbers and measured by numbers, and that controlled how the selling system worked. But times have changed."

"Oh, I hear you, Connie, if he catches me describing a program or explaining a system in a little too much detail instead of selling it, he shoots me down, saying, 'that's not your job Derek. Get the production guys to do that.' I have given him sound reasons for doing it, such as 'if I don't understand the system, how can I sell it?' But it's the same every time, 'Stick to your job, sell the product. The details can be laid out later.' It's nonsense!"

"I've explained that buyers are getting smarter with sales people focusing on value and making the buying experience enjoyable. His remarks are based on stereotypical sales staff saying anything to close the deal, that tactic is no longer effective. Fundamentally, people have changed the way they make business decisions, however a lot of sales organizations, like this place, have not evolved in line with the change. When I told Gibbons that prospects and customers are becoming increasingly selective in the businesses they trust, he told me that our customers are loyal and have trusted us for many years, 'they know what they get and how they get it.' He is missing the point, marketing and sales teams need to work together cohesively and focus on attracting qualified leads and closing the right customers. It's Gibbons' divide and conquer attitude that makes this whole company backward."

"You're right, Connie. In my previous job all departments worked together, and it worked so well."

"Exactly. And it's the basis of inbound marketing. This business could be so much more profitable if only he would see the advantages. So why did you leave the other place, Derek?"

"They bought a large office building in a much larger city, where tax benefits and a build to suit were too good to pass up. I could have got relocation expenses, the whole works, but my wife and kids did not want to leave family, friends and schools so here I am. In hindsight it would have been the better option."

"Wow that sucks."

"This place looked good on paper, all the right buzz words, if I'd known the advert was through an agency, who knew how to grab potential employee's attention, I'd not have applied. In retrospect I should have done more research into this company or better yet tried harder to persuade the family the relocation was a great opportunity, but desperation took hold – bills to pay and unemployment looming.

"Why did you take this particular job?"

"It was the first company to offer and seemed great and the fact anxiety had taken hold of course. I took the position in haste now I'm paying for that decision. I really should have held out for something better. Keep it under your hat but I'm looking elsewhere."

"I hear you, I was naïve and fresh out of college, when I took this job, I thought it was a great start for my career to build a marketing strategy from scratch. Now look at me! Good luck in your search. Well I'm going to grab a strong coffee in preparation for the meeting. See you later."

Derek walked away as Connie got up and headed to the vending machine. She remembered being so excited about this job, making plans to revolutionise the dated marketing plan, keeping up with all the new developments and implementing them. *Sucked in just like Derek, more fool us.*

She thought back to how keen she'd been to implement inbound marketing, a process of understanding what it takes to sell your product or service, in essence the key to business success. In her courses she had learnt we live in a world of new sales and marketing, a consultative world. A place where leads find you, where prospects perform research and educate themselves on your product or service long before speaking with a member of your team. As she knew from Derek's comments the roles of sales people have dramatically changed. Rather than being attached to the phone 24/7, inbound reps are advisors, who shared thoughtful answers and insights to questions, while modelling business process change. She knew today's sales professionals help prospects decide how, what and whether to buy. Sales is no longer about closing, it's about helping. Even giving old Gibbons reliable figures he was resistant. Connie told him, 65% of the buying process is completed by B2B buyers before reaching out, his reaction was typical of course, dismissive that such methods could work.

Further explanation did not sway him, but Connie made a point of getting her thoughts across even though the meeting was in his office and she felt cornered. "The key ingredient to the inbound marketing process is having context regarding who your key buyers are. It is all about understanding their interests, being able to identify their pain points and finding a solution that will add value to their lives. The inbound marketing process is much more personal." Gibbons had started to laugh at pain points and understanding interests.

"Why are you so focused on sales, Connie, your position is in marketing?"

"That is exactly my point, sales and marketing should be working together rather than in isolation. In the past, sales reps were the gatekeepers of information between your business and potential customers. They held all the product information and pricing and controlled the ordering process. In real terms they held all the power. There was no transparency and it meant that the buyer was forced to trust them. We now live in a content-centric world, where you can find anything and everything on the internet. This has stripped the sales reps of their power and given it to consumers. They can educate themselves independently – there is no need to speak to a sales rep to find information on the product or to determine how our pricing compares to that of our competitors."

Gibbons exclaimed, his eyebrows shooting upwards.

"Exactly why we need to keep all that information to ourselves, Connie. Why would we display it for all to see?"

She explained.

"Consumers can find the information on their own and will use it to their advantage."

Again, Gibbons was shocked.

"And why would we give them an advantage? We are the ones needing the advantage."

"It is to our benefit, Mr. Gibbons if we embrace the new strategies. Due to the sheer volume of content available, consumers simply don't need to reach out to sales early in the buying cycle anymore. That is why our selling strategy needs to change. We need to transition our sales arsenal from one that is filled with outbound sales tools to one that is made up of inbound-selling tactics."

Connie watched Gibbons face closely waiting for some positive reaction to inbound selling techniques, but he shook his head, motioned her to go with one hand while picking up the telephone and making a call. Connie had left the office despondent and frustrated. *He is unwilling to make any changes.*

Later that evening talking with her husband, Bruce, he made an observation that surprised her.

"Have you thought that he is resistant to all this new stuff because he feels he has no control over it? That he has no point of reference and therefore feels his position is threatened."

"Gibbons threatened! He stomps around making everyone uneasy."

"Yes, I know that, but it might be a bluff to hide his insecurity. It's just a thought."

Connie pondered this idea and began to review her interactions with Gibbons. It was true he was always quick to shoot down any new idea, clinging to what he knew best. It gave her an idea.

"I'm going to the study; Bruce I need to make up a presentation. Enjoy the game."

Taking two large note pads, she placed them side by side and wrote two headings.

Traditional versus Inbound Marketing

Current sales and business development methods:

Tradeshows

Messaging

Pitch decks

Cold calling

List building

Elevator pitches

She knew that currently the team was using these methods 90% of the time. However, these methods did not have to be scrapped altogether only adjusted, if they were not making the ROI. By reallocating some of the time, budget, training and strategy on new models they could be more effective.

On the other pad, she wrote.

New World of Selling

Blogging

Social Selling

Content Offers
Landing Pages
Sales-ready Webinars
Live Facebook sessions

She worked on how to improve, revise and merge these two strategies that would give Gibbons an illusion of control but also energize the teams. Bruce's hand on her shoulder startled her.

"Okay bedtime love, you have been in here far too long."

"What time is it?"

"It's after eleven and the game ended hours ago. Come on leave that for now."

"No wonder my eyes hurt but look I have made some progress."

"Looks impressive to me, Hun, now bedtime."

She passed Mr. Gibbons office the next morning and even though the door was closed could hear him berating some poor soul on the phone.

"It's not about making the customer happy, Tom its sales targets you should be focusing on. See me after the meeting. Of course, you have to be here – no excuses." Gibbons slammed the receiver down. *Oh, great he's already worked up into a frenzy and the meeting hasn't even started. There goes any success for my pitch.*

With her coffee in hand, Connie walked through the open plan office with its partitions corralling each staff member into a cubical. *Treated like chickens and paid less!* Her smile attracted Mr. Gibbons' attention as he walked out of his office. She had forgotten to go the long way around.

"Connie, what's so funny?"

"Nothing, Mr. Gibbons. I'm just looking forward to a good cup of coffee."

He raised his eyebrows and walked away, his face flushed and a vein throbbing in his temple. *That doesn't bode well at all.*

Tradeshows Traditional

Back at her desk she browsed through her emails. Gibbons had sent a companywide email. She clicked it:

Trade show – September 16th & 17th – New York.

All staff will be allotted two-hour shifts for each day. Smart attire expected. Brochures will be available for distribution and there will be a sign-up list for follow up contacts. A draw box for six bottles of wine will be displayed – ensure you encourage visitors to enter with their business cards, which can be utilized for cold calls.

Connie read the email in dismay, yet another trade show, which would cost a small fortune and probably not pay for itself in revenue. In her experience trade shows cost between $12K and $35K just for the booth, then there was travel and business costs on top of that, employee and operation costs and then the 'give away' prize. By Gibbons' own omission trade shows were 80% of his marketing budget. It would mean another two days of aching feet, boredom and false smiles. Even she had seen the deterioration of attendance in the last three years of these glorified industry shows. They were ineffective as a sales vehicle, costly in terms of extra employee pay, and printing of brochures that would be stockpiled afterwards on top of the venue costs. She texted her husband, Bruce.

Another trade show horror Sept 16th & 17th. 2 hour shifts both days. Kill me now!

His reply was swift.

Another one – what is that man on? I'll make a note, don't think it clashes with anything work wise for me or on our planner. I'll buy you a flask LOL

A notification flashed on her screen – Meeting in Board room in ten minutes. She grabbed her notes, drunk the last of her coffee and decided to grab another one before the meeting. *Maybe the caffeine will keep me from dying of boredom?*

Gibbons sat at the head of the board room table, several file folders to one side and a frown on his face. Once everyone was sitting down he looked around the room and stared at Tom for several moments. Tom lowered his head and flicked through a notebook.

"We have several items to go through this morning so the fewer interruptions the better. Firstly, sales targets are once again down from last quarter. This trend is unacceptable. I expect not only to make up for these dismal figures but exceed next quarter. We are not in the business of paying sales staff for resting on their laurels. I will give each of you a target for this quarter; if you do not realize that target or better still increase it there will be consequences. Do I make myself clear?"

Derek and Tom looked at each other as the other two sales representatives looked in horror at Gibbons. Connie could hardly hide her shock. *He's threatening them with dismissal?*

Connie knew without marketing and sales alignment, growth was a constant uphill battle. If Gibbons would allow the two teams to work collaboratively towards a common goal the barriers would come down and company growth would quickly accelerate. She jotted down a quick note to formulate a discussion on it later. The first step in building an inbound marketing team and executing new strategies is to create a dialogue between sales and marketing rather than the historical operating on completely separate wavelengths. She knew sales complained about the quality of the leads and marketing were frustrated by the lack of follow up and leg work put in when engaging with prospects. She could clearly see the lack of visibility between the two departments. There just weren't clear data points to measure, and therefore neither team could see the other delivering (or not) on their agreed upon metrics. Without understanding they were back to the starting position and laying blame at each other's door. She wrote SLA – service-level agreement. That would be her starting point.

Traditional Method - Buying Contact Lists

"The second item on the agenda - we are not making as much progress on the 10,000 strong contact lists we purchased. Why is that Jen and Peggy?"

Both women drew in deep breaths and spoke over each other.

"We are sending out the letters as fast as we can, Sir, but it would be quicker if we used email."

"The compiling, printing and putting in envelopes takes such a long time. Can't we email instead?"

"Emails get lost in that junk folder, a letter of introduction and the leaflets are much more personal. If the recipient sees their name on the letter they are more likely to read it rather than a mass impersonal email. I will discuss a daily target with you both after the meeting."

Connie could not hold back and said.

"May I say, Mr. Gibbons that there is no way to know if the person the letter was addressed to actually received it and we have no way of knowing what they do with it. There is no way to track the effectiveness of the letters."

"That is where you come in, Connie, you follow up on them – that's how we track it."

She sighed. Jen and Peggy looked defeated. Connie felt sorry for them. Emails were certainly more cost effective than hundreds of envelopes filled and sealed and then taken to the post office. Once again Gibbons refusal to adopt new technology was crippling the company's success.

Traditional Website versus Inbound Marketing Website

"Item three is the website and its effectiveness. Connie, we embraced your idea of having a website but to date it has not returned even a quarter of the $25,000 we invested in it. Can you explain why not?"

Connie's stomach rolled. *Take a deep breath and keep calm.*

"Mr. Gibbons the website I proposed would certainly have paid for itself by now. We did not integrate buy online, direct links to each department for Q&A or create a blog."

"Wait a minute, we paid a substantial amount of revenue on that website, it has all our products on it and a fill in form, and surely that is more than enough?"

"Unfortunately, not, we need to engage our customers and make the site much more interactive. For example, a simple Q&A can cut down the majority of phone calls fielded by the IT department, which are basic in nature and taking them away from more serious queries. The online buying app would have enabled product to be ordered, processed and sent out in half the time and a blog is a great way to give our customers an insight into the company, its staff and new developments. Involvement is key."

"Firstly, the IT department's role is to help our customers, why are we taking work away from them? Secondly, our product is not a cheap pair of shoes or a DIY table to be bought online and this blog you are talking about is just a waste of time, it doesn't increase sales."

"Mr. Gibbons the website as it is now is just a glorified brochure, nothing more. We could utilize it so much more to the benefit..."

"A glorified brochure! So, you are telling me all that money we spent was wasted?"

Connie tensed realizing her comment was ill advised.

"No, Sir we fell short of my initial concept, we need to integrate the website with these other features to make it successful. Research shows that inbound marketing that is focused on bringing in revenue is an important part of any companies' online presence; we can generate additional revenue and build customer loyalty. Customers can easily engage via a channel that plays an important role in their everyday lives. It is proven that 97% of consumers use the web to search for local businesses. We need to access that potential."

"What about our customers, Connie? Most have been with us for decades and are more than happy to continue to use the phone to call for technical support or upgrades. I can't see many of them going to this blog and reading it, it is a waste of time in my opinion. It's seems to me you are happy to spend the company's money on schemes that are without merit. Now item four."

There it is the dismissal; even with proven statistics he is resistant to all modern methodology. Why am I banging my head against this wall, over and over again? Connie sat for the remainder of the meeting feeling unappreciated and frustrated with only half an ear to the conversation. When Gibbons stood up she realized they were all dismissed.

"I expect a massive increase in sales figures next quarter. Make it happen people."

Later Connie tapped her pen against her desk looking despondently out of the window through the raindrops. The grey gloom outside matched her mood. Once again, her ideas to improve the company's profile to attract new customers had been pushed aside. No matter how she 'packaged' her ideas, the marketing director, Mr. Gibbons rejected them as 'modern foolishness.'

Her frustration went from simmer to boil. *Why can't he see the benefits?* She answered her own question – he's a dinosaur, unable to move forward and relying on the 'old' methods. Her cell phone trilling broke into her thoughts; it was a text from her husband.

Heh, are you working late? I've got tickets for that blockbuster movie you were excited about. It starts at 8pm.

Sure, would be great to get my mind off Gibbons and why stay late? She texted back.

Sounds great, I'm leaving in 40 minutes.

Connie glanced over her tidy desk before switching off the desk light and walking out of the office building. Even leaving as early as 6:45pm she was the last to leave. *Why am I putting so much effort into this place? Gibbons will never accept his marketing methods are obsolete.* Previous staff meetings replayed in her mind. Maybe she should not have been so direct but cajoling and tiptoeing around the subject had not worked either.

Traditional versus New Website Usage
"If we don't use more up to date methods, such as focused social media advertising, we will be left behind our competitors."

"You really think that would work? I have heard negative reports on it."

"I admit that the digital advertising ecosystem is far from perfect. It is plagued by inefficiencies like ad fraud, rent-charging intermediaries that add dubious value, defensive user/customer behaviors prompted by abusive legacy marketing practices, malware, and insufficient campaign efficacy reporting, all this makes digital advertising experiences increasingly frustrating for both advertisers and consumers. Those are exactly the same old Black hat strategies used for SEO and more. So, spending all of our marketing dollars on online Ads, just to bring them to a fancy new website, is a complete waste of time and money. 60% of the Ads will not hit the proper targets, either due to miss design or having Adblockers. 40% of our target demographic will simply see the same message hitting them again and again and again. However, we can tailor-make our campaign to avoid these pitfalls."

"Black Hat? Target demographic? Sounds like a case of 'Big Brother' is watching you to me. You are talking gibberish! All that texting and posting and God knows what will soon go out of fashion, you mark my words. Mail shots, advertising in the newspaper and our industry magazines, along with persistent cold calling has worked for us for many years and will continue to do so. Stick to the tried and tested methods, Connie. Our established clients don't need these newfangled methods."

"Mr. Gibbon's methods are improving every day. We can ensure we are communicating and reacting as well as compiling data on the number of 'clicks' we receive. We need to be responsive to potential clients. We need to let the brand pay for itself through ROI."

"And what exactly is an Ad Blocker? Why would we block our advertising? And clicks, what are you talking about, Connie? Seems to me you are not taking into consideration the substantial costs we invested in the 10,000 strong contact list we purchased two years ago or indeed the upgrading of the website. Emails to those ten thousand contacts will bear fruit, mark my words,"

"Mr. Gibbons these programs work by caching and filtering content before it is displayed in a user's browser. We can target what advertising is viewed. Yes, I am aware of the investment, we need the marketing strategy to be accountable for revenue, companies are in a transformational era and we cannot afford to be left behind."

"Left behind! We have a website, which is more than enough technology for our business – it showcases our products with glossy photos and descriptions and has that contact link. I think you are forgetting that I, as CMO and Timothy as CIO worked on that website for quite some time with the developer."

Yes, but you made sure I was not part of that development, didn't you? It could have been instrumental in sales increases by now. You took my notes and only used the parts you understood that's for sure. This recalled yet another pitch that failed on a subsequent occasion.

"Mr. Gibbons I quite understand your views, but machine learning is stepping into marketing departments across the globe, either using Chatbots, Analytics Lead scoring, Email send time suggestions, Fraud Detection, Web search results, Real-Time Ads on web pages and mobile devices. Text-based Sentiment Analysis, Credit Scoring and next-best offers. Even prediction of a buyer's next move as well as email spam filtering, new pricing models and..."

Gibbons looked over his glasses at her and Connie knew there was no hope of persuading him.

"I think you have a case of technology overload, Connie. Now can we get back to the reason for this sales meeting?"

She had once again bit her tongue, looking around the room at resigned faces, there was never an argument won against Gibbons. As the most senior staff member apart from the CEO, he ruled his 'empire' with manipulation and an underlining threat of 'toe the line or else'. A vision of Gibbons' look came into her mind. He had berated her in front of the sales director, and sales staff, a look of 'I know best' - you have little experience compared to my thirty years in the business. She swore under her breath as she unlocked her car. Driving home, she listened to a meditative podcast to calm herself, she couldn't go home riled up again, although Bruce was understanding and listened to her rants, it was not fair to spoil their home life with constant complaining. Bruce would offer options and suggestions but with his own high-profile career he had his own struggles. *Tonight, will be relaxed and no talk of work.* She repeated the mantra playing on the podcast three times while taking deep cleansing breaths. As she drew up to her home's driveway, Bruce was at the kitchen window. He held up a hand in greeting. I'm lucky to have him, we are so well suited. Our careers and goals are equally important, I have to make a change, and this constant frustration is not good for me or Bruce or our future.

The movie date was enjoyable, and Connie and Bruce relaxed over a late supper afterwards, chatting about the movie, its plot and characters. Work was a banned subject.

GDPR Data (General Data Protection Regulation)

The next morning, Connie felt refreshed and determined to make a difference. Bruce's words replayed in her mind. 'Don't give up, Connie you are better than that.' An article had caught her eye earlier on her alerts, once it was booked marked she responded to several emails. With her responses made she read the article with interest. It concerned GDPR Data (General Data Protection Regulation). A new EU regulation, which replaces the 1995 EU Data Protection Directive (DPD) to significantly enhance the protection of the personal data of EU citizens and increase the obligations on organizations that collect or process personal data. Connie noted the date the new regulation will come into force - May 25th, 2018 – keeping current with these regulations is vital for all marketing managers.

The article continues that while the current EU legislation (the 1995 EU Data Protection Directive) governs entities within the EU, the territorial scope of the GDPR is far wider, in that it would also apply to non-EU businesses who a) market their products to people in the EU or who b) monitor the behaviors of people in the EU. Again, she noted the impact the regulation could pose even if a company was based outside of the EU but has controls or processes with data of EU citizens, the GDPR would apply. She shook her head wondering how she would relay this information to Gibbons. She already knew his response would be that it was not at all relevant to a Canadian or US company. Jotting down a few ideas she thought of the impact this new regulation could have and if they were not compiling what ramifications there might be. Gibbons would dismiss it as not relevant if she did not explain it properly. Now how to do that!

As she walked to the coffee vending machine, Sally caught her eye.

"God were you on fire yesterday. I thought Gibbons was going to explode."

"All the good it did. He will resist any and all technological advances."

"I understand your frustration, Connie even the simplest gadgets that would make my job easier he resists. It took me six months to get him to authorize a digital drawing pad."

"Do I really have any chance then of improving the digital footprint of this company? Can it be brought into the 21st century and beyond?"

"With Gibbons holding the strings I would say it is highly unlikely."

"Great my masters in e-commerce, an MBA and a marketing degree all wasted because of one man's opposition to change. It's getting me down."

"I don't blame you for feeling that way. You are young and ambitious."

"Don't you want more Sally?"

"I keep my head down, do the work and go home to two wonderful kids, Connie that's what keeps me sane. I'm left alone for the majority of the time and that's the way I like. No serious responsibility, I just design graphics for promotional stuff."

Connie shrugged and walked to the vending machine. As the brown liquid filled the paper cup, she felt sorry for Sally, having no ambition, no drive. Just going through the motions just wasn't for her. There had to be something better. She sat down at her desk and browsed her LinkedIn profile. She updated a few items and added a couple more search related words. Knowing Microsoft acquired LinkedIn for $26.5B a while back; Connie knew the effect of merging the information had had on B2B organizations and how marketing managers utilized it for their strategies in gaining business. This was another important advance she had to get across to Gibbons.

Service Level Agreement (SLA)

At home, Connie read through one of her manuals relating to SLA. She refreshed her knowledge making notes as she thought about the best way to approach the subject.

A marketing and sales SLA is an agreement, almost like a contract, between the two teams, designed to help them work cohesively but putting in equal effort in the process and holding each other accountable for the results. In an SLA, marketing commits to generating a certain quality of qualified leads and sales agrees to follow up those leads and opportunities appropriately. An SLA is all about the numbers and makes it easier for the two teams to work together. Engrossed in the chapter, Connie was only vaguely aware of Bruce leaving for a night out with friends. Having the apartment to herself gave her solitude to become engrossed in the manual. She knew if she could make the strategy all about the 'numbers' she might be able to convince Gibbons this method was worthwhile

How to Create a Marketing and Sales SLA
1. Calculate the Marketing Side. To calculate the marketing side of your SLA, you need the following four metrics:
a. Total sales goal in terms of revenue quota
b. Percentage of revenue from marketing versus sales-generated leads
c. Average sales deal size
d. Average lead to customer close percentage

Taking a clean notepad page, she wrote out the equation.

Sales quota x % revenue from marketing leads
= Marketing-sourced revenue goal

$$\frac{\text{Marketing revenue goal}}{\text{Average sales deal size}} = \text{\# of customers needed}$$

$$\frac{\text{Customers}}{\text{Avg. lead-to-customer close \%}} = \text{\# of leads needed}$$

2. Calculate the Sales Side

   The sales side of the SLA details the speed and depth of follow up of marketing – generated leads. If you have the time and resources to analyze and determine the optimal number and frequency of follow-up attempts for each lead, it is definitely worthwhile. The first five minutes are critical to higher contact and qualification rates. If leads are responded to within the first few minutes, the odds of contacting them are 100 percent higher. The recommended number of follow up attempts is between six and nine calls.

3. Set Up Marketing SLA Reporting

   Now you have your SLA goals, it's time to put those metrics into a report where your teams can track their progress against their goals on a regular basis. If you want to go daily; start by creating a graph for your goal line by multiplying 1/n (n+#days in the month) by your monthly goal this will determine what portion of your monthly goal you need to achieve every day. They create a waterfall graph to track progress throughout the month.

4. Set Up Sales SLA Reporting

For the sales SLA reporting, you'll need to create two graphs – one monitoring speed to follow up, and the other monitoring depth of follow up. To graph the speed of follow up, you'll need the data/time the lead was presented to sales and the data/time the lead got its first follow up. The difference is the time it took sales to follow up. To graph the depth of follow up (i.e. number of attempts); look specifically at leads that have not been reached. Create a bar graph to track the percentage of leads being followed up with. This will help you see how your sales team trends over time. For leads over a certain timeframe (one week, one month, etc.) that have not been contacted by sales, look at the average number of follow up attempts made. Then graph the number of attempts made for each week or month against the SLA. It is important to keep in mind that not all leads generated by marketing will be ready to be sent to sales. Some may need further nurturing or qualification.

Connie underlined the next few sentences.

You also want to make sure that your business connects with each lead, whether sales or marketing is making the contact. The first moments after a lead converts are critical in maintaining a relationship with that prospect and encouraging his or her excitement about your company.

When creating your SLA, you also need to factor in sales bandwidth. While six to nine follow-up attempts are ideal, it might be that your sales reps are simply unable to follow up with every single MQL. Therefore, try to factor in your inbound lead velocity, how much time they spend on marketing-generated leads versus sales-generated and how much time they have to spend on each lead.

Finally, you should be reviewing these metrics on a daily basis in order to monitor your progress. The end goal is to generate more qualified leads and accelerate business growth, and the first step is to bring marketing and sales teams together to create a high-functioning working relationship. Once marketing and sales align, you can focus on building and strengthening your internal sales team.

Stretching out her shoulders, Connie realized the information had stuck with her and after her conversation with Derek knew he would be the perfect partner to show Gibbons how this strategy would benefit everyone and gain valuable income and growth. Now to convince Derek to join her and how they would get the tactic across using the 'numbers' and 'goal' ideals they knew Gibbons liked. She rewarded herself with a glass of wine and let her mind relax watching a mind-numbing reality show on TV.

The next morning, Connie laid out her notes and read through them again, thinking about the best way to approach Derek and get him on side before tackling Gibbons. At that moment Derek walked up to her smiling.

"Good morning, Connie. How's it going?"

"Good thanks, Derek you must be psychic I was just thinking about finding you. I have an idea I think we could pitch to Gibbons together."

Derek looked side to side and crouched down beside her chair.

"Actually, my days of suffering old Gibbons are numbered. I'm sure it's a great idea Connie, but I've been offered a great new job so will be keeping my head down for the next couple of weeks until my notice is over. I handed in my resignation letter to him earlier. He didn't give any indication he was pleased or otherwise. I wish you luck though. If nothing else, you do your utmost in the face of indifference."

As she watched Derek walk away Connie's mood changed from eager to half-hearted. Her scheme pinned on Derek's sales experience and her marketing knowhow. How would she persuade Gibbons now? *Why am I striving to make this place better? I'm tired of being dismissed over and over. Derek's lucky, he's got out.*

A ping on her cell attracted her attention. A job posting for a B2B company flashed on her LinkedIn alert. She scrolled down the company details and the job description. As she read her mood changed to cautious excitement. This was a job she could excel in given the chance. The company was only five years old but seeking a person with dynamic marketing ideas and enthusiasm to make a difference. It couldn't be a coincidence that this opportunity appeared at that very moment. After her discussions with Derek and Sally, she knew to stay would erode her vitality, her drive and eventually her enthusiasm for marketing. Not wanting to wait, she quickly read through her current resume, made a couple of revisions and wrote a cover letter. Then pressed send as the sun broke through the clouds lifting her mood even further. *If that's not a sign I don't know what is.*

That evening she enthused about the new position over supper, showing Bruce the advert and ticking off the requirements against her qualifications and experience.
"It's meant to be, Bruce."
"Certainly, seems to be a job made for you, Connie. Just don't get too hopeful okay?"
"I need to make sure I'm prepared for any question they come up with. Will you help?"

"You know I will. Let's browse through the Internet for marketing interview questions and do some more role-play. When the interview request comes through you will be more than ready."

"Thank you, you are always so supportive. I love you."

"Love you too. Now shall I pour more wine before we start?"

A couple of hours later, Connie's responses were casual but informed but most of all did not seem rehearsed.

"Well I'm for bed love, I have a breakfast meeting so will have to be out of here by 5:30 am."

"I'm so sorry, Bruce you should have said. Go on I'll be right there."

Connie admitted defeat when she couldn't keep her eyes open. She was shocked to see the time was 12:45 am. *I'll sleep in the spare room I can't wake Bruce up now.* After checking the locks, she changed, brushed her teeth and slid into the cold sheets. Her thoughts followed her into her dreams, a brand new corner office of her own, a supportive and forward thinking team and a boss who appreciated her.

Two days later Connie received an email requesting she attend an interview. She immediately text Bruce the news, 'I've got an interview!' and a happy face. His reply was a big thumbs up and smiley face emoji. After checking the date and time of the interview, she walked to Mr. Gibbon's office and requested time off for a dental appointment. He nodded without looking up, missing Connie's smile. *I have to get that job!*

Once back at her desk, it took her some time to concentrate on the follow up leads from the massive contact list Jen and Peggy had been spending weeks on. *I could be so much more productive.* Several sheets of paper landing on her desk made Connie jump.

"Sorry, Connie I didn't mean to throw those, I'm just fed up with old Gibbons. He told Jen and me, we have to send out fifty more letters a day - each! It's not possible by the time the letters are personalized, printed, folded and inserted in to envelopes with the leaflets and then sealed we could have sent hundreds via email."

"Take a seat, relax a while."

"I can't take the chance Gibbons will see me 'not working'. My husband has told me I'm putting stuff in envelopes in my sleep, that's how bad it's got. Sorry to rant, these are the few queries from last week's batch. Pathetic if you ask me. See you later."

"Yeh, see you later."

Wow that's not good, poor Peggy. Connie looked at the papers before her, only five queries from God knows how many mail shots. *Maybe I can use these as proof we need to embrace better methods, like email to Gibbons?* An hour later she had formulated a tactic and made her way to Gibbons office. She knocked on his door and waited.

Traditional Bought Contact Lists

"Yes, come in I haven't got all day. What can I do for you Connie?"

"It may be what I can do for you and the company, Sir."

"Alright, I'm listening."

"Well, Sir, Peggy just handed over the queries from last week's mail shot batch and it is rather poor."

"Well that's exactly why they need to be sending out a lot more!"

"I understand that, Mr. Gibbons but there is a way to make the process a lot faster and not have Jen and Peggy spending so much time and intensive work on the lists."

Connie kept her cool as Gibbons brow furrowed.

"We can email..."

"I told you that isn't going to work."

"But, Sir if I can explain. We can use a mail merge from the lists. It will put the contact's name on the email header, so it will look like it is sent to that person rather than a mass email, which you rightly say could be put into the junk folder and lost."

"Do you know how this merge thing works?"

"Yes, Sir, I can show Jen and Peggy and their numbers will be off the charts."

Best play along that Jen and Peggy do know how a mail merge works, I need to keep him on side.

"Well, alright but don't send everything at once I want to monitor if this merge thing is successful before using it for the remainder of the lists. Send five hundred and keep track. I will be waiting for exact figures, do you understand?"

"Yes, Mr. Gibbons. I will implement it this afternoon and make sure we keep tallies."

Her victory over Gibbons shone in her smile as she walked over to Jen and Peggy.

"What the heck did you do?"

"I convinced Gibbons we can use a mail merge for the lists."

"You're kidding right? If this is some kind of sick joke, I'm not laughing."

"Honestly, Peggy he agreed, only 500 names for the moment but it's a start. We have to keep track of sent emails, and the number of responses but once he sees the benefit you won't have to stuff envelopes anymore."

The two women embraced Connie.

"You are a miracle worker. Now what do we do first?"

"We need to select 500 names and enter the list into the document folder then we can set the mail merge up."

An hour and a half later all the information was entered and ready.

"We think you should do the honors, Connie, you made it happen after all."

"No, really you should do it together."

"Okay that's settled all three of us need to do it. Ready? Push that button."

The screen flickered as the command processed the mail list.

"This calls for a celebration come on let's get some good coffee from the place around the corner, so much better than that vending machine stuff."

The three women walked out of the office buzzing with expectation and Connie could see the relief on Peggy and Jen's faces.

"No more envelope stuffing, thank heavens."

"Well hopefully, we need to prove the mail merge will get results to Gibbons first."

"Oh, that's going to happen. Have you seen the recycle bin by the post box? Full of leaflets, flyers and 'whom it may concern' envelopes. I'm certain that's what happens to the majority of the letters we send out."

"You are most probably right, Jen. Now I'm buying so what do you want?"

"Thanks Connie but we agreed, we are buying as you saved us from envelope hell."

Over supper Connie relayed her small victory to Bruce and how Peggy and Jen were so grateful.

"You would think I'd just released them from purgatory."

"Well I'm sure to them you had. I can't imagine spending all day, every day stuffing envelopes. It's piece work."

"I hadn't thought of it that way, you are right it was like piece work. Well, let's hope the responses are proof enough for Gibbons to let them send the remainder of those contacts via email. Cheers."

"Cheers on a job well done."

With her success still boosting her mood, Connie went into work with high hopes. Peggy and Jen were all smiles as she passed their desks. If I can make a success of this I can use it as an example in the interview.

Bitcoin - Crypto currency

An alert was flashing on her computer screen as she turned it on. She had made up a list of marketing phrases, insights, updates, SEO's and latest marketing news so any new developments would be linked. She clicked the link to find an article on Bitcoin. She was immediately engrossed in the information. It detailed how bitcoin is a worldwide crypto currency and digital payment system, allowing peer-to-peer transactions directly between users without an intermediary. The transactions are verified by network nodes and recorded in a public distributed ledger called a blockchain. It can be exchanged for other currencies, services and products. As Connie read the figures she was amazed. As of February 2015, over 100,000 merchants and vendors accepted bitcoin as payment and even more interesting it can also be held as investment. The next set of figures, she read were astounding. In 2017 between 2.9 and 5.8 million unique users had a crypto currency wallet, most of which used bitcoin. *This is the future of business, I just know it. I need to know more. This will affect all aspects of a company and its business through all departments from sales to IT to marketing.* As she pondered the information, Connie tried to think of a way of explaining the need to incorporate this knowledge to old Gibbons – it would be another hard sell and most probably rejected out of hand. If only she could find a company, who would embrace all she was learning and allow her to integrate it into policy.

Chapter One: Lessons learned

A) How to communicate new Ideas to the leadership team, especially if they are new to out of the box thinking

a. First understand their background and their own personal agenda

b. Do not share tactics, they will get lost. Make sure you keep it high level strategy focused

c. Understand your audience and adjust your message accordingly

d. Agree on the goal and the destination even before the strategy

B) It is not who you are but what you do that defines you.

a. It is not the number of MBA master's degrees. Not even your 30 years versus 3-month experience. What really counts is what you can bring to the table

b. Stay humble in your approach and eager in your learning to achieve the 100X more

C) Culture - eat strategy for breakfast

a. The culture of your organization is the key to unlock the potential of your human capital. Do you have a culture code, does it reflect externally as it reflects internally? As a marketing manager you will need to communicate some of that

b. General Manager, Marketing Manager, CMO or CEO. Your mission is to be a factory that creates leaders and those leaders will create other leaders. At some point in time your organizations will all become leaders. 80% of them will be leaders without a title. Make sure that this is your core hidden mission if you want to see 100X growth in 7-10 years.

c. Please remember that 100X growth is not only a reflection of your top line revenue or product line revenue, not even your net profit or your EBITDA only. It is the effectiveness of your brand internally and externally. When was the last time you reviewed your brand strategy and brand extension?

D) There are 5000+ Marketing automation tools out in the market place as of 2018 will be followed by even more; it is not about the tool. It is about the strategy that will then dictate the tool or the platform that will integrate with the group of tools. It is the old 80/20 rules. Spend 20 of your time figuring out and selecting and learning the platform or the tool. But 80% of the time tuning and adjusting your strategy to get results. Remember marketing is quickly evolving from Activity based➔ to lead generation to the next generation of marketing framework, which is revenue marketing.

E) It is the journey that counts not just the destination. While you are climbing the steep mountain to the summit, I promise you it will get even steeper sometimes, less oxygen on the way up with even more gravity that will pull you down. You need to remember that only at that time your true self will raise to the occasion and hopefully you are in the correct organization that has the healthy culture to drive you and your team forward. If not push hard to build the culture.

Chapter Two – Meeting the Mentors

In contrast to Connie's workplace management experience, another company's leadership team were conversing in an office across town, highlighting their unique culture and a different involvement.

"Morning, Dan how was your weekend?"

"Good thanks, Mike we were out at the lake. Manage to catch several good fish. How was yours?"

"Not as exciting as yours, we took in a show after a day of yard work. Are we still on for the meeting at ten?"

"Yes, we are - we need to discuss your proposal and get everyone on board."

Mike winked as Dan rolled his eyes. Both knew Greg would be agreeable but Miriam; their CFO would be a harder nut to crack, when it came to extra financing.

Later as the four main staff members sat down together, Mike relayed his proposal.

"Good morning everyone, I will just get straight to it. We need to make radical changes to our marketing strategy over the next few years to improve ROI value to our company. I've watched how inbound marketing is outperforming traditional marketing. Every day we hear about another brand leader growing their business due to inbound marketing."

"Have we not adopted some of these new techniques, Mike?"

"We have, Dan but only pieces and to be honest they are not enough. We need to shift resources around to make the changes needed to increase lead generation, reduce costs, and grow new markets."

"If we can reduce costs, then I'm okay with that, Mike."

"Thanks, Miriam but to implement these changes needs some investment."

"You just said we can reduce costs not increase them."

C-Suite - Top senior executives positions tend to start with the letter C, for chief, as in chief executive officer (CEO), chief financial officer (CFO), chief operating officer (COO), and chief information officer (CIO).

"Let me explain. For more effective marketing we need to engage all the C-suite and get everyone on board and become excited about and endorse the strategy. In short with inbound, everything's digital and its analytics play a major part in attributing dollars spent to revenue generated. Today, we are spending as much as 10% of our annual budget on marketing, but by applying inbound marketing, we can put hard numbers against marketing performance. We have to embrace such concepts as brand awareness, impressions, and followers."

"So, you would have figures available to track its effectiveness?"

"Exactly right, Miriam you would have cost versus effect figures at your fingertips."

"Would these figures align with the profit and growth objectives for the company I am projecting? I'm not just talking bottom line profit, but return on investment, remember we have a five-year target to achieve for the venture capital investors. Can we find and pursue the right growth strategies, while measuring and monitoring business performance and, as Miriam said, control spending and in essence do more with less?"

"With a dedicated approach to inbound, Dan, we can provide greater returns. The longer we wait to do it, the longer it will take to get those results. By building a partnership in inbound marketing, we will increase profits and revenues through greater efficiencies because inbound marketing is measurable, predictable, and attributable. Look at the diagram, it shows our pressures and concerns.

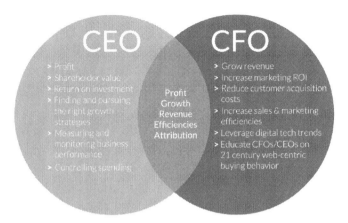

CEO
> Profit
> Shareholder value
> Return on investment
> Finding and pursuing the right growth strategies
> Measuring and monitoring business performance
> Controlling spending

Profit
Growth
Revenue
Efficiencies
Attribution

CFO
> Grow revenue
> Increase marketing ROI
> Reduce customer acquisition costs
> Increase sales & marketing efficiencies
> Leverage digital tech trends
> Educate CFOs/CEOs on 21 century web-centric buying behavior

"All these marketing terms you are using, such as brand awareness, impressions, or followers do not align with my financial targets of profit, revenue, and indeed growth generation. My job is to safeguard this company's fiscal future."

"That's exactly why inbound marketing is the way to go, Miriam. We can identify and track metrics for marketing that can be directly attributed to profits and revenue. In real terms we will have hard data for LTV, CAC, MQLs/month and ROI. It gives us a formula for cause and effect, put simply - spend this dollar, get these dollars back. With these predictable models to attribute (<— aka "track"), measure, analyze, and improve we can show marketing adds value to the company's bottom line."

"Alright I'm listening, Mike."

Note *This section is rather technical, so it is okay to skip it and come back dear Reader.*

"Let me explain in financial terms rather than marketing terms, Miriam. This will help you too Dan. In inbound marketing, the content we create is an asset, just like the workflows and processes we create to go with them. Inbound marketing's methodology creates assets that have a compounding effect because they continue to generate value (leads) over time without additional investment. It also has a compounding return. As you know Miriam, compound interest is interest added to the principal of a deposit (or loan or credit card) so that the added interest also earns interest from then on. It is like making deposits to different savings accounts. I read an example, which explains it quite well. The savings accounts are held by Google's search engine and various social media networks. Our deposits are the assets we create and publish (blog and other content, including processes, systems, and workflows). Our assets constantly earn interest, which shows up as higher search engine rankings and ever-growing social media networks that share our assets widely. They in turn provide us with on-going income in the form of traffic and leads that we can nurture until they're ready to hand-off to sales. In reality collectively, these assets have a lasting return with no additional cost."

"So, if I understand this correctly, we would receive returns on these systems for quite some time."

Pay-per-click (PPC), also known as(CPC) cost per click

"Yes, Miriam we would. With our PPC campaigns we have advertising that is a reliable and predictable tactic. We instantly generate leads, which over time are easily tracked and measured to accurately predict sales and revenue. However, a study in 2015 by a MIT Sloan MBA student on ROI on using HUBSPOT's marketing software Highlights showed:

3.15X more visitors per month within one year
4.77X more leads per month within one year

72% of customers saw increase in Sales revenue within one year

Mike continued as Dan and Miriam listened closely.

"The first month we may only do 4 posts blogs that attract 10 new followers on social media. The second month, we may publish another 4 blogs that will add two content offers with 40 new followers and increase our search engine ranking for eight keywords and generate 20 leads. By six months, we may have published a total of 30 blog posts, created 10 content offers, have a total of 200 followers, and are showing up on page one of Google for five keywords, and generated 100 leads. The compound effect from creating those assets over time don't just double the leads the second month, they generated 10x the results in only a few short months. This is all reliant on how much content we produce and how quickly, the competitiveness of the keywords we choose, the value of our content offers, and our conversion and close rates."

Cost per lead, often abbreviated as CPL
"Can I ask then, Mike what would be our CPL?"

"Good question, Dan. As you know CPL is how much we spend to acquire one lead, which we can acquire by dividing marketing costs by total leads generated. Marketing costs and leads can be as granular as a specific asset or campaign or based on all costs and leads in a particular time period. CPL shows how cost-effectively we invest marketing dollars. The more granular we get (e.g. content, landing page, CTA, campaign, etc.), the faster we can determine which ones are more effective. Tracking the CPL helps us continuously improve for greater efficiency. It can also help isolate which assets are better at converting leads at different stages of the marketing funnel. Let's look at **CAC = Sales & Marketing Costs/New Customer Acquired.** CAC is the total sales and marketing cost divided by the number of customers acquired, over a specified period of time (a month, quarter, or year). For example, if we spent $300,000 on Sales and Marketing in a month and added 30 customers that month, then that month's CAC is $10,000.

Mike saw Miriam's wide-eyed look at the mention of $300,000 but continued.

"With tracking we have a Marketing and/of CAC= M-CAC/CAC ratio and can calculate marketing CAC (M-CAC) and Marketing's percent of CAC. We then have traceable figures to show how much more efficient and effective inbound marketing is at delivering qualified leads to sales than traditional marketing. As we begin to reallocate budget from traditional marketing to inbound, M-CAC will eventually decrease because inbound brings in more qualified leads at a lower cost."

"This is interesting on the finance side for sure, Mike but what about the LTV?"

"That's my next point, Dan and something I'm sure Miriam is wondering about too. I'm sure that LTV's are one of those metrics that keeps you up at night, Dan, the estimated revenue that a customer will generate during the entire span of their relationship with our company. We should already be tracking this metric and I think Miriam and I should work on a formula for it as it provides a good indication of the maximum amount we should invest in CAC."

Here is how we calculate the Customer Lifetime Value (LTV)

It is an estimate of the average gross revenue that a customer will generate before they churn (cancel).

"Now you ask, 'why should I care about LTV'? Primarily to apply a limit to your Customer Acquisition Cost (CAC) - if you're spending more on acquisition than you anticipate you will earn
from the customer in revenue, you're going to be in a bad place very soon (unless you have a bottomless pot of money to spend on acquisition)."

Customer churn rate and LTV

"Customer churn rate is the rate at which a business is losing customers due to cancellations (proactive churn) or failures to renew (passive churn) and is usually measured on a monthly basis. Other ways to account for varying churn in your LTV calculation are adopting a more advanced LTV estimation formula by using statistical models such as Bayesian Probability, which take a probabilistic approach to predicting LTV or calculate LTV per customer segment. Different customer segments can have widely varying LTV. It's a good idea to segment your customer base to get more meaningful results, e.g. calculating LTV separately for customers paying monthly versus annually is highly recommended."

How churn rate affects LTV

"One difficulty with estimating LTV is factoring in customer churn rate. The "simple" LTV formula assumes that churn happens linearly over the lifetime of a customer. However, this is never really the case in most real-world scenarios."

Adjusting your LTV formula for varying churn patterns

"Let's take for example, if our customer churn contains a mixture of Annual Renewals,
Constant, Declining and Cliff patterns, there is an easy way to adjust our simple LTV formula to account for the variance by applying a discount. This leads to a more conservative LTV estimate."

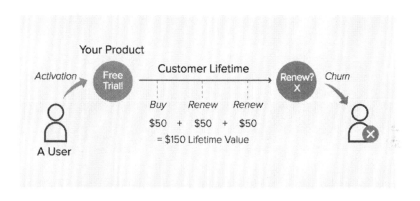

ARPA Customer Churn Rate x 0.75
Your business model leads to a steady expansion in MRR for existing customers, e.g. because you're billing per number of users.

Accounts for basic (linear) expansion

$$LTV = \frac{ASP}{Cust.\ Churn\ Rate} + \frac{m\,(1 - Churn\ Rate)}{Cust.\ Churn\ Rate^2}$$

Now back to how to truly calculate the ROI. Here is the formula.

***Note for readers. This is just a suggested model. Your business model might vary but this will give you an example from which you can build from. ***

Sales quota x % revenue from marketing leads
= Marketing-sourced revenue goal

$$\frac{Marketing\ revenue\ goal}{Average\ sales\ deal\ size} = \text{\# of customers needed}$$

$$\frac{Customers}{Avg.\ lead\text{-to-}customer\ close\ \%} = \text{\# of leads needed}$$

ROI - The return on investment

"Sounds like a good plan, Mike but now I need ROI information for this inbound marketing strategy you are proposing."

"Obviously, you want the highest ROI in the shortest period of time possible. The reality is that inbound marketing isn't instantaneous, but we should see significant results in about six months. The PPC however, is an immediate investment play. We put money in and immediately get leads out but only as long as we keep buying PPC. Think of it as the equivalent of renting space (on someone else's website). We don't own that space and we have to keep competing for it (pay more to stay in that same space). Think of PPC as a lead factory we rent, whereas inbound is a lead factory we build, own and can resell with the company."

"A good analogy Mike, I agree rented versus owned is a much better prospect."

Yes, Mike I also agree, rented assets don't generate long-term value. So, am I right in thinking PPC's can increase in cost daily, if not hourly, to generate the same number of leads but only if we constantly invest?"

"That's correct, Miriam. In contrast, inbound marketing has a much higher ROI than PPC. Yes, it takes time to build the lead generation factory to produce that higher ROI. But by owning that factory we can look forward to an on-going higher ROI than PPC even if you stopped producing content for a period of time."

"And why should we adopt this new marketing strategy now, Mike?"

"As I've said inbound marketing builds a lead generation factory. We create assets we own that keep delivering value forever with no additional investment. Although it takes longer than PPC to ramp up, IM delivers a consistently higher ROI. As with all assets, it takes time to build them, so the sooner we get started, the sooner we'll get a return."

PPC versus Lead Generation Factory

"But the PPC has been working up until now. Mike. Why change?"

"Well, Dan, PPC has an important place in our overall marketing mix. However, we don't want to become overly dependent on PPC, it is not an investment. It's pure expense. In fact, PPC can be extremely volatile depending on how competitive keywords become. We would either hold spending steady and get fewer leads or have to increase spending to get the same number of leads. If we ran out of money for PPC, leads would dry up. With inbound, the more assets we build over time, the easier we can withstand any budget crises with minimal harm to our lead generation factory."

"I like the idea of averting budget crises for sure, Mike but how reliable is this strategy?"

"Dan, the methodology has been proven. The system works. Obviously, we need time to put content, processes, and workflows into practice and gather our own data, but with enough trend data, we will be able to consistently execute and deliver results based on data-driven formulas."

"So how predictable is this strategy? What's the expected ROI?"

"Well Dan, we have access to an ROI calculator that is based on an annual report done by MIT's Sloan School of Business. It predicts the average 2-year rates for traffic and leads based on 13,500 customer's actual usage of HubSpot. However, we need at least six months of tracking our own data, using our original content, offers, processes, and workflows before we can accurately gauge and commit to a performance range for ROI, Marketing CAC, traffic, conversion, lead generation rates, and cost per lead. We won't be able to say with 100% certainty what one individual blog post will do, but we will know monthly averages over time. We'll be able to figure out that if we produce about X blogs per month, we will generate about X number of leads. This is where we need to fill in our own estimates."

Dan's next question was one Mike had been anticipating.

"Will inbound marketing work outside the US? What regulations / problems can it cause, EEU privacy laws, for example?"

"Dan, it works outside the U.S. The methodology has been widely adopted throughout the EEU and Canada. We have GDPR to worry about, but this will be a different story for a different time. I know that any marketing automation tool or marketing agency, who understand GDPR, would be ready to adopt it. For example, HUBSPOT/Marketo and other platforms are ready for GDPR. I heard about this company Flawless Inbound www.flawlessinbound.ca, they are not your traditional inbound marketing partner. They have worked with at least 100+ B2B Tech/VAR/MSP organizations to help unlock their business potential in marketing, sales and customer service but before we even think about engaging them. We will need an internal resource from the organization to orchestrate all the activities

"Is it possible to test this system first?"

"Miriam, this is where someone with inbound marketing experience can help. To engage with our organization and help with strategy and planning to ensure that all the components are in place."

"So Mike, can we produce enough content that people would be interested in and even read it? Do we have enough interesting things to say?"

"I believe so, Dan. No industry is boring to the people within it. Our industry is growing and there are competitors out there, so we need to stay ahead of the game. There are many topics we can write about. We don't only have to write about our products or services. We'll be writing about the concerns and issues our customers and industry face and talk about trends, innovations, and new ideas. We'll publish strong point-of-view articles that demonstrate the depth of passion in our company for what we do and why we do it. We can publish our interviews with leading experts and also take other people's content and do reviews or summaries of them. There are a thousand and one ways to produce content that people are interested in and will find valuable and useful. That's our job - our expertise. It's the art of marketing and why we should compete with what our competitors and industry trade associations are doing."

"How long will it be before we see results with inbound marketing?"

"If I can get the resources I need, Dan, I estimate six months before we have significant results. It will take somewhat longer before we see reliable and predictable data we can confidently use though to accurately predict future marketing performance."

Mike waited for Dan's next question, the one they had engineered earlier to get Miriam onboard.

"What resources will you need exactly, Mike?"

"I admit I am on a steep learning curve with this inbound marketing, but I believe if we hire a designated marketing professional we can go from the $3M we are achieving now to the venture capital company's target of $12M in the five years you need, Dan."

Both men waited for Miriam's reaction.

"Wait after all this you want to employ someone else? Can't we make do with the systems we have now, Mike? I don't think paying another salary is going to achieve what you think it will."

"Miriam, that's exactly my point. Someone with knowledge and experience of these new strategies is what we do need. I can fudge my way through, but it will be time wasting and I cannot guarantee I will be making the right decisions or implementing the correct strategies. We need a modern thinker."

"I agree with Mike, Miriam, we need to move forward with new marketing techniques and as Mike is being so brutally honest about his ability in them, I think we should hire."

Miriam looked from one face to the other. With resignation in her voice she agreed.

"I will be keeping a close track on this person's fiscal effectiveness and if they don't deliver to target I'll be expecting consequences."

Miriam stood and walked out of the room. Mike and Dan breathed out deep sighs.

"Greg, you've been quiet all through this meeting. Do you have any questions in regard to the product and technical department view of this strategy?"

"I'm not sure I can add much, marketing is not something I understand or really get involved with. I focus on aiding customers with installations and subsequent updates. What benefit would I derive from this inbound marketing?"

"Actually, you will become very involved because each department will cross reference the others. It becomes a cohesive force bringing knowledge, expertise and experience to the mix."

"I'm open to it of course but not entirely sure how that will work, most sales people do not understand the intricacies of the software we supply, leaving us to explain the technology."

"That is the strength of inbound marketing, Greg to have all the information available to the customer."

"Well, count me in. I'll be interested to see how it works."

Greg stood and left the room.

"It went better than I expected, that's for sure."

"You did a good job, Mike. Now we need to make sure we hire a miracle worker."

"It will have to be someone with drive and enthusiasm that's for sure but also have an inquiring and resourceful mind but with the relevant educational background and experience of inbound techniques and who is keen to implement them. I'll work with HR to come up with a job posting for LinkedIn. It has been successful in the past in finding us great team members. I've listed some points for the interview we need to keep in mind:

- Uses easy-to-understand language
- Is articulate and can clearly communicate his or her point of view
- Is punctual and responds in a timely manner
- Does research and comes to each conversation prepared
- Has an entrepreneurial spirit and isn't afraid to make decisions
- Is transparent and open–this can help build trust
- Stays up-to-date on trends and happenings in your industry

- Understands the big picture and can work with diverse teams
- Has a strong curiosity and interest in learning
- Is knowledgeable of your product or service
- Has an active social-media presence and online reputation
- Naturally enjoys helping people

"An excellent list. Make sure to send me a copy. Good work, Mike, now I have to go, I have three more meetings today all of them in different parts of the city. Catch up later; I will want to see that advert before it goes live."

Mike gathered his notes and went in search of Cameron, their HR department manager. After compiling the job positing, Mike emailed it to Dan. He hoped the title would attract the right kind of individuals –MarTech, Marketing Technology Manager required. We are in search of a marketing maverick. Dan's response was almost immediate.

"Go with it!"

Once the posting was live, Cameron kept track of responses and related the submitted cover letters and resumes to Dan and Mike. Within six hours they had ten responses. The two men read through them at their leisure after work and emailed their thoughts on each. Eventually they had three candidates they felt worthy of interview and instructed Cameron to send out the invitations to interview. Two were younger candidates and one with more experience. Cameron noticed that Connie Ryker was the first to accept the date and time and informed Mike.

"Well, let's see if she is as keen when we give her our expectations of her role."

***

With three days to prepare for the interview, Connie spent her evenings reading the new B2B company's website; their blog had only incorporated one marketing video. As she understood these were becoming more effective than just basic blog writing content, she noted down her action to improve upon that aspect. The client reviews were impressive. It was apparent they had embraced some inbound methods; exactly what she had been trying to convince Mr. Gibbons was the way forward. The company's client base was in Canada and the USA and from the data she gathered they had grown significantly in its five years of operation. The website was clean, informative and attractive. She also recognized their use of Account Base Marketing, the new strategic approach to B2B organizations. As she viewed the site she became more excited at the possibility of working in such a business. The job title had appealed a great deal - MarTech, Marketing Technology Manager – she knew it was the new job title emerging in the marketing industry. If they needed a marketing maverick she was determined to give them just that.

"You are really keen on this job, aren't you, Connie?"

"Yes, Bruce, I am – their mandate and mission statement show a forwarding thinking and progressive approach. It's the exact opposite of 'Dinosaur Inc' where I have wasted four years of my life."

"Not wasted, Connie, just a learning curve."

"I thought after gaining my marketing degree, my career would be at a more advanced point by now."

"Honey, you have seen how not to do it, now use that experience to get it right. Now come and sit down and have a glass of wine. Too much study makes Connie weary and grumpy."

Connie swung her arm around to thump her husband, but he was too quick. He was right though pondering the website pages over and over wasn't helping. Now it was time to relax.

A couple of days later, she chose her outfit carefully for the interview and took her e-reader, which held a list of questions she wanted to ask. Arriving twenty minutes early and calming her nerves in the car park, Connie entered a sleek and tastefully decorated reception. A young woman greeted her, noted her name and asked if she would like coffee, tea or water. As her mouth was dry, Connie requested water. The receptionist handed her a chilled glass bottle and a glass and then picked up the phone announcing her arrival.

As she waited, Connie noted the framed prints of the company's' clients, awards and newspaper articles. A man walked into reception and held out his hand.

"Hello, Connie Ryker welcome to Lancett ProCloud. My name is Greg Gould, I'm the product manager. Follow me."

His grip was firm and dry; Connie hoped her nerves had not made her palms sweat.

"I'm pleased to meet you, Mr. Gould."

"Greg is fine we believe in team work rather than a system of hierarchy, everyone has a part to play and is involved."

They walked down a corridor sided with glass overlooking the river.

"You have a fantastic view from here."

"It does have it perks, Connie."

Greg opened a door and Connie was surprised to see, not the long board table with stern men facing her on a single chair as she had envisioned but several couches, chairs and tables once again overlooking the river valley. Two men were seated flipping through a file folder and looked up as she and Greg entered.

"Connie this is Dan Lancett our CEO and Mike Fisher, VP of Sales."

Well this should be interesting, all three top men interviewing me. So glad I prepared. She held out her hand and shook Dan and Mike's hands firmly.

"Please sit, Connie do you want coffee or tea?"

"Oh goodness I left my water in reception."

"Not to worry we have more here. Water then?"

"Yes please Mr. Lancett."

"Dan is fine, Connie."

He passed her a bottle of water and a glass and sat opposite her on a couch with Greg. Mike sat on a chair slightly to one side.

"Well let's begin, shall we?"

Connie nodded at Dan, breathing in slowly.

"You gave us quite the cover letter, Connie. It appears you are more than interested and seem capable from the experience you have detailed. We would like to ask a few questions to get to know you better and your outlook from a marketing standpoint."

Connie nodded and waited for Dan's first question.

"How long have you worked at your current job?"

"I have been with them for four years."

"Was it your first position in the industry?"

"It was my first full time position in a marketing role; however, I gained a MBA followed by a marketing degree prior to taking the position. I worked part time or on a practicum basis for a couple of companies while studying."

Mike leaned forward to ask.

"Why are you looking to make a change?"

"I am frustrated in my current role as traditional methods, such as mail shots and trade shows and the like are seen to be the only marketing tools that are worthwhile. Although I have presented in-depth proposals to utilize more creative methods the 'tried and tested' ones are favoured. I want to make a difference and not 'coast' along."

"There has been some animosity then?"

"Not exactly, Greg just a refusal to try any new techniques, which I found extremely frustrating. Even when I have shown comparable data with graphs, relayed SLA techniques and inbound strategies there was a resistance to change. I understand we have to keep up with the latest sales and marketing trends and work as teams rather than separate departments."

"So how do you stay up to date with new marketing techniques?"

"Well, Dan, I have numerous alerts on my cell and laptop for marketing updates and trends. I feel we can lose our revenue goal if we stand still."

"So you actively engage in the industry information?"

"Certainly, I am on several marketing forums on LinkedIn and other marketing specific online groups. I contribute to the discussions and have been able to connect with some influential people through them."

"What is your view on new marketing concepts?"

"Firstly, Mike, the new inbound marketing strategies have excellent reviews and noticeable results from the examples I have read. I have also researched SLA's in depth and feel that working as a team involving all the departments of the company is the first step in gaining a cohesive system. One in which everyone understands their role and their accountability. With a common goal we can initiate and achieve a sales target."

"Would you welcome a target then, Connie?"

"With a set goal, Dan, I feel it motivates a team. Without one we are working hard with no target to aim for and it dilutes our efforts."

"An excellent way of putting it, thank you Connie."

Dan nodded to Mike as he asked.

"Would you be willing to make decisions in relation to any marketing strategies you implemented?"

"Yes, I would, Mike. You will find I am keen to learn new methods but also that I research them in detail in order to ensure I completely understand the methodology and how to set them in motion. If I can't explain something clearly enough for others to understand I am failing myself and the company."

"Do you have a definitive idea you would like to bring to bear, if you are hired?"

"I have thought a great deal on how to improve a business' ROI. I think a two-pronged attack would gain sales. Firstly, it is cost effective to convince people who already know your goods to break out their wallets and buy more of your wares. Getting new customers is HARDER than working with existing ones. Once existing clients see the extra value then we can use that momentum and referrals to work in conjunction and forge ahead with new clients using inbound methods."

"An interesting view, Connie, where did this idea come from?"

"Actually, an article I read by Fred Reichheld of Bain and Company, in summary it asks to consider the cost of serving a long-standing customer versus the cost of attracting a new one. Customers tend to generate increasing profits with each year they stay with a company. For example, in financial services, a 5% increase in customer retention can produce nearly a 25% increase in profit. This is because returning customers tend to buy more, which in turn lowers operating costs. An added bonus is the return customers will refer others to your company. In some instances, these customers will pay a premium to continue to do business with you rather than switch to a competitor they are not familiar or comfortable about. In essence you utilize your current client base to increase sales but also have a great sounding board to promote to new clients."

"Have you read our website, Connie?"

"Yes, I have. It's clear, concise and informative."

"Would you change anything?"

"Well, I did note that you only have one video currently on the site, Mike. I think more would drive greater traffic and they are an excellent device to showcase the company."

"Indeed, and what was your impressions of the blog content?"

"May I be honest?"

"Well, of course, Connie. We are open to suggestions."

"Thank you, Dan. I feel the blogs are informative, although maybe not as detailed as they could be. The Q&A section is basic and could be improved upon. Research shows customers are more inclined to make up their minds on a company and/or product by their own investigation prior to contacting them." *I hope my views are not detrimental to my job prospect, but I know what works on websites.*

"You have shown us you are diligent in your research and knowledgeable about marketing trends and methodology. Thank you for coming in today. We shall deliberate once all interviews have been completed and send out emails."

Dan and Mike stood and shook Connie's hands. As Greg escorted back to reception, he said.

"Most of that stuff goes straight over my head, Connie, to be honest but I like the idea of improving the Q&A for technical queries, it could be a great timesaver for me and my team."

"There is also the option of live chat for queries on the website where you can develop a series of 'how to videos' and detailed diagrams. I hope I will be given the opportunity to work with you all."

"It sounds quite fascinating. I wish you luck, Connie."

She was surprised the interview had been over an hour, they seemed interested in her ideas at least. She felt confident she would be offered the position. As she walked out of the main entrance a nervous looking young man walked in wiping his brow. *Maybe he is the next candidate?* As she was walking back to her car she noticed a coffee shop on the corner. Its name, Froth or Not? made her smile, she decided to celebrate with a latte. She entered the coffee shop to find a clean but cozy atmosphere with booths along one wall and round tables scattered around. The main counter displayed an array of freshly made sandwiches and muffins. A chalkboard written in multiple colours listed drinks and specials.

"Hi, what can I get for you today?"

"Hi, a chai latte please with foam."

As the young man attended to making the latte, Connie looked around, a man sat at the farthest booth with a laptop open and ear phones in, he was talking with great animation over some point or other. Also, on the table were two tablets and a thick folder of papers and a notebook where he was jotting down notes as he spoke. His concentration was evident. *A workaholic if ever I saw one.* After paying for her latte, Connie sat at a table replaying the interview in her mind. Had she said the right things, asked the right questions, been confident but not pushy? She took out her e-reader re-reading her questions.

"Are you going into the interview or just come out?"

She jumped at the voice close to her side. Turning and looking up the 'workaholic; was standing beside her chair.

"Ummm, well I've just left, but how did you know?"

"I've interviewed enough people in my time to know that look. Not quite desperation but anxiety of 'what if."

"I had no idea I was that transparent."

"Please don't take offence, I only wanted to lessen your anxiousness, your tapping foot was a clue. If you have prepared well it will be 'in the bag'."

Connie had not realized she'd been tapping her foot.

"Well, thanks for the reassurance."

"My pleasure, good luck with the job."

The man exited the coffee shop, carrying his laptop in a smart carry case in one hand and his tablets and folder under the other arm. Connie watched him disappear around the corner then breathed deeply. I have to get a grip. An hour of yoga and meditation tonight will help. *Now back to Dinosaur Inc!* At her work desk, Connie scrolled through, read and replied to several emails then returned telephone messages. She kept her focus keeping the interview out of her mind. At home that evening she discussed her interview with Bruce.

"You will get it, Connie your whole face lights up when you talk about this new company. It sounds like they are certainly more forward in their thinking and marketing methods."

"It would certainly be a place I could grow my experience but also learn a great deal. Just the thought of somewhere that engages progressive thinking and keeps up with the latest marketing trends and technology is exciting. They did however ask some poignant questions about my decision making and how I felt about targets, am I up to the challenge?"

"Of course, you are, don't sabotage yourself before you even start."

"You are right, Bruce I know how to research and plan. It is going to be amazing."

Holding up her glass she clinked it against Bruce's. *I need to have faith in myself and my abilities. I wanted to grow professionally so now's my chance.*

Chapter Two: Lessons learned

A) It is important to understand the audience in the room, even when Mike was pointing out inbound strategy, it seemed like a focused marketing plan to Dan (CEO). His approach was very different compared to his conversation with Mariam (CFO). Understand the perspective and goals of your executive team before you delve into technical or Techy speech in your marketing approach.

B) Remember everyone will assume that they know marketing, but marketing means different things to different people. And everyone is correct. Your mission, if you choose to accept it, is to align all the definitions to the only important objective, which is revenue driven marketing.

    a. For a graphic designer marketing is about creating an aesthetic.

    b. For a UX expert marketing is ease of use and adoption of the website

    c. For a Marketing Manager it might be about campaigns, visits, leads, Webinar attendance, and trade show contact conversion.

    d. For an Inbound Marketing manager, it is all about conversion (TOFU, MOFU, and BOFU), CASL, GDPR and other marketing standards depending on the region they are running campaigns into.

    e. For a CMO it will be about branding, revenue attribution to the business, and much more... Read more in to the story.

    f. For an IT Manager, it will be about security compliance, hosting and SSL, load balancing, uptime, integration to Gmail or O365, integration with other IT or business applications.

g. For a Content Writer it will be about the Story telling to match not only the overall brand but the Why, How and What of the product/service and what it can do for the persona they are trying to attract to their marketing funnel.

h. For Social Media Managers, it is about increasing followers on all the usual social media streams (LinkedIn, Facebook, Twitter, etc.) and the engagement and amount of interactive conversation that will bring more meaningful engagement to the organization.

C) Preparing the key, even if you are expert in your field, give time to reflect on how Connie was preparing for her interview. And how she stayed collected and calm under pressure.

Chapter Three – Crossing the Threshold

"Hi Dan, what was your view on the candidates?"

"I'm not as keen on the older man, Thomas as I thought I'd be. Maybe I was expecting a more dynamic sales pitch from him. He was personable enough, but I didn't get the impression he was fired up to make a difference even though he has more experience on paper. What did you think of him?"

"Well, he was certainly professional but coming from a bigger organization, with a different growth model and it being a more mature organization, I think he will expect a large marketing team and a sizable budget to go with it. He also referred to a more traditional marketing perspective that does not add any value to revenue."

"I thought much the same as you actually, yes he has been in the selling game longer than the other two but I'm not sure that's what we need right now, especially if he thinks he has an unlimited budget. What were your thoughts on Jordan? He was fluent in marketing speak, but I'm not so sure he could put it into practice. I got the impression he is more theory than practice."

"I did like, Jordan, he had great energy but wanted to change everything! His suggestions to revise our corporate identity package for instance would mean extra costs and valuable time we need to utilize for marketing, not re-branding or indeed revising all the presentation materials. All I could see were dollar signs for layout, colours, standards and icon sets. It's great to suggest a new colour palette but its costs I am unwilling to pay, and I don't believe he understood the ramifications of doing it."

"You put your finger on it perfectly, yes he had great ideas, but we need to increase sales and marketing revenue not dilute funds for a 'picture perfect logo'. My money's on Connie. She was a real fireball and obviously did her homework on us and the company. I liked her honesty and her ability to think on her feet when given a direct question on practices she would implement. So, we are in agreement? It's Connie Ryker for MarTech at Lancett ProCloud."

"Yes, she is my choice – I think she will propel us into a great inbound marketing strategy and make a real difference to our ROI. She is a better fit for a lean operation with a small budget and no marketing team army. She certainly took on board our start up marketing approach. But she and I will need to keep Miriam on side with trackable results. I'll tell Cameron to send out the relevant emails."

Dan patted Mike on the shoulder and smiled, he viewed Connie as the linchpin to increased sales and profit and ultimately achieving the venture capital company's goal of $12 million in the next five years. He saw from her interview she was enthusiastic, willing to learn, was adept at research and capable of implementing marketing strategies. As he headed out of the office his expectations of Connie's role as marketing manager grew.

***

Connie glanced at her cell as it gently vibrated on her desk. Expecting a text from Bruce with his ETA from a work conference the notification made her heart leap - it was a personal email alert. Her hand shook as she clicked the icon.

'We are pleased to offer you the position of MarTech with Lancett ProCloud. Please confirm your acceptance and date you are available to work.'

Trying to remain calm, Connie carried her cell to the elevator and pressed the down button. When the doors opened two men were inside, briefcases in hand, they nodded at her in greeting. One asked.

"Hello, is this the correct floor for Evans and Ernest?"

"Actually, you need one down."

She entered the elevator and they stood in silence as it descended one floor. The men left thanking Connie for her help. Alone, she pressed the ground floor button but could not resist doing a happy dance before the doors opened again. Once outside the office building, she excitedly text Bruce.

"I got the job, with Lancett. I am so happy. We have to celebrate tonight. What time will you be home? I am going to love giving in my notice to old Gibbons!"

She walked back and forth for while impatient for Bruce to answer. Then realizing he could be in a meeting or traveling, she went back into the building and back to her cubicle. Knowing her days were numbered at Dinosaur Inc her mood lifted. She checked her vacation day allowance and allocated sick days left and realized she could leave in eight days. Although it was tempting, the money would be welcome and to have a few days off between jobs would give her time to plan for her new position. Her cell vibrated.

"Wow! Great news, well done, I knew you would get it. Yes, celebrations tonight. Home by 7:30. Pick a restaurant. Love you X'

She replied with several X's.

***

Mike rubbed his temples and blinked. *I've been in front of this screen too long.* After Connie's acceptance of the position, he thought about methods to keep her and the rest of the team engaged. He found an article that gave him some useful points. Some he already utilized but it was always good to refresh methods.

Encourage them to get sleep:
It's hard to stay focused when you are sleep deprived. A lack of sleep will result in not only a less focused employee, but also a less motivated, less effective, and less articulate one. Encourage your team to get eight hours of sleep every night and set an example by doing it yourself. You'll see an instant improvement in morale, efficiencies, and win rates.

Educate them on your product:

As the world continues to go inbound, the way people make business and purchasing decisions have changed. To compensate, sales people must know what they are selling top to bottom. For efficiency, set up a training program to get sales reps up to speed quickly so they can better understand your product. This training will help them have more meaningful conversations with prospects.

Mike wrote: staff training days?

Set goals:

Most sales reps are motivated by reaching monthly numbers. To keep them engaged and working hard, set goals at both the team and individual level. Think about setting goals that are lofty but still attainable. With this strategy, you will see which of your reps rise to the top. A sign of a successful sales rep is someone who wants to blow his or her metrics out of the water each month, not simply reach them. Keep your eye on the reps that keep working hard once they've hit their quota; these are the ones you'll want to think about promoting or giving your larger deals to.

Mike jotted down: Are goals visible to everyone? What format would work best? How do I gauge each team member?

Instill core values:

It may be hard for your reps not to let a loss break their motivation. As a manager, don't focus too much energy on lost opportunities. Sales reps also need to be open and honest with their prospects. An extremely powerful result of honesty is trust. When your sales rep truly understands the pain points of your potential customers, your product transforms into a solution.

His next note was: research typical pain points for our industry. Find examples to showcase.

Leverage sales enablement tools:

Empower your team with tools that can help it organize, prioritize, and sell better. The last thing you want is for your sales reps to be so busy that they're overwhelmed, missing meetings, and losing track of proposals.

Once Mike had noted the bullet points, he stood up, stretched and entered the living room; his wife turned around and held out a cold beer.

"What are you a mind reader?"

"Of course I am honey. Come and sit by me and watch some mind-numbing TV to relax that brain of yours."

He kissed her on the cheek, took a long swallow of the cold beer and exhaled. The next morning Connie would start at Lancett ProCloud and he knew he would need to be rested. *Follow the article's advice and sleep!*

Mike was the first to arrive at the office and set down a notepad on his desk. Once his computer was turned on he created a spreadsheet and entered the team member names down one column, next he made headings and on the far-right goal figures. It was not until Cameron knocked on his door did he realize how much time had passed. The office was full, and everyone engaged in his or her work.

"Morning, Mike, I have Connie in my office, we are just going through the usual paperwork, so I thought I would ask where you want her once she has filled in all the forms?"

"Hi, Cameron, yes send her over to me and I can walk her around and introduce her to everyone."

A while later a gentle knock sounded on Mike's door. He turned to see Connie dressed in smart but casual clothes and a tentative smile on her lips.

"Do come in, Connie, good to see you. Now I promise not to bombard you with too much information on your first day. Let's grab a coffee and then you can meet the team."

"That would be great, thanks, Mike. I'm really excited to be here. Coffee sounds good."

Connie was pleasantly surprised to find that there was no vending machine but a couple of real coffee machines in the communal kitchen. There were tables and chairs but also sofas placed looking out of the large window.

"Wow, this is nice. I've been drinking vending machine coffee. This is a nice space, Mike."

"We like to encourage proper breaks for coffee and lunch, Connie; sitting at your desk eating a sandwich is discouraged. We also use this space for more informal meetings or brainstorming."

A young man and woman entered the room.

"Good morning, I'd like to introduce Connie Ryker. She is our new MarTech Manager. Connie this is Ethan and Mia, they are part of the sales team along with Noah."

"Hi, nice to meet you, Mike has told us you have a new marketing strategy that is going to revolutionise our marketing."

"Well, I wouldn't say revolutionise, Ethan but yes I have some ideas on a strategy that I feel will make a significant difference."

"Don't let Ethan spook you, Connie, he likes to see what new people can offer up front."

"Thanks, Mia I know I have some large expectations to realize but feel everyone has a part to play in it and want to work with everyone to make it work."

"See you two later for a proper greet and meet. Now Connie, let's go and say hello to Greg and his team."

"Is that the Greg I met when I came for the interview?"

"Yes, he is the product manager and a tech wizard."

Connie recognized Greg as he stood looking over a man's shoulder. A complicated array of figures flickered on the screen.

"Hi Greg, I think you know Connie from a couple of weeks ago."

"Yes, hello again Connie, welcome aboard."

"Thanks Greg."

"This chap is Mark; he develops the upgrades to enterprise versions of our software and then installs onsite. Over here are Rachel and Colin, who monitor and resolve technical issues within the cloud-based version. We all deal with customer queries and explain the mechanics of the system."

Connie greeted each member of the tech team. *I will need to sit down with them all and get my head around the ins and outs of this system.* She made a mental note of their names, feeling excited to learn more in-depth.

"Now I can show you your work station and let you settle in for an hour or so. If you need anything just shout, okay?"

"Thanks, Mike that would be great."

The office was compiled of seating areas much like the communal kitchen with monitors on raised stands and low storage units. Mike directed Connie to a desk with a glass partition on two sides. It held two ergonomic chairs, one with a normal looking seat and back but the other with a ball to sit on and also a small twin seat couch.

"This looks different, Mike."

"We were not sure of your preference for seating so gave you a choice; you can test them all out and see which ones work best for you. If you want all three then that's fine too. The computer here is connected to the main frame so everyone can share information etc. You also have a laptop, which you can take home if you wish to work from there on occasion or if you are out on site. We will issue you a company cell phone and a parking pass tomorrow. See how this space works for you, if you want to move elsewhere that's not a problem."

"It is certainly very different from what I am used to, Mike, I had a small cubical before."

"That must have been awful. We have found it is more productive to have a more flexible working space. We encourage everyone to utilize the space and not feel confined to a desk all day. Here are your passwords for logging on. Now I have a couple of calls to make. If you have questions ask Mia, Ethan or Noah."

Connie thanked Mike again and looked around. The office space was bright, modern and welcoming, the complete opposite of the grey cubicles and oppressive mood she had left. She tried out the different seating, logged into her computer and clicked on the various links. Mia came over with a coffee a while later.

"How's it going? Is your brain fried yet?"

"There is a lot to take in, Mia but I think I have most of it figured out."

"Have you got any questions?"

"Well, I do have a couple on this sharing link, how do I connect to one person rather than everyone?"

Mia clicked on a couple of icons and showed Connie the procedure. She also gave Connie a quick tutorial on several other software applications, just as they finished a message popped up in the middle of the screen.

'Marketing meeting in 10 minutes – Space 1.'

Connie's questioning look made Mia smile. Oh right you need to know the spaces. We have various areas where we hold group meetings. Near the kitchen and its sitting space is for informal staff meetings, just to your left along that large window is space 1 and over there next to Dan's office is space 2. We don't have a board room as such. Any private meetings are held either in Mike's office or Dan's. The only traditional type office is along that corridor and is Miriam's domain."

"So, we go to the space and sit around? It seems very casual."

"Dan feels a more relaxed atmosphere is conducive to productivity. Staff do not feel tied to a desk or disconnected to everyone else."

"Well, I am certainly enjoying the openness after working in a cubicle for years. Why does Miriam have an office then?"

"From what I have heard she insisted on having a 'proper' office, something to do with financial records requiring security, so Dan had the office constructed for her. She can be prickly so tread carefully."

"Thanks, Mia forewarned is forearmed. Now we should get to that meeting."

They walked over and met Mike, Ethan and Noah at space 1.

"Good morning, I hope you are finding your way around Connie?"

"Yes, thank you. Mia helped with a few things."

Sales Cycles & Customer Leads

"Excellent, now I think we need to discuss two main concerns to get you on board, Connie. Firstly, our sales cycle is too long; it can be from three to six months and sometimes even as long as nine months, this needs to be shortened and I would like you to come up with a plan for achieving that. Secondly, we have to deal with multiple decision makers in regard to the sale and implementation of our programs, can you give any insight into how to make that process smoother?"

"These are intriguing problems to have, Mike I will work on them. I will need to understand the complexities of how you approach new customers and investigate the current sales cycle."

"Great we can give you figures and examples to help you with that. Our other concerns are to get more meaningful leads and make our numbers on a quarterly basis. We are open to any new ideas you put forward Connie."

KPI or Key Performance Indicators

"Thank you, Mike I know I have my work cut out for me but am more than willing to take up the challenge. Initially, I want everyone to be a part of the new inbound marketing structure I am planning to implement, which will include branding, KPI or key performance indicators, revenue growth and in-depth interaction with existing and potential customers."

"Sounds like you have a firm idea on how to proceed Connie, does anyone have any questions?"

"Could you explain the KPI, I'm not sure what that is exactly."

"Of course, Ethan, a KPI is a key performance indicator or in essence a performance measurement, which evaluates the success of an organization or a particular activity within in, such as projects, programs, products or other initiatives. We can use this system to monitor success in repeated, periodic achievement of operational or strategic goals. KPI's can be used for any department measuring performance improvement, so one for sales initiatives will differ for one, say for finance. One option is to apply a management framework such as a balanced scorecard. In its simplest form it is:

Communicate what we are trying to accomplish

Align the day-to-day work that everyone is doing with strategy

Prioritize projects, products and services

Measure and monitor progress towards strategic targets.

"Wow it seems more complicated than I envisioned."

"It really isn't that complicated, Ethan. I can lay out a few examples, which will probably help."

"As you are probably aware, Dan is more concerned with achieving financial and sales goals so how would we set about setting those goals within this inbound marketing structure?"

Revenue Growth Goals

"Well, Mike the biggest challenges marketers face today is how to set and measure goals for their departments. For SaaS companies specifically, marketing teams are tasked with lead generation, sales-pipeline contribution, and revenue generation — or what is commonly called pipeline marketing. With the Lancett ProCloud system, where organizations do not need to install and run applications on their own computers or their data centers, we have eliminated the expense of hardware acquisition, provisioning and maintenance, as well as software licensing, installation and support to a section of our customer base. So, to calculate these goals, we must work backward from our revenue-growth goals and the percentage of those goals that the marketing department is expected to source. From there, we apply our funnel conversion-rate metrics to create a model that will provide visibility into how many leads our team will need to generate at each stage of the funnel, along with the amount of website traffic needed to meet those numbers.

Think about it the way award-winning copywriter and content marketer Kathryn Aragon thinks about her marketing goals, "I always start with my end goal, and work backwards. Where do I ultimately want to be? What do I want to be doing? And why does it matter?" This process can be further refined by breaking the model down by both buyer persona and marketing channel. This breakdown will help us gain insight into the annual contract value (ACV) and conversion rates of specific marketing channels. Through these insights, we'll be able to pinpoint the most effective ways to acquire new customers."

Inbound Marketing

"So how does this inbound marketing work?"

"It is a marketing strategy, which aids capital efficiency. In fact, it has been reported that recent SaaS IPOs have been two times more VC-dollar-efficient than their predecessors due in large part to the shifting dynamics of the marketing and sales organizations as channels of customer acquisition making them substantially more efficient. Once goals and budgets are established, we can begin to explore our lead generation and pipeline marketing options. By utilizing inbound, content, and lifecycle marketing, we can aid our repeatable customer acquisition process. Inbound marketing has become a cornerstone of successful SaaS marketing for four reasons:

- Lower cost of customer acquisition
- Allows the business to scale
- Shortens sales cycle
- Increases customer retention

"What measures can we take now, Connie?"

"The first step is creating content on the website that will drive highly qualified traffic to it, so we need to start blogging. While it may be intimidating to blog on a regular basis, it's absolutely attainable. Posts don't need to be long and we can also include videos, slides, or infographics. I would like to have meetings with everyone on this as we need to include all aspects of the company, its products and staff. It is important, and I understand, we need to define our buyer personas, as well as the journey they go through from the awareness to decision stages of buying our product. I read that HubSpot found businesses with blogs that have accumulated at least 51 posts, see 53 percent more traffic than blogs with 20 to 50 posts. The second step is creating content that will help convert qualified prospects into leads by leveraging premium (gated) content. Premium content offers aid in converting visitors into leads at the top of funnel. Content can also be used to nurture leads further down the funnel by creating different assets that align with the buyer's journey."

"This is an excellent start, Connie. How do we track these buyer's journeys?"

"Mia, a good question, we will do this by carefully documenting it to ensure we are crafting content that will help address the needs and concerns of our prospect at these crucial junctures. Look at this diagram; it is the buyer journey engagement model for any B2B organization. Well, it at least covers the major cycles of how an educated buyer would review their needs, either online or offline by attending events, tradeshows or vendor events. Typically, a buyer should think about attending a Gartner/IDC or Small BNI event to know about a product or service. Then what they or the decision maker will usually do is to review and discuss internally with their team members and decision makers a strategy. This will engage either their Technical (TDM) and/ or Business Decision Makers (BDM).

Buyer Journey

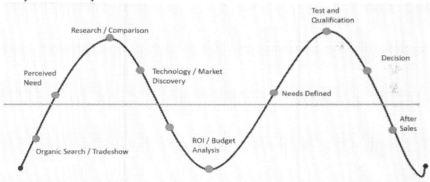

Content Promotion

"We also need to keep in mind content promotion, as publishing content alone is not enough to be successful. We must also make sure our content reaches the right audience beyond organic search. With social media publishing at a base level, it's important we promote our content through at least one key social media channel. For most B2B companies this includes: • LinkedIn • Twitter • Facebook • Google+. Using social media for content promotion increases the reach of our marketing efforts. Share and re-share new (and old) blog posts, content offers, and videos on a regular basis. Establishing a cadence in content promotion on social media can be very effective. While the life of a Tweet, LinkedIn post, or Facebook post varies, they all remain short lived — especially Tweets. We should not be afraid to post the same piece of content multiple times. In addition to using social media channels for content promotion, we need to find our buyer personas' digital watering hole to generate leads. We can do this by answering questions on Quora, sharing articles on industry-related blogs and forums, and relentless focus on adding value to the conversations in which we want our company to participate."

"Would we use paid promotion then?"

"Yes we can, Noah. It is a great way to get our content in front of our buyer personas and accelerate our content efforts. The two most effective channels, I believe, from some research I have done, are LinkedIn and Facebook. In addition to promoting Facebook posts to extend the reach of our content, we can create targeted ads, where we target people who'll love our business by location, demographics, interests, behaviors and connections. We also need to utilize influencer outreach. As influencers likely receive lots of requests, it's important to build a repertoire with them. I found a recommendation for this. We can follow Andrew Gale's four-step framework for influencer outreach. In summary it is pre-engage, personalize your email (ego boost), show you appreciate the post (ego boost) and how your post is going to make the influencer's even better (value boost), offer or give something for free (value/ego boost).

Noah nodded as Connie continued.

"Your hope for the influencer contribution is to help tell a story by focusing more on the story of the pain point. In other words, the problem they are having and then slowly show them options and eventually start showing the benefits of our solution for the buyer versus our own company story (at least do not focus on your company story as of yet). You need to put the buyer in the centre of our story and echo his pain/need of the solution and slowly from their advice educate them on how to fix it."

"Lastly, I would also encourage guest blogging, which goes hand-in-hand with influencer outreach and building our blog audience. In essence we guest blog on established blogs. Similar to influencer outreach, this can take time, but by actively commenting, sharing, and engaging with the authors and content of the blogs on which we'd like to appear, we can establish a connection prior to making a guest request."

"So are we all onboard Connie's plan?"

Connie was relieved that Mia, Noah and Ethan all nodded to Mike's query. She realized they needed to think about optimization and understood she had to implement making tweaks to the process. She knew it was increasingly more critical to have a system to track activities, deal progress, and close rates accurately. Having a CRM would not only allow other members of the team to access the contacts but would also help the sales reps keep track of what they have covered with each prospect. With such a tracking tool they could ensure each conversation was meaningful and engaging. By also leveraging the CRM tasks and reminders that could be set for the team. She knew she needed to devise a follow-up schedule that would work and that the reps could follow. *It will help everyone effectively manage all of their leads at once and ensure that nothing slips through the cracks.*

"I think we have made an excellent start and Connie thank you for your in-depth explanations. Whatever you need in terms of information or assistance we are all keen to give, am I right team?"

Again, everyone nodded, and Mia gave Connie a friendly smile. Connie walked to the kitchen and poured a large coffee. The pressure was on and she needed to keep pace with Mike and Dan's expectations. Back at her work space she opened a spread sheet and an information link headed CRM. With the definition on one side and the working sheet on the other she began creating a strategic plan.

'Customer relationship management (CRM) is a term that refers to practices, strategies and technologies that companies use to manage and analyze customer interactions and data throughout the customer lifecycle, with the goal of improving business relationships with customers, assisting in customer retention and driving sales growth. CRM systems are designed to compile information on customers across different channels -- or points of contact between the customer and the company -- which could include the company's website, telephone, live chat, direct mail, marketing materials and social media. CRM systems can also give customer-facing staff detailed information on customers' personal information, purchase history, buying preferences and concerns.'

'CRM software consolidates customer information and documents into a single CRM database, so business users can more easily access and manage it. The other main functions of this software include recording various customer interactions (over email, phone calls, social media or other channels, depending on system capabilities), automating various workflow processes such as tasks, calendars and alerts, and giving managers the ability to track performance and productivity based on information logged within the system.'

She listed various options to extend the company's reach:

- Advertise to audiences we've never previously targeted
- Create products that will target new audiences – what would this entail?
- Constantly use imagery that associates with a target customer's perceptions
- Give rewards to loyal customers?
- Partner with other companies – who?
- Expansion beyond state lines?

A couple of hours later her grumbling stomach was too much of a distraction and Connie rolled her stiff shoulders and rubbed her eyes. She realized that the office was unusually quiet. As she looked around she could not see anyone apart from Mia and Noah in the seating area adjacent to the kitchen. She walked over to them.

"What did I miss, where is everyone?"

"Lunch break, we were going to give you another five minutes then come and rescue you. You were so focused you didn't hear me talk to you."

"I'm sorry Noah, once I get into something I go into my own world. Well I need to grab some lunch then. Thanks guys."

Noah and Mia gave her friendly smiles and returned to their discussion. Connie grabbed her purse and left the building. The sun was warm on her face and the Froth or Not? sign glowed from across the road. Well that's the closest place and I know the lattes are good, now to try the food. Inside there was a queue at the counter and most of the tables were full. Connie waited in line and browsed the sandwich list as she waited. After ordering a Brie, grape and apple on pumpernickel sandwich with a caramel coffee she stood to one side. Looking around she recognised the man at the far table. Again, he was talking to the laptop with earplugs in. *I wonder what he does all day. Does he even have an office?* With her sandwich and coffee in hand she sat on an adjacent table to the man and took a large bite. Her stomach growled in anticipation. She looked up fleetingly hoping no one else had heard it but the man gave her a smile and lifted his coffee mug in salute. Connie gave a weak smile – *how embarrassing.*

"How did the interview turn out, if I may ask?"

"Oh, I got the job it's with the company across the road there, Lancett ProCloud."

"Well that is excellent news, congratulations. What are you doing there?"

"I am their new MarTech - Marketing Technology Manager. I have some large goals to achieve; I just hope I am up to it. I can talk the talk but now I've been put in charge of achieving those goals I have to admit I am feeling rather out of my depth."

"Sounds interesting, I have some experience in marketing maybe you could use me as a sounding board? If you want to that is."

"That is very kind of you, sorry I don't even know your name, I'm Connie Ryker."

"You can call me Mr. G. Nice to meet you formally Connie. So, what is your first goal?"

"Well I could say everything but maybe I can restrict it to one or two, I discussed at this morning's meeting."

"All right this sounds interesting, let's talk on these two goals first."

Connie explained the two points she had raised in the meeting and Mr. G answered.

Customer Life Cycle

"What you are proposing sounds like lifecycle marketing."

"Okay, can you explain that for me, it sounds intriguing?"

"Of course, customer life cycle is the progression of steps a customer goes through when considering, purchasing, using, and maintaining loyalty to a product or service. In essence it is sending the right message to the right person at the right time, incorporating leads and customers alike. The typical enterprise customer will have 10 – 30 interactions with a company before buying. Due to the upsell and cross-sell after the sale, more than half of the customer's revenue potential will occur after the customer begins to pay."

"So, a SAAS company needs to engage prospects and customers across their entire lifecycle."

"Exactly right, Connie, you catch on quickly. However, this is a difficult proposition, and to do it effectively marketers have to understand the two speeds of lifecycle marketing. The first speed, **"speed one,"** refers to time-sensitive campaigns capitalizing on social trends and new-product-feature announcements and are ultimately geared towards driving the most qualified traffic through the funnel as quickly as possible. In the SaaS environment this can be best understood as a free trial or demo campaign to a highly qualified lead. The second speed, **"speed two,"** is a broader content strategy that will help attract and convert leads that are not yet ready to buy or enter into a trial. This type of marketing helps to fill your funnel with leads that are not as ready to buy, are still in the awareness or consideration phases and can be nurtured with engaging content. Do you get the idea?"

"Yes, I do. I can utilize the products we already have with several new versions that are coming up in the next month or so."

"Just keep in mind, while these two speeds have the power to amplify each other, when they are used incorrectly diffusion can occur and they become less effective, just like two gears working in tandem. Think of it this way, in a traditional marketing and sales model that overemphasizes speed-one marketing alone, leads will drop off over time. However, by amplifying marketing efforts between speed one and speed two, marketers can better capture revenue from leads that may have dropped off over the same delayed or extended sales cycles. Here let me know you in a graph." Connie watched Mr. G draw on a piece of notepaper.

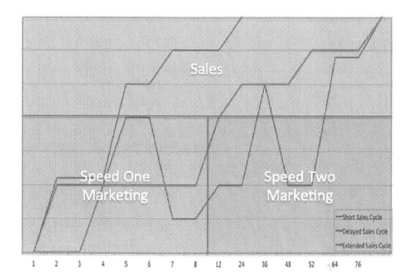

"What makes this type of marketing possible is the realization that not all visits, leads or even customers are created equal, and you have to analyze their behavior to know how to categorize them into speed one or speed two, or even to identify ongoing upsell opportunities.'

"That is so helpful, thank you so much. I would love to talk more but I really need to get back. Maybe next time I can quiz you some more the price of a coffee?"

"It would be my pleasure, I'm here a lot so don't be afraid to come over. If I have a conference call you may have to wait a while though."

"Well, of course I don't want to monopolize you. Thank you again."

Connie stood, and they shook hands. She was buzzing with excitement as she walked back to her new office. Mr. G sat at his usual table and jotted down a few notes then reflected a while before writing down some more.

With Bruce away on a work trip, Connie didn't want to bother cooking that evening and the soup on offer at Froth or Not? she had spied earlier would make for a warm and hearty meal for one. She entered the cozy store and smiled at the server and ordered a large bowl of roasted potato and leek soup with a pitta filled with chili chicken and salad. A familiar face smiled at her from across the room.

"Mr. G do you ever leave here, is there some secret you are keeping?"

"Well, the only secret is my sister owns this establishment and it makes for a more conducive working environment for me."

"That explains it then, free coffee and food all day in a warm and cozy spot. I would love it too."

"Are you on your way home?"

"Actually, I dropped in to buy my supper, my husband is away, and I wasn't going to cook."

"Would you like to continue our earlier discussion then, if it is convenient of course?"

"Are you serious? I would be grateful for your time and will buy you that coffee."

"Excellent, come over once you have your supper. We can chat while you eat if you like."

Connie gave Mr. G her full attention as he went into more detail on lifestyle marketing.

Marketing Qualified Lead (MQL)

"So to continue our previous discussion, you need to harness lead to MQL. Speed-two marketing tactics are ideal for nurturing a buyer from a lead to a marketing- or sales-qualified lead. The decentralized and content-heavy nature of speed-two campaigns are ideal to engage a contact over an extended sales cycle. Then, by analyzing his or her digital body language (viewing a pricing page multiple times or using a pricing calculator) you can shift that contact into a speed-one nurture stream and encourage him or her to sign up for a free trial."

Mr. G jotted down some notes and continued. "Let's look at a couple of methods, firstly, a free trial. With a clearly defined beginning and ending, a free-trial campaign is an ideal time for a "speed one" focused campaign that can be centred on the key features of your product and how it can help solve the pain points of the prospect. By analyzing common conversion activities and information gathered earlier on in the buyer's journey (perhaps from your speed-two efforts) you can then tailor the speed-one messaging to the unique needs of your persona to drive higher conversion rates. Secondly, customer upsell, which is when someone converts to a paid customer, continually nurture him or her (speed two) until he or she indicates he or she is ready to upgrade, then fire up the speed-one upsell campaign."

"So, if I understand this correctly we identify leads and customers and use these methods to target them?"

"Correct, Connie. At the end of the day, winning lifecycle-marketing strategies will be those that provide your leads and customers with the information they need, when they need it. By understanding the core principles and messaging behind these two speeds of marketing and combining them with digital body language and product-usage information, you can be sure that you're delivering this information to your prospects with the right message at the right time."

"So, a free trail would be my initial plan?"

"For SaaS companies, speed-one marketing strategies can include a free trial. While much of the focus is on driving leads into a free trial and further nurturing them with email communications, it isn't enough. You must be able to look further down the funnel and see the impact that your free-trial marketing efforts have over the entire lifetime of a customer. The messaging and communication within your free trial should be customized to the unique needs of your buyer personas, the exact same way your marketing messages got them into the free trial in the first place. For example, an e-commerce company could change its free-trial messaging for someone, who is just starting out with e-commerce compared to someone, who is an experienced e-commerce user. This is because the key features to which he or she needs to be introduced will be entirely different. Advanced users might be more interested in the reports they can run on their store performance, while someone, who is just getting started needs to be instructed on how to add a product to his or her store to begin with."

"I can see I have a lot of homework to do to get to know the current customers and identify potential ones for Lancett. You have given me such a boost to my confidence, Mr. G, thank you."

"My pleasure, I can continue if you have more time but totally understand if you have information overload."

"Not at all, I was feeling guilty about keeping you."

"Well, then let's wrap up this method and then we can say job well done. Once personalized free-trial experiences are in place for each of your buyer personas, you can analyze the results. Instead of looking at a temporal analysis of your free-trial conversion rates and lifetime value, monthly recurring revenue and churn, analyze all these different factors with a better understanding of the actual users behind the numbers. You will also see how they are converting in your trial and how valuable they are to your business over their entire lifetime. To accomplish this, you can use a cohort analysis to improve user on-boarding and free-trial conversion rates. Many SaaS companies use cohort analysis to measure customer lifetime value, revenue per customer and churn to ensure their customer-acquisition strategy is effective. One of the best ways to understand and optimize free trials is to break them down by different buyer personas. This analysis can have a profound impact not only on the effectiveness of your marketing efforts and which customers can be acquired the most efficiently, but also on your product itself and which users are finding the most value."

Connie jotted down several key points before Mr. G continued.

Speed Two Marketing Initiatives

"Let's look at speed two marketing initiatives. You will come across leads that are a perfect fit for your product but aren't ready to buy. That doesn't mean they won't ever buy. By implementing a broader content strategy through a series of small conversations, you can help nurture and onboard new customers. For these customers, enrol them in contextually relevant drip nurturing campaigns. Let's say for example, one vice president recommends setting up a drip campaign to resell the value prop, re-educate, and offer incentives for users to come back. His campaigns go as far as creating a 12-month drip campaign. The frequency will depend on the trial length, but it typically goes: Day 1, 4, 7, 14, 21, 30 & 45 days, and then every two weeks after that.

Another method is user onboarding. Often, software-based solutions require coaching, education, and insights for your personas to experience the value and maximize a given functionality. When it comes to lifecycle campaigns, you want to create your strategy around key moments in the lifecycle. Your emails should convey value and be as helpful as possible, rather than be a vehicle for self-promotion. To begin, spend time identifying the flow of your on-boarding process and align your emails with the actions you want recipients to take for them to become activated users. Write these down, Connie."

"There are many different lifecycle emails you could employ, but to get you started, here are four of the quintessential emails you should be leveraging:

• The welcome email • The getting started email • The milestone email • The upsell email

Welcome Email

Your welcome email should be actionable, informative, and clear. While you want recipients to engage by viewing or clicking on it the goal of your welcome email is to move users through the onboarding process (and get them to use your product).

Best practices:

• If you include an introduction, make it brief. • Build momentum; your email should reflect what you want users to do next. • Include a clear, compelling, and enticing call to action.

Getting Started Email

Your getting started email takes the welcome email a step further. Now it's time for them to dive into your software. The goal of this email is to move them from the inbox to the app or platform as efficiently as possible. The sooner users take action, the sooner they'll garner value from your product.

Best practices:

• Focus on benefits, not features. • Include a deep link; don't make users jump through hoops to get to the feature you suggested they check out. • Use data to your advantage by not asking people to do something they've already completed with your software, such as setting up profiles. • Educate, educate, educate.

Milestone Email

The milestone email should reinforce the value your software is delivering by speaking to the recipient's accomplishment. In doing so, you make your customers feel good about their experiences and get them excited to get back into your product.

Best practices:

• Make users feel awesome for using your product by employing upbeat, positive language. • Use micro-CTAs to deepen your relationship, such as referring a friend or following on Twitter.

Upsell Email

At this point, customers have been using your product for some time. Now is a perfect opportunity to add even more value for your customers.

While "upsell" generally holds a negative connotation, many users welcome these emails. If executed strategically, customers truly appreciate you letting them know about something great they may have missed before.

Best practices:

• Again, focus on the benefits versus the features. • Weave an upsell through a communication you would have sent anyway (i.e. product update, shipping confirmation, etc.). • Include personalization so the recipient feels good about his or her relationship with you and recognizes that you're paying attention to his or her experience.

There are many more on-boarding emails that you should strongly consider adding to your lifecycle marketing and customer success strategies. These examples are designed to get you started and onboard customers sooner, rather than later. Does this give you enough information to get you started, Connie?"

"Oh, my goodness this is pure gold to me, thank you so much Mr. G. I think just buying you a coffee pales into insignificance. I should be taking you out for a fancy dinner."

"I don't think that is necessary, Connie, it is a joy to converse with someone, who is not only interested but totally engaged in this methodology. Now, if you will excuse me I do need to connect for an international conference call. I am happy to give you pointers any time. Have a good night."

"Connie resisted hugging Mr. G, he had given her so much fuel for her inbound marketing strategy, but a cup of coffee and a hand shake were all she could give right now. With his help she felt confident she would make a difference to Lancett ProCloud and reach Dan and Mike's targets.

Once she was at home she read through her notes and created a document with bullet points, graphs and strategic targets. At eleven o'clock she gave in to tiredness and fell into bed dreaming of her future success.

The following morning, Connie couldn't wait to begin her plan and arrived forty-five minutes early. Luckily, Mike was just pulling into the parking lot.

"Well, there is an early bird, couldn't you sleep?"

"Actually, I slept really well but once I heard songbirds outside my window, I was wide awake. I have a plan for the website I want to work on."

"Okay, sounds good. Let me know when you are ready to share." Mike held the door open for her and Connie strode into the office space eager to begin. With further research given to her by Mr. G, she read through the steps required for website optimization on a link he'd written down for her. She clicked the link and read eagerly.

Website Optimization

The primary objective of your website is to attract visitors, turn them into trial users or leads, and win those users as customers. Your website needs to be an online lead generation machine that is fine-tuned to convert and engage visitors. To do so, you need to keep visitors on your website longer; the longer they explore, the greater the opportunity for conversion. We'll cover how particular design elements can keep visitors around longer and turn them into paying customers.

5 Must-Have SaaS Web Elements

Value Proposition

As a rule of thumb, you should aim to communicate your value proposition within ten seconds. This is a statement on your homepage that clearly defines your solution for your personas and why it is the optimal choice over competitors in your industry.

muHive, a customer-engagement solution, went through multiple rounds of site revamps. Prior to beginning the process, the team received feedback that its homepage didn't clearly state what the company does, resulting in a high bounce rate. To remedy this, the team created and tested different copy options. An effective value proposition can increase your ROI by approximately 15 percent. Ultimately, muHive was able to decrease the bounce rate of the homepage through a clear, concise value proposition.

Pricing Page

As buyers spend more time researching before contacting sales, the pricing page of SaaS websites have reached critical importance in the buyers' journey for enterprise SaaS sales and especially for companies, who have a lower monthly subscription cost or annual contract value. Why? Because it's the place where people go to decide if they want to use (and pay for) your service or not. For SaaS companies, it means you need to:

• Have a pricing page. • Make it easy to find and navigate. • Include different packages or options that speak to your buyer personas.

When designing your pricing page to its full potential, keep these lessons in mind:

• Create different tiers of plans that speak to each buyer persona you are targeting • Structure pricing that scales with usage through value metrics but keep this simple enough so customers understand what value they'll actually derive from your solution. • Don't skimp on design or user experience, but don't go over the top. Make the design of your pricing page clear, concise, and specific.

Free Trial/Demo Calls to Action

Take advantage of your inherent ability to let your potential customers use your product before they buy it. An effective free trial can increase lead qualification and lower customer acquisition costs.

The first step to getting visitors into a free trial is to promote it on your site. You can do so by creating and placing calls to action for the free trial/demo throughout your website, particularly on your homepage. A free trial/demo CTA needs to be strategically designed or no one will ever convert into a user. In fact, the conversion rate from visitor to trial is just 8.4 percent.

Bizible's solution for increasing free-demo users was to implement the persistent demo form. It added a global request-a-demo form on every page, including the blog. It leveraged HubSpot's inline form, which also fills in your information if you've downloaded content previously. This addition increased demo requests by 40 percent.

Other ways to increase free trial/demo conversions:

• Add "free" to your CTA copy. • Have the form scroll with the visitor. Make the form short. • Test different colour buttons. • Add a human element (imagery). Include social proof.

Pop-Ups

Pop-up and exit intent forms are a great way to capture leads and actionable, direct feedback from your website visitors.

For example, Office Drop was able to increase its pricing-page conversion rate by 40 percent by incorporating user feedback. It asked users, who stayed on its pricing page for 40 seconds or more, questions through a pop-up.

Exit intent pop-ups capture leads from content offers and build your subscriber list or newsletter. The key to success with these pop-ups is to ensure they are presented when users do not feel their experience is being interrupted, but rather enhanced. According to mageworx, the best time to display a pop-up is 60 seconds after a website visitor has entered your site.

Live Chat

Add live chat to your site to allow visitors to reach out directly to a sales rep at their convenience. Dave Rigotti of Bizible has recounted that although Bizible's live chat does not generate a large number of leads every month, the leads sourced through the live chat contribute more than 25 percent of its new monthly recurring revenue. That makes it one of the business's top three sales channels in terms of revenue generation. This is a great example of effective pipeline marketing and a strategy all SaaS companies should consider investing in.

Conversational Marketing

Live Chat and Chatbots have become one of the more lead conversion effective techniques as of late. Pay close attention to companies that start to combine Sales playbooks with Chatbots and start building an automated escalation process to insides sales managers. This is an easy approach to implement and it can help immediately to prove that you can bridge marketing and sales while applying this tactic.

Watch for what HUBSPOT have been doing lately with their Chat and Unified conversation box. Also, with what Drift and other companies have been bringing to the marketing place.

We live in a world where we carry our phones everywhere and send messages constantly. People love messaging because it's on-demand, real-time, and actually feels like a conversation.

Now, think about the way B2B businesses communicate with their customers. Does it look anything like the way people actually like to communicate?

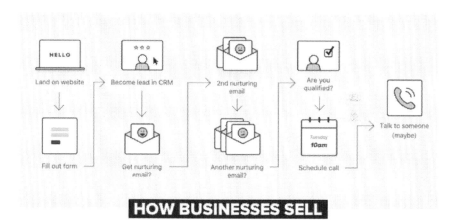

HOW BUSINESSES SELL

Nope. Instead, the best-in-class B2B approaches to communicating with customers looks more like this:

Unlike traditional marketing, conversational marketing uses targeted, real-time messaging and intelligent chatbots instead of lead capture forms — that way leads never have to wait for follow-ups and can engage with your business when it's convenient for them.

A single marketer can set up a chatbot that automatically greets hundreds or thousands of visitors and asks them qualifying questions. The best part? Once your sales reps connect their calendars, chatbots can automatically book demos for them. There's nothing like waking up to a calendar full of high-quality meetings that got booked while you were asleep.

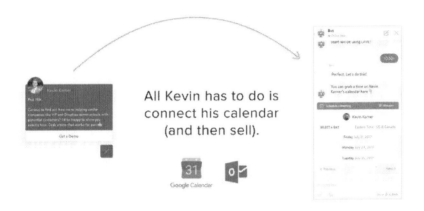

All Kevin has to do is connect his calendar (and then sell).

Conversational Marketing Is the Playbook for the Modern World

Conversational marketing finally gives sales and marketing teams the playbook they need to create the on-demand buying experience customers have come to expect.

Fortunately, making the switch doesn't have to be a massive undertaking

The Conversational Marketing Methodology Phases

Conversational marketing is built on a proven three-stage process we call capture, qualify, connect. It enables companies to take people from website visitors to qualified leads to customers faster than ever using real-time selling.

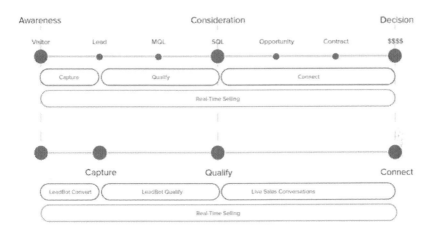

4 Ways to Optimize Your Website

With these elements in place, it's important to continue to optimize your website over time by running strategic A/B tests. To do this:

• Begin with a foundation of analytics and define reporting requirements, the tools (platform) needed, and the personnel structure required to undertake a CRO effort successfully. • Identify the key benchmarks for existing performance (visit-to-lead conversion rate, bounce rate, time on site, etc.) that you'll be measuring and form a clear and measurable hypothesis on how these can be improved. • Set clear goals on what you're hoping to achieve.

A simple and proven framework to start a program like this can be bucketing your pages into a quadrant looking at both the conversion rate and the amount of traffic each page receives.

High Traffic and High Conversions

These are your top performing pages and can be prioritized last for optimization testing. However, they've been the cornerstone of lead-generation efforts for months. Start by assessing these pages and understanding why they do well. Are they featured prominently in your navigation and driving lots of direct traffic? Are they SEO-optimized and ranking well for a high-volume search term? Are the CTAs on this page clear? Is the content so compelling that someone couldn't possibly not convert?

With this in mind, determine how these elements can be carried over to pages that aren't performing as well.

High Traffic and Low Conversions

These should be the first pages you begin to test and prioritize.

• Test imagery. Looking at a CTA will help improve the click-through rate. • Action at the top of the page is taken more than action at the bottom of the page. • Limit CTAs (ideally limited to one per page). • Evaluate content.

Low Traffic and Low Conversions

This is the toughest segment of the lot. Not only are they not driving conversions, they're also not getting traffic. It's going to take more time for those pages to reach a statistically significant volume of conversions to reach conclusions on any test.

• Figure out how to drive more traffic. • Incorporate what you've learned in your other tests.

Low Traffic and High Conversions

These should be your second priority.

• Drive more quality traffic. • Start with optimization via paid and organic search. • Improve navigation to drive more traffic.

Now that your tests are up and running, continue to measure and optimize them.

Once Connie had read through and made notes, she created a summary of the main points. These she would relate to Mike and the marketing team. She also needed the web designer to initialize and add several programs she knew were missing on the current site to make the strategy work. Confident she had all the information to hand; she walked to Mike's office and knocked on the open door.

"Come in, Connie you were certainly focused this morning. What do you have for me?"

"I would like to make some revisions to the website to enable us to utilize inbound marketing techniques."

"Are these revisions going to require significant expenditure? You know Miriam has the purse strings so to speak."

"Actually, I don't think they will be expensive in themselves, it may take Roger sometime to action them and input the necessary software, but I can go through each item with him and report the costs."

"If you could, that would be great. I know Dan is happy to give you the lead on this to some extent, but it certainly isn't carte blanch to spend without limit. If we can prove the costs will create income, we should be on safe ground."

"Thanks, Mike I will get on to that right away."

Connie found Roger sitting in front of an array of screens each one with either imagery or code scrolling on them.

"Hi, Roger this looks impressive. How do you keep track of it all?"

"It comes naturally, it's like anything the more you do it the easier it gets. What's up?"

"I would like to go through some changes I want to make to the website and track what the specific costs would be on each. Do you have time now or shall I comeback?"

"I have time now most of what you can see is automatic, I just need to input occasionally. What's the plan?"

"I've written a list, here take a look."

- Build as many links as possible to make the site rank higher
- Keyword rich content
- Concentrate on links, good code, and content
- Adding pages to encourage more traffic

- 'Blanket' keyword strategy to increase ranking on keywords whether directly related to field or not.
- Written content for backlinks
- Limit images used

Roger read through the list.

"So, we are cramming in as many keywords and backlinks as we can?"

"Yes, the more we have the more traffic – don't you think? We can utilize the SEO better that way."

"Well, I'm sure you know what you are doing. I can build more SEO and create more pages by splitting some of the existing content, will that help?"

"Sounds great, thanks Roger; I will keep you posted if I find more 'marketing' improvements."

A while later Mike approached her.

"Connie, do you have a moment?"

She turned to face Mike and smiled.

"Of course, what can I do?"

"I just had a discussion with Roger; he relayed the actions for the website you discussed with him."

"Yes, we should have a fully interactive SEO website in no time."

"I commend you for taking the initiative but maybe you are getting ahead of yourself? We do have methods in place and it might be best to improve on them first."

Connie's heart and stomach sank, *please don't say these are traditional methods, I just left another position because of that!* Her disappointment must have shown on her face as Mike quickly replied.

"I'm not saying these are not great improvements; just don't change everything overnight. Okay? Why not come into space one and we can chat?"

As they sat Connie stifled a sigh and waited for Mike to talk.

"I'm not dismissing what you are doing, Connie but I do want some effort put into the existing marketing already in place. We can't change overnight. Do you understand?"

"Yes, Mike of course, sorry I got caught up in the excitement of implementing inbound marketing and all its benefits. What so you need me to do?"

"We need to start planning for one of our annual trade shows. And it would be an excellent experience for you to have a 'hands on' role. You can use it as a research foray into our competitors and what methods they use."

Connie smiled and swallowed her disappointment. With Mike's directive ringing in her ears, Connie initially stifled her resentment of going back to basics but resolved to follow Mia and Ethan's lead regarding organizing the trade show. As with her past experience she knew it would be literature, draw prizes, fancy banners and the direction that all staff approach all and every passing attendee with a 'sales' pitch.

"Yes, it will be a good way to investigate what other companies are doing. Who's in charge of the organizing of the trade show?"

"Currently, Mia and Ethan share the load, but I really think with your insights the three of you can make something great."

"I'll go and talk to them now, Mike. Thanks."

As she walked over to Ethan and Mia, she reflected on the trade shows she had suffered at 'Dinosaur Inc' – the poor attendance, ridiculous expenditure and minimal return on the investment. *I have to make a difference to show hiring me was the right choice but maybe Mike is right, not all at once!* She made a mental note to list KPI's – Key Performance Indicators – to measure her initiatives.

Key Performance Indicators (KPIs) are measurable values used by marketing teams to demonstrate the effectiveness of campaigns across all marketing channels. ... Track your marketing goals with these marketing metrics and KPI examples.

Trade Show Success

She joined Mia and Ethan working at a series of computer screens, each one displaying an array of trade show promotional literature, a map of the venue and a booking form for a nearby hotel.

"So, what's the plan so far for this trade show?"

"Hi, Connie, well we have attended for quite a few years and have been reasonably successful in generating sales leads."

"Are the other vendors known to us?"

"Yes, quite a few are but we did notice on this year's list a couple have not signed up and two new companies are registered."

"So, we need to find out why those two didn't re-register and what specific products the new ones have compared to us."

"Oh, I didn't even think about that!"

"Well, if we are going to attract new customers, we need to know what other products are being offered and why a business has dropped out. Let's look at the new companies first. You both have better product knowledge than me, so you can guide me through it."

With a specific task to concentrate on Mia and Ethan became more enthused. For the next couple of hours, the three of them worked diligently and discovered the reasons for the non-registration and a similar product to Lancett ProCloud's from the other two companies. Armed with this information Ethan went to talk to Mike and Greg to make sure there was no conflict or cloning of the company's product line.

Connie and Mia continued to develop an eye-catching display and enrolled Roger in developing an interactive touch screen for Q&A hung on the rear wall. Mia was intrigued with this idea of Connie's.

"So, we let visitors to the booth click through the Q&A themselves?"

"Yes, it may seem odd to let them use this kind of method, but most people are intimidated by several 'sales staff' crowding them as soon as they come near the booth. This way they can click through and if they are interesting they can approach us. People like to take their time to decide on their level of interest instead of being pounced on."

"I know we have been sales motivated in past year's maybe you are right, Connie."

"I do have a couple more ideas, if that's okay?"

"Sure, let's see what you have, a fresh outlook is always good."

"Well, I know we have literature handouts but if we have the time and funds could we also hand out stickers and even wearable's or light up trinkets. If people see them they will be intrigued to visit the booth and get their own. We could number them and have a winner at the end of the show."

"Wow, what a great idea. I think we had some rubber bracelets one year that were ordered but never used as they didn't arrive until a week after the show. They're probably in storage somewhere."

"They would be perfect as long as they don't have a date on them."

"No, it was the company logo entwined with a graphic design."

"Now this idea might seem counterproductive, but I understand we work closely with a couple of firms that have complementary product lines, right?"

"Yes we do, we sometimes collaborate, why?"

"I will pass this idea by Dan and Mike but maybe we can trade leads and contact information prior to the show and invite them to our booth. I've read it is a great show booth tip in terms of ROI and doubles sales opportunities."

"Do you think that's wise? Wouldn't we be trading with our competition?"

"No, we would partner with brands selling different products and services that happen to have the same target market."

"Oh, now that sounds like a great idea. Heh, Ethan come and listen to these ideas of Connie's."

Ethan joined them, and Connie relayed her new ideas. He was impressed and thought about her next question.

"Our brand isn't easy to display so how can we make it more interesting?"

"Well, I think with the interactive screen we will have an advantage this year from past years and we could load a couple of laptops with sample programs to demonstrate the systems."

"Yes, that would work well, Ethan great idea. Not only will it generate interest but will give visitors a better understanding of our value proposition. We will need to ensure all trade show staff are well trained before the show and create a strategy going in and how they can utilize the resources provided. However, we shouldn't have the staff start a conversation with trying to sell the product first, unless a visitor is interested in it. They should begin with a sincere interest in the visitor and their company and its needs first."

"Most of us will be at the booth so we can work on the strategy together with Mike."

"Yes, sounds good, Ethan. Now do we have tickets for our best clients? We should give them a VIP experience."

"Now I hadn't thought of that either, Connie."

"What better way to wow our best clients, Mia than by getting them into one of the biggest trade shows of the year? The best part is it will likely have an automatic return on investment when they attend and have special passes. Do we have tea/coffee and snacks for the booth?"

"We usually have some refreshments, nothing fancy though. What were you thinking?"

"Well, I know that the coffeehouse across the roads does magnificent muffins and just the aroma will entice visitors. I will ask if they would be willing to bake us a large batch."

"I for one will be happy to eat them!"

"Well, Ethan they are for visitors first."

"Now, we should also decide on how we will measure the success of the show. We need to measure the marketing techniques and their effectiveness as well as ensure we follow up all leads within a day of the show. Each visitor will have engaged with multiple vendors, so we need to be contacting them as soon as possible."

"We can have a list of visitors drawn up the next morning from business cards collected and requests for more information sheets."

"Great that will give us a good start, thanks Mia."

With the trade show organization going smoothly Connie, Ethan and Mia rewarded themselves with a nice lunch at a local Italian restaurant. Connie enjoyed their company and lively banter so different from the resigned faces of Dinosaur Inc.

Chapter Three: Lessons Learned

As you embark on a new journey to convert your website and marketing asset from a fancy brochure to a real marketing asset; that is converting for you on daily, weekly and monthly basis, please take the following into consideration:

You must start with a strategy. I would like to call it a business strategy that will match your overall objective for your fiscal year. From there the marketing needs to align, so you need to figure out the proper marketing Playbook that will be allocated to the business strategy to achieve the overall business outcome.

As we have done with lot of our clients before, remember you will need a foundation and not just borrow playbooks with no marketing foundation in place, if you do so you will be creating a nightmare and a marketing train wreck that you will not be able to stop.

So here is what we would recommend:

Five Stage Process

1) Marketing Strategy Build: Sales and Marketing must agree on the persona with a max of three. Please note we are not discussing ABM (account-based marketing) yet. If you decided to go the ABM route, then check future chapters in this book. We have a full chapter on ABM.

   a. Persona Creation

   b. Buyer's Journey Canvas

   c. Editorial calendars

   d. Omni Channel Strategy

e. Keyword Strategy

f. Competitive analysis

g. Picking a marketing automation that can do at least 7 to 8 different functions from our platform. If you are dealing with 15 different marketing automations, you are setting yourself up for failure.

2) Fundamentals

a. List Segmentation if you have one

b. Social media connections

c. Database clean-up and continued review

d. Website that is not built as a traditional fancy with bills and whistles but built from an Inbound perspective.

3) Content Marketing

a. Blogs

b. eBooks

c. Whitepapers Case studies

d. Video, Video, Video (everywhere, landing pages, LinkedIn post, social media, even Instagram if you can.) website explanations, customer testimonials and so on.

e. Infographics.

4) Alignment

a. Lead Generation stages

b. Which CRM Marketing and Sales can truly adopt in their day to day operation

c. Media buy and budget on which platform

d. Reporting (we will cover more of that in future chapters)

e. What is expected as revenue attribution from Inbound marketing, versus ABM (account-based marketing) versus traditional LeadGen, versus helping the sales team work on existing opportunity that will take from six to nine months, if you are B2B organization.

Learn more about conversational marketing that includes Live Chat, Chatbots, and Sales Playbooks in our chat scripts. That will be the trend for the next few years. I am also seeing that it will eventually evolve not only in your sales and marketing department but will quickly spread in other lines of business, such as call centres/customer service or customer success departments. As well as in other lines of business such as M&A and financials and back office, it will help you grow your company exponentially.

Chapter Four – Road of Trials

With her hope that she had found some inbound marketing approaches to the trade show situation, she still had the nagging feeling her SEO for the website was not right, she visited the coffee shop midafternoon. Her mind was full of SEO articles she had read and re-read, had she made the right choices?

She mentally lists the SEO directions she had discussed and put into action with Roger.

- Build as many links as possible to make the site rank higher
- Keyword rich content
- Concentrate on links, good code, and content
- Adding pages to encourage more traffic
- 'Blanket' keyword strategy to increase ranking on keywords whether directly related to field or not.
- Written content for backlinks
- Limit images used

A tap on her shoulder brought her out of her thoughts. She looked up to see Mr. G smiling at her. She gave a weak despondent smile back.

"Well, that's not the sort of smile I usually get from you, what's going on?"

"I think I've messed up and have idea how to fix it."

"Well, I'm sure it is fixable. I'll grab a coffee and we can chat. Do you want another?"

"That would be great thanks. Chai tea please."

Connie felt slightly better knowing she could talk with Mr. G. His help previously was worth its weight in gold.

"Now here you are."

Mr. G sat opposite Connie and sipped his coffee waiting for her to start. She relayed her actions for the website SEO in detail then fell silent. Mr. G nodded and then lifted out a tablet from his briefcase.

"I understand the reasoning behind your decisions, but they are not the most up to date methods. Let's go through them one by one."

"Creating more links to rank higher is good but without analyzing the linking domain it does not give you important feedback. According to search metrics, building links is still in the top five of the most important ranking factors, but you must build links in a different manor now. Around Penguin 2.0, which was released in May of 2013, all of that changed. Nowadays, it is important to focus on the quality of links you are obtaining, rather than the quantity. Sometimes less can be more if you know how exactly to build links the proper way. Secondly, writing keyword rich content for better ranking can work but now Google uses latent semantic indexing (LSI), which was conceived around February 2004 and became more and more prominent within search through every update. With this type of indexing, the contents of a webpage are crawled by the search engine and the most common words or phrases are combined and identified as the keywords of that page. LSI also looks for synonyms that related to your target keywords. Today, it's important to optimize your page for the user experience; so in other words you do not have to place your keywords word-for-word in the content. Write the content for the user. By using synonyms and related terms, the search engines will still understand what your goal is."

"So, although I am applying SEO rich content I need to track its effectiveness and centre around a goal?"

"Yes, Connie that's correct but you should not focus on links and content alone. About five years ago, SEO used to be all about getting tons of links, good code, and okay content. These days, most of the websites that are ranking really well have a large social following. People argue whether it directly or indirectly affects rankings, but either way it does have an impact. Think of it this way, the more popular your website is socially, the more eyeballs you will draw to it. The more people see it, the more backlinks and traffic you will receive. Additionally, social media is a great way to send out content and get the traction you are looking for."

"Now I knew that social media was becoming important, why didn't I remember that?"

"You are on a steep learning curve Connie, and it takes time. Another item on your list – creating more pages – will not actually help. What you need to do is make sure you are focusing your content on quality, not quantity. If you do not have good content, you will not rank well and all those pages you created will not help your cause. Take the introduction in February 2001 of Google's Panda algorithm updates that have been getting better and better at detecting bad content. Nowadays, if you have poor content it is possible you may face a Google penalty, so make sure you are creating great content that users want to read. There is also a big misconception that higher rankings mean more search traffic. It is true that people will see your listing, but it does not mean you will get more click-through. There are a couple of reasons for this:

1. You do not have the correct keyword strategy because you are trying to rank for keywords that are unrelated to your field.

2. Your meta descriptions are not appealing and inviting for the user.

To solve these problems, I suggest you try using Google Ads to create a great keyword strategy relating to your business and be sure to use enticing meta descriptions to get people to the site. It is a good rule of thumb to think about what would entice you to click through."

"That's great advice, Mr. G as usual. I've made a mental note to research them."

"Another way to build SEO authority is to guest blog at a large scale. Before Penguin 2.0 in 2013, people used to write content, whether bad or good, to anybody that would listen, with a link back to their site. A lot of the time, it was content that had nothing to do with their actual industry; they were just trying to get a backlink. Guest blogging has changed immensely since then. Now it is important that if you do end up getting one or two guest posts here and there, that they are high authoritative, relevant websites. Guest posting on a smaller scale can be beneficial if you do it the correct, ethical way."

"So, from what you are telling me the keyword stuffing I proposed is not going to give me the results I was hoping for either?"

"Well, I can tell you that Google's own, Matt Cutts, warned us in 2007 against stuffing our pages with keywords to rank higher in the search results. Some webmasters did not take this to heart, until Google continuously came out with new algorithm updates, like Panda, every year that were meant to target bad content. Keyword stuffing is 100% against Google's webmaster guidelines and is a dangerous game. Because of Google's algorithm getting more advanced each year, you are likely to get your website penalized."

"Oh, now that wouldn't bode well with my new bosses would it!"

"You can change the priorities of the keywords and utilize them more effectively. Another point I would like to make, is that for a long time, it was okay to neglect the images on your site and still rank without using alt text and image file names to boost your page relevance. On-page SEO is more important than ever, so excluding images will prevent your website's SEO from being the best it can be. However, as search engines cannot see images on websites, it is important to give the image an alt text and relevant file name to ensure Google knows what the image is about. By not creating this text, you lose a huge opportunity to be as visible as possible online."

"Now I know that is a requirement I can instruct Roger to implement those changes. Thank you."

"Something else to avoid is getting listed in lots of directories that fill your backlinks profile. On April 24, 2012 Google released the first Penguin algorithm update, which targeted websites with unnatural links and has since gotten more sophisticated. It is important that webmasters and marketing ensure they are not just getting a ton of links from low-quality spammy directory website. You should, instead focus on niche related directories that have strict standards and high authority that will benefit your personas by getting quality information about your company's mission and website. It is pretty easy to decide which directories are natural and which are unnatural, so take the time to investigate them. I hope this gives you some direction, Connie."

"Once again you have been so helpful, and I am in your debt. Thank you so much. Oh goodness, I must get back I had no idea how much time had passed. See you soon, I hope."

Connie ran from the coffee shop waving as she exited the warm atmosphere and a new revitalized enthusiasm.

She went straight to Roger and asked him to stop his previous directive.

"Roger, we need to rethink and get this website more productive. The first is something called muHive, a controlled automation framework for real time customer engagement."

Connie watched Roger's face light up as he turned and smiled.

"Oh, now this is more like it, I have been itching to use more dynamic programs. What's next?"

"We need a pricing page; I will get the sales team to work on the figures and a 'free trail' option, which I'm sure the techs can devise."

"This is going to be exciting stuff, Connie."

"So, in the hopes I am not talking out of turn can I go through what I know about a SAAS pricing page with you? Just kick me to the kerb if you feel I'm talking down to you."

"A refresher is always a good thing, Connie. Fire away and I'll interject when I can."

"Okay then, well from what I have researched the anatomy of pricing pages highlight best practices in aligning products, pricing, design and messaging to help educate our site visitors and will enable our sales process."

Roger nodded in agreement.

"They should generally adhere to this basic structure." Connie sketched out a diagram.

Basic	Pro	Enterprise	Custom
High Level Value Prop (Who it is for)	High Level Value Prop (Who it is for)	High Level Value Prop (Who it is for)	Beyond Basic, Pro and Enterprise OR a Customized Version
Threshold (# of Users, Transactions)	Threshold (# of Users, Transactions)	Threshold (# of Users, Transactions)	Above Enterprise Threshold
Price/Month or Contact	Price/Month or Contact	Price/Month or Contact	Contact or Schedule
[CTA BUTTON]	[CTA BUTTON]	[CTA BUTTON]	[CTA BUTTON]
Additional Thresholds	Additional Thresholds	Additional Thresholds	Additional Thresholds
Key Features	Key Features	Key Features	Key Features

"We then take advantage of our inherent ability to let our potential customers use our product before they buy it. With effective free trials allowing for increased lead qualification and ultimately lower customer acquisition cost. So the first step to getting visitors into a free trial is to promote it on our site. We achieve this by creating and placing calls to action for the free trial/demo throughout our website, particularly on the homepage. But more than just throwing a button on the site with some basic microcopy, a free trial/demo CTA needs to be strategically designed or no one will ever convert into a user. In fact, I read that the conversion rate from visitor to trial is just 8.4 percent. Take for example; Bizible's solution for increasing free-demo users was to implement the persistent demo form. It added a global request-a-demo form on every page, including the blog. It leveraged HubSpot's an inline form, which also fills in your information if you've downloaded content previously. This addition increased demo requests by 40 percent."

"This is all great information, Connie. I've also looked into the new methodologies for websites and some other ways to increase free trial/demo conversion are to add "free" to our CTA copy, have the form scroll with the visitor, make the form short, test different colour buttons as well as add a human element (imagery) whilst adding social proof."

"That's great, Roger, we seem to be on the same wave length, this is exciting - now how about pop-ups? I've read pop-up and exit intent forms are a great way to capture leads and actionable, direct feedback from our website visitors. For example, Office Drop was able to increase its pricing-page conversion rate by 40 percent by incorporating user feedback. It gathered feedback by asking users, who stayed on its pricing page for 40 seconds or more through a pop-up. Exit intent pop-ups are a great way to capture leads from content offers and will assist in building a subscriber list or newsletter. The key to success with these pop-ups is to ensure that they are presented at a time where users do not feel their experience is being interrupted, but rather enhanced. According to mageworx, the best time to display a pop-up is 60 seconds after a website visitor has entered your site."

"That's an area I will have to research, Connie but I'm sure it won't take me long. Are we adding live chat too?"

"I would love to have that option; it will allow visitors to reach out directly to a sales rep at their convenience. Dave Rigotti of Bizible has recounted that although Bizible's live chat does not generate a large number of leads every month, the leads sourced through the live chat contribute to more than 25 percent of its new monthly recurring revenue. This makes it one of the business's top three sales channels in terms of revenue generation. That is a great example of effective pipeline marketing and a strategy in which all SaaS companies should consider investing. So, if I have understood it correctly there are four ways to optimize a website. With these elements in place, it's important we continue to optimize our website over time by running strategic A/B tests. To do this we begin with a foundation of analytics and define reporting requirements, the tools (platform) needed and the personnel structure required to undertake a CRO effort successfully. Identify the key benchmarks for existing performance (visit-to-lead conversion rate, bounce rate, time on site, etc.) that you'll be measuring and form a clear and measurable hypothesis on how these can be improved. Set clear goals on what we're hoping to achieve. A simple and proven framework to start a program like this can be bucketing our pages into a quadrant, looking at both the conversion rate and the amount of traffic each page receives."

"However, as they've been the cornerstone of the lead-generation efforts for months. We should start by assessing these pages and understanding why they do well. We need to question are they featured prominently in our navigation and so driving lots of direct traffic? Are they SEO-optimized and ranking well for a high-volume search term? Are the CTAs on that page clearer than those on the rest of our site? Is the content compelling enough that someone couldn't possibly not convert? With this in mind, we need to determine how these elements can be carried over to pages that aren't performing as well."

Roger jotted down a couple of suggestions, further encouraging Connie's enthusiasm.

High traffic and low conversions – test pages:

Test imagery, a pair of eyes looking at a CTA will help improve the click-through rate.

Action at the top of the page is taken more than action at the bottom of the page.

Limit CTAs on the page (ideally limited to one per page).

Evaluate content.

As Roger writes the next few sentences he remarked.

"This is the toughest segment of the lot. Not only are these pages not driving conversions, they're also not getting as much traffic. This means it's going to take more time for those pages to reach a statistically significant volume of conversions to reach conclusions on any test."

Connie nodded her agreement as Roger wrote.

Low traffic and low conversion – test pages:

Figure out how to drive more traffic.

Incorporate what you've learned in our other tests.

His next note concluded, and he stated.

"These are our second priority after we have tests up and running on our high-traffic, low-conversion pages."

Low traffic and high conversions.

Drive more quality traffic.

Start with optimization via paid and organic search.

Improve navigation to drive more traffic.

With a series of improvements and additions to the website Connie thanked Roger for his help and made her way back to her space, her mind raced at the possibilities ahead for her at Lancett ProCloud. This was what she had always wanted. Now she had to tackle the trade show and how to make it a better resource. She listed the main reasons trade show attendance failed she found on an internet search:

1. No one knows you are attending

With literally hundreds of exhibitors at these shows often attendees try to plan their days beforehand. Without a notification from you of your show stand number and position they will quite literally pass you by and you lose the chance to speak to them and capture their interest.

2. No one knows your company like you do

Traditional trade show marketing tactics teach us to prepare a pitch, sell people at the trade show, and get leads! However, as things are moving at top speed, often, passers-by do not have the time to stop and watch a demo or hear your canned spiel about what sets you apart. Although valuable, you need to give attendees options and provide them information that most interests them.

3. The trade show follow up is a nightmare

With attendees receiving several product-centric emails from the trade show exhibitors or follows up from given business cards. Setting yourself apart is difficult, you need a way of optimizing each step of the process to ensure high-quality leads and overall great return from tradeshow attendance.

> Connie sat back and pondered these points. *How do we overcome them?* After clicking several links, she found one that answered some of her questions. She wrote copious notes as she read.

Tradeshow tradition way versus the Inbound way

Inbound sales and inbound marketing enable you to create an entirely different trade show experience
and will transform how you think about trade show marketing. The truth is that trade shows don't execute themselves. You need to plan for your shows and do so aggressively.

That's why you should consider an eight to 12 week planning period to get ready for an upcoming show. In addition to figuring out the logistics of the event, you'll want to focus on how to get more marketing qualified leads (MQL's) to visit your booth.

When preparing, ask yourself some questions about what you hope to take away from the show. Specifically, how many leads will you need to get from the show to make it a winner from an ROI perspective? How many of those leads must close, and for how much revenue? How many per day? How many per exhibit session? This makes the event a fully quantitative exercise and takes subjectivity out of the equation.

You also need to know what your big story at the show is going to be, and how to use content to help deliver that message. Instead of handing out stress balls or pens, provide your visitors with an exclusive e-book that's only available at the event and that will never be available again. If they want the e-book, they have to register with you at the show. This way, you get leads that are actually interested in what you do, as opposed to just your promotional products.

Once she finished writing she thought, *these are great points and I'm sure I can get the team onboard to action them.* As the article continued she began to feel more confident in her part in organizing the trade show.

What To Do Pre-Show With Inbound Marketing

Hope is not a strategy. Waiting for people to show up and find their way to your booth is a recipe for underperformance. Instead, get access to the registrants, and make sure there is pre-show communication that highlights your educational offer. Create a short series of communications that lead up to the show. Build excitement by teasing the educational experience. Highlight your speaking event (because, you are speaking at the event, right?). Or draw attention to your educational offer or the education that your experts are going to provide during the event. Turn your participation into an opportunity instead of the standard "stop by and say hi" activity.

What To Do Post-Show With Inbound

Unfortunately, none of the work above means anything unless these leads turn into revenue. So, make sure you have a clear lead nurturing plan in place before you go to the show. As soon as the event is over, people get back into their routines, and they're going to forget all about you. To prevent that, create a lead nurturing campaign that launches on the day the show ends. Think about the experience your new fans will have when they get an email from you with the follow-up you promised, plus some additional educational material. What about when they get another email one, two or three days later? And how about when you follow up again in a week to close out the conversation? The answer is: They're going to be impressed.

Connie made another list of the following points too.

If you insist on going to trade shows and conferences, insist on putting an inbound strategy behind your investment. Here are five tips to help you plan and execute your trade show using the inbound marketing methodology.

1. The marketing manager should know before booking the tradeshow what kinds of personas are going to be attending the show. That way you can appropriately adjust their inbound marketing tactics leading up to the event to fit the types of individuals that will actually be present. This will in turn allow for more MQL's to show up on trade show day.

2. There needs to be at least 45 days of social media posts prepared in advance of the tradeshow.

3. Use tradeshow hashtags. This will help to improve the reach of your posts, which will allow more people, who are planning on attending to read about your involvement in the show. Your company should follow the tradeshow's Twitter/LinkedIn/Facebook accounts and be actively engaging with them before the start of and during the tradeshow. All the blogs prior to the tradeshow day (at least 30 days before) need to highlight that you will be in the tradeshow and inform people of why they should attend.

4. Create a CTA for each blog, landing page, social media post and eBook that will take the visitor to your website to arrange a pre-booked meeting before coming to the tradeshow.

5. There should be email campaigns sent to your existing prospect lists announcing that your company will be at that trade show. Let them know that you are pre-booking meetings, and perhaps consider some sort of special offer to get them to attend.

6. Design a dedicated landing page for "progressive profiling" of whoever wants to pre-book a meeting with you during the trade-show. This will catalogue what they are looking for, when they want to engage, and if they're the decision maker. Find out what the big challenge they are facing is and why are they looking to your company. This information is gathered so your sales associate or marketing coordinator that meets with them during the trade show, will be more prepared to act as a trusted advisor. This will also allow them to build a deeper relationship during the trade-

show; instead of just giving some goodies or flyers away that will end up in the recycle bin after 48 hours.

If you have a show coming up in less than a month, you're probably too late. The worst thing you could do is rush it. But, if you have shows or events lined up for three months down the road, now is the perfect time to get an inbound marketing event plan in place.

Work out the schedule first. Start backwards from the day of the event, and plan your pre-show, in-show and post-show marketing tactics. Once the plan is complete, assign the individual tasks to your team or have your agency help with the implementation. The results should include doubling the leads gained from the event and producing real revenue from your trade show program.

Connie looked up at the calendar, they had just over two and half months before the show. She knew she would need to be proactive and get these inbound methods and actions started right away. She turned to her laptop and looked at how she could action mass marketing to enable them to catch up using social media but also the more traditional methods of the trade show promotion, such as newspaper and radio adverts.

<u>Mass marketing</u>: a market strategy where a firm ignores market segment differences and tries to appeal to the whole market with one offer or one strategy. This system entails broadcasting a message to reach the largest number of people possible. Traditionally mass marketing is focused on radio, television and newspapers media. The idea being by reaching the largest audience possible, exposure to the product is maximized, and in theory should correlate with a larger number of sales or buys into the product. This method is however the opposite of niche marketing, as it focuses on **high sales and low prices** aiming to provide products and services

with appeal to the whole market. Niche marketing targets a very specific segment of market; such as specialized services or goods with few or no competitors.

With a plan to flood as many media avenues as possible, Connie sat back. *If I can action all this in the next few days, we can make the trade show a success. It will show Mike and Dan I can make a major difference to the company's ROI.* She stretched and rolled her shoulders realizing how tense she had been focusing on the tradeshow literature. A text alert sounded on her phone.

Working late, sorry Hun. Don't wait up. X

She replied with a sad face emoji and then a heart and kiss. No worries I might be here late too. Love you X

Mike's farewell as he left the office made her conscious of how quiet the office space was.

"Oh goodness is that the time? Night Mike, I will pack up and be on my way. Sorry."

"No hurry I left a key on your station, so you can come and go as you please. But don't work too hard, you need to relax and rest as well you know."

"I promise, Mike and thank you."

Once the door shut on Mike, she looked around although it was such a great space to work in she missed the background noise so decided to drop into Froth or Not? before going home. As she entered the warm aromatic atmosphere of the coffeehouse she was delighted to see Mr. G at his usual table. He raised a hand in greeting and she nodded and smiled back.

With a bowl of soup and a thick sliced sandwich balanced on a tray she approached Mr. G.

"If I am intruding I can go."

"To be honest I need a break, you can get too focused on something and your thoughts begin to become unclear. Have you had a better day today?'

"I have actually although I have found out that our next trade show is just over two months away and with the inbound method you have informed me about, we might be struggling with adequate pre-promotion. I will have to flood all media avenues with promotion for the next few weeks to catch up."

"What is your intention, to promote multiple avenues with the same advert, offers and text?"

"Well yes, it is the fastest way I can think of."

"There is a better way, Connie. It is the difference between mass marketing and ascension marketing, in essence marketing to help you 'rise above the noise'. It is more effective. Let's look at the ways that digital technologies are changing the environment, the opportunities, the challenges for business, across different continents and markets, types of industries, types of products and so forth. What can we learn from what is in common across these different kinds of industries? You need to tap into digital marketing and how it is changing in this digital era.

There has been a broad shift from mass marketing to customer networks and this should lead us to rethink the marketing funnel. What is the role of a marketer within the organization?"

Connie took an intake of breath, but Mr. G shook his head.

"There's no need to answer Connie as there are many different answers to that question. When I ask different marketers, I'll hear a variety of statements about building a brand, reputation, connecting with customers, driving demand, working with the sales team. So, there are a lot of roles that you may play, but a really interesting response I heard to that question came from Jonathan Becker, who was the Chief Marketing Officer of SAP at the time and he said to me that he thought that the fundamental role of a marketer is to keep the organization focused on the customer. Wouldn't you agree it is a really unique role to marketing as a discipline within the organization?"

She nodded her agreement her spoon half way to her mouth.

"Don't let that soup get cold now. Do you want to finish before I continue?"

"Oh no please carry on, this is fascinating."

"Okay, we think about the many different things that marketing may get involved in and touch on, really all of them, whether it's driving marketing insights, assisting in the development of new products, driving and supporting communications to customers, using service and data to try to maintain a customer relationship after purchase, metrics and feedback from the market, even thinking about where the business model is going. All these different aspects of the business that marketing may support all have one common goal that is that customers are at the centre of them all. However, the interesting thing is the nature of customers today is changing – it is the nature of their relationship to organizations. I find very often when I start talking to businesses about digital marketing there are a lot of questions that come up that have to do with the different technologies because there are so many and they're changing very rapidly, so it's understandable. Companies are fixated on what's our YouTube strategy or are we using Facebook effectively or not. How should we be using Instagram? Well, some of our customers are now on Snapchat, right? Should we be there as well? We have many different tools and technologies to consider and utilize.

It's easy to get side-tracked in starting to think from a point of view of how all these different technologies fit together and work or don't work together, but I think it's more important to begin the process by thinking instead about how these technologies are changing the way that the customers connect to you and the way the customers connect to each other, even outside of your organization, and that's really changing the dynamic and the paradigm within which we operate. It really is a world where we're moving from thinking about customers as a lot of individuals, who we are marketing to and rather as a network that is very dynamic and interconnected within which we must operate as a business."

"What do you mean by customers as networks?"

"A good question, Connie, let me explore this idea with you a little bit through three stories. The first story is about some of the new risks that we face as organizations as customers become much more connected and have a voice in a way that they didn't have before about their experience of us as a business. So, this is a true story about a musician named Dave Carroll. He's a singer/songwriter from Canada. Dave rose to internet notoriety through an unusual experience he had as a customer of a major business, an airline, which I will not name. So, Dave was a traveling musician and he was taking a trip flying from Halifax, Nova Scotia to get to a concert and had to go through Chicago. On this trip he had a bad customer service experience. So, pretty common experience, right? Not something unusual. Airlines always deal with customers, who have had a bad experience and they manage it as best they can. It's an industry where there are a lot of variables out of your control. Well, Dave had a particularly bad experience. First of all, they actually damaged his guitar in transit to the gig. So, as a musician, that's kind of about the worst thing that can happen, but that wasn't all. When he went to the airline at the end of the trip and said you broke my guitar, what are you going to do about this, they said I'm sorry, Mr. Carroll, you have to speak to someone in the other office, the other airport."

"Oh, that is poor service!"

"Yes, it is but after six months, he finally spoke to someone at the airline and they said I'm sorry, Mr. Carroll, but it's been six months and you can no longer file a complaint. He was understandably very frustrated, and he told this person, if I were a lawyer, I would sue you, but I'm not a lawyer, I'm a songwriter, so I'm going to write a song. And he did. "

"He did? He wrote a song about it? That's genius!"

"Actually, he wrote three songs and got together with some friends and recorded a video. Now he was, I should point out, not a musician with a huge social media following at that time. This is not somebody with scads of fans all over the world. He didn't have a record label contract, just a working musician, traveling, playing gigs, singing his songs. They shot the video in one day with no budget, just something fun."

"Oh, I would have loved to have seen that."

"Okay, let's watch the first 30 seconds or so of it." Mr. G held up his tablet and clicked a link. The screen came to life and Connie could see the musician and his friends.

"It's kind of catchy, right? Airline Breaks Guitars, sort of sticks with you. Well, as you can see he put this video online and a lot of other guitarists with the same experience saw it. People connected with that experience. They started sharing it with others. It grew very quickly and so it moved from being in the local press to being something that was on television and all the sudden everyone was paying attention. Millions of people watch this video on YouTube. Last time I checked, it was over 15 million people I think had seen it."

"Wow, that's amazing."

"Well, when it got to about a million or two and was really growing quickly, the airline reached out to Dave and said we're sorry, we'd like to pay for your guitar repair. And he said no thank you, you had your chance. This is not extortion. I'm just telling my story. That's what I do. I'm a songwriter. If you want to give some money to charity, that's fine. But, the airline felt bad and they said well, we'd love to make it up to you somehow. Next time you're in Chicago, please let us know. So, the next time he was traveling through Chicago he did let them know and they met with him at the airport."

"So, from one video he made a huge difference?"

"Exactly, his voice was heard above the noise. Another story about customer networks that shows that customer networks can be not just a threat or a challenge to your business and your brand, but they can also be a boom or a benefit. If you look any multimillion-dollar brand, you can go on Facebook any day and see it has millions and millions of fans. People have reached out and liked the page from all over the world. The size of a large country, 10's of millions of people. And you can see them connecting with the brand every day, writing comments in all different languages saying how they like that product, where they just tasted or tried it, post a picture with it, share a memory of the first time they had tried it, who gave them their first one, et cetera. It's this really striking repository and connection point of all these people, who have a positive association and connection with the brand. But, the interesting thing about the Facebook page for one particular product was it was actually not created by the company's marketing team and it wasn't created by their advertising agency. It was created by two customers, Dusty Sorg and Mike Jedrzejewski, a couple of actors, who were out of work, between jobs in Los Angeles. They had a little free time on their hands and were both fans of a particular product and decided to create a Facebook page for it - one of their favorite brands. This was in the early days of Facebook, when it was just opening up beyond being open to students at colleges and high schools and becoming open to the public.

"I always thought it was the company's Facebook page, I didn't know that."

"So, there are multiple pages about this product, but there was something about their page. They got their friends to sign on and their friends of their friends and they were sort of actively on it. So, what happened was as Facebook was really growing and taking off, as new people were coming on to the platform and they searched, this seemed to be the most interesting kind of exciting page related to that brand and so that was where folks gravitated to. It quickly became the second most popular page in the entire network with millions of fans. And then one day Facebook reached out to the large company at their headquarters in the USA and said we just want you to know that the page is hosted by Dusty and Mike, don't worry about it, we're going to take it down on Tuesday. And the company said what are you talking about? We have millions of fans on that page and Facebook said oh, well, you know, our lawyers have been looking into this and they've discovered that a lot of people have been creating pages for brands and properties that they don't own. They are not the intellectual property owners, they don't own the trademark, and so we don't want to create any false impressions, so we're just going to shut all those pages down and you can start whatever you want on Facebook and it'll be your thing because we know brands like to control their own image. Now, what would you do? What would be your response if you were them? "

"I'd tell them to leave it alone; it was too popular to discard."

"Yes, my feeling as well Connie, so, this was an interesting stage in this product's evolution as a brand because traditionally it has been a brand. It was for many years. It was built in the traditional fashion, where brand and its image were very carefully constructed by the company. Think of popular jingles and packaging and the well-known logos as well as all the advertising you are familiar with. It was all about creating and sculpting a brand yourself. But, the company C-suite has started to realize that in the digital era, as customers networked together closely, there were going to be some areas where they needed to take a more hands-off approach. So, they actually got back to Facebook and said look, can we do something a little different and they worked out an agreement, where in this case the page was not shut down. Instead, Facebook simply took control of the page away from Dusty and Mike and gave control, administrative privileges of it to the company. And then the company did a very smart and interesting thing. They reached out to Dusty and Mike and they said hey, you guys are some of our favorite customers. How would you like us to fly you out to LA and give you a tour of the headquarters? They said sure, that sounds great. They flew them out and they visited the company's headquarters, which is actually a top tourist attraction. There's a whole museum to the history of the company and all kinds of things to see. They had a great time visiting that day and seeing the headquarters and meeting with the folks there and they said, you know, we love what you've done on Facebook. Would you like to stay involved as part of this Facebook community? And they said sure. We can give you administrative privileges and you can continue to be involved and that is what they did. Dusty and Mike continued to be involved and really kept the voice of the customer as part of how the community continued to grow. It's a very different way of thinking about what makes, nurtures and sustains a brand in the digital era."

"What an opportunity for Dusty and Mike, from a small page on a social network."

"That's the point, Connie, customer networks can do more than just impact your image and your reputation and your brand, the way that people feel emotionally about you. They can also impact the core of your business with innovation and value creation and they also influence businesses of different kinds, including a B2B business in the info tech industry. One is well known as the hardware maker of much of the hardware that powers the internet and all sorts of networks in the world around us. It is a very large company and one of its challenges each year is how does it sustain a level of organic growth. Growth that is not just through acquisitions of new technologies and new companies, but how does it build and incubate new businesses of its own. In order to develop this, they've taken different approaches trying to get everyone in the organization involved in innovation, saying, look, you don't have to have innovation in your title to have a great idea for where the company could grow next. And they've used idea markets and other kinds of tools to bring in and surface ideas from anyone throughout the organization that the company could look into investing in. And they'd had some success, when they decided to broaden the scope. Why should it just be our employees having ideas for the company's next opportunity? Maybe our customers, folks outside the business, could also identify a growth opportunity for us?"

"They opened it up to everyone?"

"Yes, they launched something called the I-Prize. It was a year-long process where it was basically a business model competition. Anyone in the world could apply and submit an idea for proposal for a new business by the company. And they gave some guidelines. They said we want something that is really tapping into some adjacencies for our business. So, it should be an area we're not currently operating in, but maybe we can sell into existing customer relationships or we can tap into some of our existing technologies that could be made relevant as well.

"How successful was it?"

"They got thousands of applications due to a large and attractive prize. They said the winner at the end of the year would get $250,000, quarter of a million, and also have the chance to work at the company on the new business if they wished to. As you can imagine that got a lot of interest! There were teams around the world developing ideas, and then they went through a series of stages in the competition, where they narrowed down the field and gave feedback and asked for more development of the business plans. At the end of the year, the winning team was actually three people. It was Anna Gossen, her brother Neils, and her husband Sergey Bessonnitsyn. Interestingly, all three of them were graduate students and had never written a business plan before. None of them had an MBA. They were computer science and mechanical engineering as I recall, but they came up with a proposal for the company to go into the smart grid frameworks business."

"What is a smart grid framework?"

"Let me explain. Think of a large building or campus like a university or a corporate building. There are many different points of power consumption within that facility. It could be lights in the ceiling; it could be projectors or all kinds of devices, then late at night everything is shut off in the building or the campus. In actual fact all those individual points of power consumption are still drawing a very small amount of electricity from the grid. It's called the passive consumption of electricity. So, what a smart grid framework does is actually a technology for managing and reducing this passive consumption, which, again, in a large facility can really add up and be significant. So, the company really thought this was a brilliant idea and they were happy to give the prize to these three students. Of course, they were thrilled; they got the $250,000 and a chance to work there. The company in turn was happy to give them the prize because they identified and evaluated this business plan and said it could be, within five years, a billion-dollar business. They had a new billion-dollar business opportunity that they only found because they went outside to their customer network."

"It was obviously a major boost for the company."

"Yes, and the research, compiling, auctioning, prototype building etc. had no direct cost to the company from those numerous participants. When we look at these stories we understand there's a fundamental shift happening between customers and organization relationships. It really poses a daunting question. You have to ask yourself what role will your customer have? Will they be a challenger? A threat? Or perhaps, in some ways, your biggest competitor to your success? Or will they be a business driver? An enabler? An evangelist? Or even a source of innovation that's going to help create new value for your business in the future? We can think about the shift to customer networks in terms of a fundamental shift in the nature of markets. Throughout the 20th century, businesses grew based on economies of scale. They really operated and grew under a model of mass market and in this model the company is the source of all products, ideas and innovation and communications, and the customer is very passive.

Really the only role for the customer was either to purchase or not meaning customers were treated as an aggregate - a collective, who were waiting to be persuaded to buy. This was the mass market model and it worked very effectively, throughout the 20th century. Businesses around the world grew and succeeded in that way, but I believe we're in the middle of a fundamental shift, a long-term shift from a market based around mass markets to a model of markets that we can think of better as a customer network model."

"Am I taking from this that my mass marketing plan is not the way I should proceed then, Mr. G?"

"It can make the promotion look 'busy' but in fact not give you a solid return on your efforts. In the customer network model of markets, you'll see the company is still deeply enmeshed is the largest circle within the diagram because the company is still the biggest source of innovation and ideas. You're still responsible for your brand. I would say you are the steward of your brand, but the company recognizes you're not the only actor and that the customers and potential customers out there, have access to all the same digital platforms for communicating, creating, innovating, sharing and connecting with others, just like the companies do. In fact, the customers have a lot of influence on things like the future of the company and its image, reputation and brand. In this model, the role of the company is somewhat different. It is still important that you innovate and create value and distribute it and push it out to the market, but, at the same time, within the network the company needs to be listening in. You need to be observing and learning from these different interactions within the network to identify new opportunities, understand where customer needs are going, and also to spot those customers— the certain customers, who are going to do more than just buy your product, who are going to be like a Dusty Sorg or like an Anna Gossen, who are going to take a more active role and actually help to catalyze new opportunities for your business in that network."

"It is a highly interactive relationship then between customer and company. That makes a lot of sense now I think about it."

The Science of Customer Network

"To understand customer networks a little better, let's sit back and comprehend a bit about the science of networks, where it comes from, and some of the lessons we can learn. The science of networks started in the 18th century with a Swiss mathematician named Leonhard Euler. And the origins of what was at that time called graph theory. It started with a puzzle that he was trying to solve. It was a longstanding puzzle in the European city of Konigsberg, which had many rivers and bridges within it and the puzzle was, 'how can you cross all seven bridges of Konigsberg without repeating one?' Now, no one had ever figured out a path that would do this, so it was assumed there wasn't a solution, but of course, as a good mathematician, Euler wanted to develop a proof. Could you know without a doubt it was not possible? He started thinking about the different landmasses and the bridges that linked them together and he said 'what if I could simplify this into a simpler model' so he translated it into a diagram where all the landmasses were shrunk down to single points, a node, if you will. The bridges became links between them. This was the first time, we started to use graph theory or what later became called network theory to take a real-world phenomenon and simplify it into a model of nodes and links. When he did that, in this case, it became a clear mathematical solution. If you were going to be able to cross the seven bridges, then all the non-terminal nodes are the landmasses you go through in the course of your journey that would need to have an even number of links so that you could go in and out of them without repeating the same bridge. But, once you made it into a simple - a graph diagram, it was very clear all of the nodes actually had an odd number of links and therefore you had your mathematical proof there was no solution to the Konigsberg bridge problem. Although it started as a mathematics paper, over time it led to a whole branch of mathematics developed by such mathematicians as Paul Erdos and Alfred Renyi and has been applied over the years to many different fields of science and industry, using networks to understand and map out transportation and what kinds of transportation infrastructure and networks are more or less effective. It has been used in communications, biology, even social organizations looking at the spread of ideas in religion and language, each of these fields has been marked and shaped by applying the ideas of networks and how they operate to better understand the underlying mechanics."

"So how do we apply this science of networks to marketing?"

"I knew you were a thinker, Connie. If we think of customers as a network, what does that mean? Well, a definition that I'll offer is that a customer network is the set of all your current and potential customers of an organization linked to that organization and to each other through a web of digital tools and interactions. When we think about this, what goes into that network is really going to vary from business to business and it may not just be one kind of customer. Really any key constituency can be a customer within your customer network. So, for some firms it might include business customers, channel partners, or end consumers. It could also be investors, who influence your business, or analysts in the press, or regulators as well as any employee. In fact, any constituency that is critical to your business could be in your model of your customer network. Even if you're in a different kind of organization, for example, non-profits, they still have members, large donors and small donors. Again, we include the press, partner organizations, and volunteers. Any constituency, whatever it is that is critical to your business, and also the relationships between these constituencies, is what you want to be thinking about applying as you model the idea of a customer network for your own business."

"So, can you explain more of this science? I am finding this fascinating."

"All right, as long as you are happy to listen and learn. Let's look at some of the science of networks and see some principles that have been developed elsewhere, which can actually be applied directly and help us understand the dynamics of customers as networks. One of those principles from network science is Metcalfe's Law, which is a measure of what's also called network effects. What Metcalfe said was basically, if you look at a network with many different nodes on it, as you increase the number of nodes in that communication network, (that was what he was focusing on) the number of possible links increases exponentially and therefore the value increases exponentially. The classic example he gave was if you think of a fax machine or telephone. If you only have one telephone, there's really no value to it. However, if you have two telephones, you now have a private channel of conversation between two people. Then, of course, as you add more, the number of possible connections increases, and it actually increases as a factor of n times n minus one over two. So, what happens is we see this actually play out in a lot of dynamics, in the social media we use, and in a lot of the ways that we communicate now as businesses. Using these digital tools, we get the network effects. The more people using a technology or platform, increases its value and its potential influence grows rapidly and tends to lead to participation tipping points, but after a certain number of people get onto a new platform, it starts to become much more attractive to new folks. For example, another really interesting finding from the history of the science of networks is from Stanley Milgram, the American sociologist in 1967, who did a famous test called the Small World Hypothesis. The idea was that people within their personal relationships were in fairly tightly meshed networks. To test this theory, bearing in mind it was before we had the internet, email, or anything like that, he used the technology at hand and devised an interesting experiment. He found 160 people in the Midwest and gave them a postcard and then asked them a question. He said 'Do you know this lawyer in Boston, and he gave a name, everyone said no, I don't know that lawyer. Then he asked them to take the postcard and think of whomever they might know who might be most likely to know a lawyer in Boston and send it to them. Then when they get it, if they know the lawyer, they'll send it to that lawyer and if not, they'll make the same educated guess."

"It seems such a long drawn out process now but a clever way to test his theory."

"It certainly was although it was rather a rough and tumble experiment. Obviously, people would not necessarily know what the shortest path was, they would just intuit it based on their best hunch and there was a lot of chance, of course, the next person might just get this postcard and throw it out and say, 'Well what is this? I have no idea.' But in actual fact, out of the 160 postcards that he started with - well, let me ask you, Connie. How many do you think made it to the lawyer?"

"There must be a probability in there somewhere, but my guess would be maybe 9 or 10."

"It turned out 42 of the postcards made it to the lawyer, despite all of the challenges and possible chaos that could come in-between starting and reaching him. That's more than 25%."

"That number is a lot higher than I imaged."

"And the other really interesting finding was that of all the ones that made it to the lawyer, they took on average five and a half steps to get from the originator to the ultimate recipient. Stanley Milgram took that number, round it up, and thus was born the phrase "six degrees of separation" which has later been used in a play by John Guare and a movie, and lots of ways that we think about the interconnectedness of our world. It was an early experiment, but really pointed to the fact that as digital technologies now make it much easier to find each other on something like a Facebook, rather than through using postcards kind of randomly sent, is that ideas and messages, brands and value, can transmit quickly through these densely meshed networks connecting us to each other in this world."

"I suppose it's on par with the dying art of letter writing, everything is now immediate through social media and text. There is no waiting time."

"Yes, it is, Connie. Now am I keeping you too late? I do have a couple more points I can go through if you would like but please don't feel you are obliged to stay."

"I am more than happy to stay, I learn so much from you, and it is me, who should be apologizing for keeping you from your work or home life."

"Not at all, we have maybe another hour before they close up the coffeehouse and once I'm on a role I like to keep going."

The Power law Distribution The 90-9-1 Rule

"My next piece of science is the 90-9-1 rule. In a lot of natural phenomenon when we measure them, they tend to follow what is commonly known as a bell curve distribution. You've probably seen this in textbooks and situations you can think of it. The thing about a bell curve is that most phenomena cluster around the mean. So, you've got that center of the bell, where most people are closest to it. Think of, for example, the height of adult human beings. You know, there's an average adult height in a population and most people are within a couple inches of it, right? Even with a world with six billion people on it, there is no one who is 15 feet tall, for example. Right? As you move away from the center of the distribution, the likelihood of the frequency becomes extremely small extremely quickly. And a lot of things, including biological phenomena follow that. Other phenomena, though, follow what's called a power law distribution. In a power law distribution, there is no clustering around the mean. There's no average that most things are close to. You have a few rare cases of an extreme high value, if you will, and then many more cases as you go towards the opposite end. We can see this, for example, with the size of grains of sand on a beach. You have a few larger ones and many smaller ones. Power law distributions apply to oil deposits. There are a few very large and very valuable lucrative oil deposits underground around the world and there are more smaller ones and there are many, many more oil deposits, which are much too small to actually be economically usable. Vilfredo Pareto, the Italian economist made the power law famous, when he looked at the distribution of wealth in many societies and coined what's known as the 80/20 rule, which is that 20% of the people own 80% of the wealth. And we see this same phenomenon playing out in a lot of behaviors and dynamics within networks.

So, one of the ways this has been applied to social behaviors networks was by Jakob Nielsen, a usability expert, who looked at how people participate in online media and forums and coined this 90/9/1 rule, as he called it. Say you look at something like a Wikipedia or a discussion forum or a blog network, you'll find that there are basically people who go there, but there's 1% who are really the active participants. These are the people, who are starting a new article on Wikipedia, who are posting content, original content, of their own, for example. Then you get roughly an order of magnitude higher, so about 9%, who are the semi-active participants. These folks comment on the content, on a blog post, or who make a small edit or a slight contribution to an existing Wikipedia article. And, lastly, the largest group, another order of magnitude higher, the 90%, roughly, if you will, are what Nielsen called observers. These folks are not actually commenting, writing or taking on an active role, but they're looking, they're reading, they're watching what is being created there and they're being influenced by it. It's a very important rule to keep in mind as you look at network behaviors as a business. To understand there's a real divergence between those who might be very visible as active participants versus the number of people who are being shaped or influenced by what they see going on in these networks."

Mr. G smiled as Connie made a couple of notes regarding the 90-9-1 rule. He then continued.

1-To-1 Communications Tools to Many-To-Many Communication Tools

"So, the question is what is driving this shift towards more network behaviors among customers? We can really understand it in terms of shift in the tools for communication that are available to us because customers have always had the ability to communicate and express themselves. Word of mouth has always been really important to businesses, but the tools we've had for communicating as individuals were things like phone calls, writing a letter, communicating face-to-face, giving advice. In each of these, one person is communicating at a time to one other person. So those opinions and feedback from markets can spread, but they do so in a more step-by-step fashion from one person to the next. What's broadly happened is numerous new technologies have become available to everyone, which is a different kind. There are many-to-many communication tools now rather than one-to-one. So, it means everyone, who has access to this tool can behave like a broadcaster, right? It's not like radio or television, where a few entities or people, who have a lot of influence, have access to this broadcast medium. If you're on email, or using a blog, or posting a comment about a product on a review site, or if you're uploading a video to YouTube, with any of these tools, everyone who's on it becomes a broadcaster. Everyone, all of the many, have access in the moment to all of the many and so each person can spread an idea simultaneously to numerous others. What happens is it allows any idea, opinion, and value, to spread rapidly throughout a network in a much quicker fashion.

That's how you get something like Dave Carroll's video and his funny song, suddenly spreading from an un-famous musician to be seen by millions of people using digital tools and that's really driving the shift from how companies relate to customers from the mass market model, where we are pushing our messages and our products out to them to a dynamic method, where we are enmeshed in a network with them. We are communicating reciprocally and each of them has access to these same platforms for communication themselves."

"So, allowing interaction not only between customers and employees but other customers create a communication hub, where ideas and experiences can be shared?"

"Yes, that's right, Connie."

Rethinking the Marketing Funnel

"One more way of thinking about this shift is in terms of its impact on or reshaping of the marketing funnel. Now, the marketing funnel is a tool used by businesses all over the world as a way of thinking about their marketing objectives and the tactics they're going to apply to them. It actually dates back to psychological research from the 1920's into what's called the hierarchy of effects. And it really is a psychological model and that's why the marketing funnel is still applicable or can be used even as the context around it and our behaviors change quite dramatically because you still, as a business, need your customers to go through these different psychological stages. The first goal, of course, is you need to achieve awareness. People need to know that you exist as a business or that you have a new product on the market. Once you get some people to the stage of awareness, you need as many of them as possible to come to the stage of consideration.

That's where they see the value in your product and, after consideration, say okay I can see I might want to make use of this product or service from this business. Then, of course, you want as many of them as possible to the stage called preference. This is when you decide on the company you want to do business with or the product you intend to buy. It's typically measured by marketers as purchase intent, but, of course, as good marketers, we know there is a difference between purchase intent and actual purchase and that's why in the funnel model there's another stage, which is action. We have to get the customer from preference to action. Action is to buy, but it can also be to subscribe to a service, or even cast a vote, if this method was applied in political marketing. It's that key action you're trying to drive as a marketer. We can use this marketing funnel to understand and think about the impact and use of a variety of traditional marketing tactics. We can use some pre-digital broadcast marketing tactics such as television advertising, or out of home advertising, print magazines, et cetera. Even direct mail."

"That was one of the methods used at my previous job. It was painful to watch hundreds of envelopes stuffed and mailed day after day."

"Yes, I remember you mentioning it. These methods tended to be applicable or influential at one or more stages of the funnel. For example, television has traditionally been seen as useful in driving awareness. In fact, it still is. If you are trying to drive awareness rapidly to a large segment of the population, with maybe a new product or service, if of course you have the budget, television is certainly a powerful tool for doing that. But, let me ask you to reflect. In your own experience in your industry and your markets, what do you see happening with these broadcast marketing tools? What's happening in terms of their use and their influence or efficiency in your industry or your market?"

"Most television advertising in my mind is ignored. It is an opportunity to leave the room if nothing else."

"So, in reality the impact of customer networks on these broadcast tools is varying depending on the markets using them. However, depending on which customer segment you're trying to reach, some of these broadcast tools, such as print advertising, are simply not reaching your preferred audience. For instance, products that focus on a younger audience will not be as successful in this medium due to the mobile-focused audience. In some markets, television advertising is still effective, but with the price going up per 1000 people you want to reach; even here the audiences are shrinking. So, while it is powerful, the efficiency per dollar spent is actually declining. Broadly speaking these tools still have a role, but at the same time, we now have customer network dynamics, which have their own influence. We have to rethink our influence at each stage of the funnel. In short, television was the old way of driving awareness now one of the most powerful ways of driving awareness or powerful influencers is search. It is common for everyone to use a search engine when looking up an idea, topic or a product category and thus discovering a business for the first time. When you get to the stage of consideration, we are often influenced by product and customer reviews. Our opinion is swayed by what other people are saying about a business or product and the ratings it is receiving."

"I am often persuaded by a good review myself, Mr. G. It is a great tool for anyone purchasing or investigating a new product."

"Exactly, and once you get to the stage of preference, for a more considered or in-depth purchase, such as an automobile, a vacation or even a refrigerator, you're more likely to go to people you know and actively reach out to your social network on Facebook or Instagram for their review. Ask them hey, has anyone been to this destination recently and have a recommendation for a hotel. Has anyone bought this refrigerator? I'm thinking about buying it and I'd love to get some feedback. Right? Then, when we get to the stage of action, the actual purchase, there are also more dynamics at play. You might be purchasing still in a physical store, you might be buying online, or it might be digitally delivered to you or some combination of these. This has changed loyalty too instead of the key cards, which you'd stick on your keychain for your loyalty points, when you went to the supermarket or the pharmacy, now using social media, businesses can keep in touch with a customer and keep that communication going and hopefully nurture and sustain that relationship. But, the biggest change actually to the marketing funnel, because of customer networks and their dynamics, is actually now one more stage. So, once we get as many people as possible to that stage of the first purchase, and then we get as many of those as possible to the stage of loyalty where there's an ongoing relationship, we now want to also get as many of those customers as possible to a stage that I call advocacy. "

"I haven't heard this term used in this way before. Who would be the key people for that?"

"They are the people who actually write a customer review on websites, who answer that friend's question on Facebook about the refrigerator, who take the picture of themselves at your vacation destination and share it on Instagram. These people are feeding those comments, images, answering answers and giving points of view and because of the nature of search engines and social media, they wind up reaching the top of the funnel and influencing the next customer from the very beginning of their journey, from awareness all the way through because, in social media and in search engines, what your customers are saying about you is actually much more visible and much more influential than what you're saying about yourself. So, the power of customer networks is really changing and shaping how we get the most out of this marketing funnel."

"So, in a way the influencers or advocates are doing your marketing for you by conversing with potential customers for your product."

"Yes, exactly. It is a 'free' marketing tool; however, it has to be monitored and 'fed' with your own information, guidance and interaction."

Chapter Four: Lessons learned

- There is a shift from a mass market approach to marketing to a customer network. We've gone from a world where marketing as a discipline was really based around mass marketing, mass manufacturing, mass messaging, really a one size fits all outlook. Marketing was done using blanket broadcasting to the customer.
- The traditional method was about interrupting customers to gain their attention. This advertising model and the most effective selling at the time was done by the company itself through mass advertising. Really the goal was to persuade the customer to a single action - to purchase and the dominant tools were really about driving awareness and differentiation from other offers in the marketplace.
- The customer network approach to marketing is really quite different. It's a world that focuses more on niche than mass, where each customer chooses, perhaps even creates and modifies an offering to suit their own needs. Where companies are both sending out, but also receiving information.
- Learning from, and connecting with, a customer enables you to earn attention by providing content that's valuable, utility and experience, and where often the most effective selling is done by the customers themselves. Where you can instigate and inspire advocacy, reviews, and positive words of mouth. The goal becomes, not just to persuade; but to inspire.
- When you inspire confidence in your brand, trust, loyalty, and the dominant tools of getting there are really about innovation, often collaboration, and finding points of shared value where the customers feel that they connect and have something in common with you as a business.

Chapter Five – Confronting the Shadow

Mike noticed Miriam's stone-faced look as she walked past his office en route to Dan's. *That doesn't look good.* He turned slowly to see her close Dan's door – *that really isn't good* she's *obviously got something she's unhappy with.* Turning back toward his laptop he waited only a few moments before a message popped up from Dan.

'My office now.'

With a hesitant knock on the CEO's door, Mike entered to find Miriam tapping one foot and glaring at Dan.

"Good morning, what's up?"

Before Dan could speak Miriam began a tirade leaving both men speechless.

"You told me that the new marketing person would make significant improvements to our ROI and that is the reason and only reason I gave my consent to hiring her. We are now 90 days in and all I've seen is expense after expense and certainly no increase in income! I think it's time you fired her and stopped this hemorrhaging of funds."

Dan looked at Mike tilting his head to one side with an expression of expectation.

Mike swallowed hard.

"I understand that there have been some extra expenses but..."

"Some, do you call increased overtime and the IT budget exploding some?"

"If I can explain, Miriam the expenses in IT are for specific software to enable the website to be more interactive. To implement those changes, we have been working extra-long hours. There has to be tests for the links and how the site performs."

"I think you have been taken for a ride, Mike. That girl has no idea what she's doing so throws money at anything and everything. If there is no significant improvement in a month I expect her gone."

"Miriam please, if you could just listen."

"I've listened long enough – I need absolute proof in the account balance before I change my mind. And Dan I suggest you keep a close eye on the expenditure."

Before either man could reply, Miriam left the room blustering as she went through the work space. Unfortunately, for Connie they met face to face on the corner to Miriam's office.

"And you had better get results or you're out!"

Connie stood open mouthed, her heart thudding and hands shaking. She had given Miriam friendly smiles and good mornings, but they had never been reciprocated. Now she experienced the full force of the woman's temper. *Oh my, what was that all about?*

As she turned away Mike was walking towards her without his usual friendly smile.

"Do you have a moment Connie? We can go to my office."

Now Connie felt uneasy. She was well aware that Miriam had been against them hiring her. Was this the end?

"I take it you saw Miriam?"

"Yes, I did. What happened?'

"Well, you happened. She is pushing for real returns on the expenses she has seen 'flooding', her words not mine, across her desk and no real rise in income to quantify it."

"Mike, I am doing as much as I can to make the company's brand and profile stand out from the crowd. It takes time."

"That is just the problem, we are in Q2 and not achieving anywhere near the numbers Dan wanted or expected and Miriam has made the point abundantly clear. We need to reassess our tactics and get those numbers. You need to come up with something to prove your success."

"I'm looking at a system to measure the results to date and will get figures to you as soon as I can, Mike, I promise."

"Okay, well I won't keep you then."

Connie walked out of his office her mind reeling. *How do I measure my results? Where is Mr. G when I need him?* She laughed at her own question – the coffee shop of course, that's where I will find him. Grabbing her coat and tablet she left the office, it may only be mid-morning, but this was important she needed help, her job may depend on it. Her relief at seeing Mr. G's familiar figure at his usual table must have shown on her face because his smile vanished.

"Goodness you do look worried, what happened?"

"If I don't find a way to measure and report my results so far in this campaign there is a real possibility I will be let go."

"Alright, so let's grab a strong coffee each and get to work."

"You are my life saver, Mr. G really you are. I can never repay you for all this expertise."

"Let's call it a mentoring thing for me and leave it at that."

Once they were sitting down Mr. G began explaining how Connie could measure her results but also build a full end to end goal for her B2B marketing campaigns.

"You need to build a marketing funnel end to end but more importantly build decode metrics to help measure the performance of those campaigns, with these you will be able to communicate back to your leadership team and the indomitable Miriam."

"Yes, Miriam is my fiercest opponent. If I can give her actual figures, hopefully she will switch to my way of thinking and strategizing. What's the first step?"

B2B Marketing Guide line to Decode Metrics

"All marketers should know how critical it is to understand how their marketing efforts contribute to the bottom line. There's a lot that goes on behind-the-scenes to generate sales pipeline and ultimately revenue, as I'm sure you are aware. By becoming a data-driven marketer that's in tune with the right metrics, you can demonstrate marketing's contribution to both. The use of metrics will enable you to illustrate the impact that you and your team are driving in the organization, which is critical to ensure you have the budget and resources you need to deliver optimum business outcomes. Without metrics, it's nearly impossible to measure the success of your activities and identify elements to optimize in future campaigns. And without them, there's no way to determine your return on investment (ROI)."

"Exactly Miriam's point, she wants proof that I am worthy of the salary they are paying me."

"So, CEOs and business leaders need to understand how to evaluate campaign effectiveness and demonstrate how their efforts impact revenue growth, these include:

- Defining the revenue model

- Modeling the revenue cycle model in the marketing automation platform

- Measuring early-stage, mid-stage, and late-stage indicators of success

- Tracking campaign and channel success

To prove how marketing contributes to business growth, you need to know how to connect the right data points together; however, it is not always straightforward. I read that according to B2B Marketing and Marketscan, only 32% of marketers pursue a data-first strategy, and less than half of marketers feel prepared for a data-driven marketing future. Understanding how to analyze your marketing efforts has never been more important and obviously that is clear on a personal level for you."

Why are Metrics Important?

"I have a favorite quote by Peter Drucker, the founder of modern management, who said, 'You can't manage what you can't measure.' Marketing metrics are essential to understanding which campaigns or channels are the most effective and illustrating the ultimate value that they drive. Now, many marketers measure soft metrics (sometimes known as 'vanity' metrics), which include brand awareness, impressions, clicks, organic search rankings, and reach. And while these types of indicators are valuable for understanding the early-stage impact of a campaign, oftentimes, they are not what the C-suite cares about and I get the idea that these are not what Miriam and Dan are interested in either. In today's economy, most CEOs and CFOs want to hear about growing pipeline, revenue, and profits, and soft metrics are tricky because, in many cases, they measure activity rather than results — quantity over quality. Instead, I feel you should hone in on quality metrics that prove the revenue impact of your campaigns."

"This sounds like the best option for me, Mr. G. What do I need to do?"

"Let's look at some questions you should be asking. Make a note so you can go back to them later."

Connie jotted down as Mr. G spoke.

• How is your lead database growing this quarter versus last quarter? What about this year versus last year?
• How does the pipeline look for this quarter and next?
• How much profit did we make year over year? And how much of it is contributed by marketing?
• How much revenue and profit do we forecast for the next quarter? And what resources do we need to accomplish our goals?

"Now to answer these questions with authority, you need to:

- Know the revenue of each marketing campaign investment across channels
- Understand how quickly leads are moving through the funnel
- Measure and forecast results
- Make a strong business case for marketing investments

"Goodness how do I identify these from all the data I have compiled?"

"Its true marketers can drown in a sea of data, but you can shut out the noise by focusing on the right set of metrics. This is where marketing automation tools, like Marketo, which has robust reporting capabilities. Once you're measuring and tracking each campaign's return on marketing investment (ROI), you can confidently answer questions from the C-suite, giving credit where credit is due and demonstrating marketing's role as a revenue driver. I am going to give you some pointers on how to do just that."

"I'm ready fire away I will make notes as fast as I can but if I get muddled I'll stop you."

"Sounds good, Connie. Firstly, let's set up a solid framework."

Set Up A Solid Framework For Measurement

"Step one is to define your revenue model. This important step for campaign measurement requires an agreed upon revenue model with defined stages and definitions. Essentially, it's an internal version of your buyer's journey, as defined by marketing and sales, starting from when a buyer first becomes aware of your business to after they become a customer and beyond. While a buyer's journey is self-directed, having clearly defined revenue stages helps power the health of your marketing funnel. Importantly marketing and sales need to collaborate to formally define each stage in the revenue model, the business rules that determine a prospect's movement from one stage to the next, and at which point a prospect should be handed off from marketing to sales.

This builds a foundation for a comprehensive set of metrics that creates accountability for each team and helps optimize the flow of leads towards a purchase. It can also help you monitor the trends for each stage and discover where there may be bottlenecks in your lead management process, allowing you to make forecasts and optimize how leads flow through each stage. Depending on your organization, your revenue cycle model may look different."

"I have an idea how I can make a framework for Lancett ProCloud, let me make another note."

"I'm in no hurry, Connie."

"Thank you, I have to jot this down while it's fresh in my head."

"Right, are you ready?"

"Sure, I'm ready for the next step."

"It is helpful to break up the revenues stages into three parts.

Top-of-Funnel (TOFU), Middle-of-Funnel (MOFU), and Bottom-of-Funnel (BOFU).

"Prospects, who are starting their buyer's journey map to the TOFU stage, engaged leads and qualified leads map to the MOFU stage, and leads that are sales opportunities map to the BOFU stage. But marketing doesn't end after the sale. The customer journey extends from awareness to acquisition and all the way to brand loyalty. If your marketing strategy includes targeting specific accounts via account-based marketing (ABM), your revenue model may vary but let's say in this case, you've already identified key accounts that are most likely to generate revenue or have other strategic importance, and your efforts are focused on identifying and engaging with the right people in those accounts. While your funnel may be smaller at the top, it will yield more qualified leads in the long run. In either case, the measurement of your campaign and channel success will be the same, except with a focus on either leads or target accounts."

"I have set identification and engagement of key accounts already. I hope I have done it the proper way though."

"Well let's continue and you can determine that."

Revenue Stage: Top-of-Funnel (TOFU)

"Prospects in this buying phase have just entered your sales and marketing funnel. They are aware of your product or service but are not ready to buy. To enable that shift you can even break this Stage down to sub-Categories, such as:

New Names: This is the number of buyers, who have officially entered your database, but have not engaged with your company yet. This could be someone who was acquired through a business card at a tradeshow.

Lead: A lead has been determined to potentially be a qualified buyer based on your buyer profile and is opted-in to your marketing communications through engagement with your brand. This could be someone who downloaded an eBook and officially entered into your database. Leads will begin to be nurtured with the goal of eventually becoming marketing qualified leads (MQLs).

Revenue Stage: Middle-of-Funnel (MOFU)

"Prospects in this buying phase have the right demographics and behavior and have engaged with your content or offers, have displayed buying intent, and are potentially sales leads. These can also be broken down to two Sub-categories"

Marketing Qualified Lead (MQL): At this stage, a lead officially becomes a marketing qualified lead (MQL) based on scoring criteria that you have defined. For example, this could be a VP of Marketing, who watched a demo and has previously engaged with you multiple times.

Sales Qualified Lead (SQL): Once a lead becomes an MQL, sales should evaluate whether the lead is qualified through a phone call or email based on interest in your product or service and whether they're a good fit. If they are, then the lead becomes a sales qualified lead (SQL). But if a salesperson decides to reject, or recycle, an MQL, it goes back to marketing for further nurturing.

Revenue Stage: Bottom-of-Funnel (BOFU)

"Prospects in this buying phase are close to becoming customers. And again, there are two sub-categories.

Opportunity: Opportunities are the number of SQLs who fit the BANT criteria:

Budget: This lead can afford your product or service.

Authority: This lead has the authority to purchase your product. He or she is the decision-maker. Need: There is a pain that your product or service can help solve.

Time: The lead's purchasing timeframe aligns with your sales cycle.

"The number of opportunities for each campaign reveals how valuable your leads are in regard to your primary internal customer – the sales team. If your campaign leads are not converting into opportunities, one reason could be that your sales team doesn't see value in the leads you generate, and your campaign may not be as valuable as you thought. If this is the case, you'll need to refine your campaigns to target the right audience."

"This is certainly something I have not thought through, I will need to look at that, Mr. G."

"The other sub category is,"

Customer: Customers are closed-won deals who have purchased your product or service.

"Remember though, Connie, the buyer's journey with your company shouldn't end post-sale. Plan a strategy around customer base marketing — retention, cross-sell, and upsell — to maximize the value of your hard-won customers. Now, let's look at step two. Are you still following me?"

"Without a doubt, thanks Mr. G."

Set Up A Solid Framework For Measurement

"Step 2 is to model the revenue cycle in your marketing automation platform. Your revenue cycle model will be used to direct the rules in your marketing automation platform. Look at this example on my tablet; it is from a marketing automation platform, showing how you can build a full lifecycle. Can you can see how each stage of the revenue cycle can be defined in your marketing automation system, where intelligent rules govern where someone is in the buyer journey at any given time — based on their behavior across channels, their engagement with your campaigns, their lead score, and even data changes in your CRM system (such as someone getting disqualified because they left their company or becoming part of an opportunity).

"Can I ask the, how can I use a revenue model to do more effective marketing?"

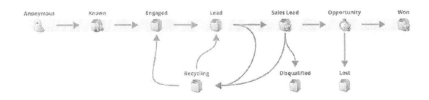

"You can build a Success Path Analyzer, which enables marketers to visualize the movement of prospects through each stage in the journey. As you can see the important metrics that are indicating how leads are flowing through the funnel are easy to identify, giving you figures on how many leads are in each stage, the average time in each stage, the conversion rate for leads going from one stage to the next, and more. Why does this matter you ask? This system allows you to see where leads get "stuck" and where to focus your marketing efforts in content and campaigns, that will then help nudge them to the next stage. Breaking the sales cycle into distinct stages allows you to track movement of buyers through each stage–which in turn lets you answer key questions to optimize your campaign accordingly.   These questions include, but are certainly not limited to:

- How long is the purchase cycle from initial awareness to a closed deal?
- Is there a stage where people get stuck?
- How much pipeline coverage is needed to help sales hit their targets for this quarter?

"Once you set up your revenue model, you can begin to measure throughout the different stages you defined. Identifying your goals and what metrics you will measure is critical to achieving buy-in and setting expectations. When planning any marketing investment or campaign, your first step is to forecast your expected outcomes. What does success look like? Do your key stakeholders have the same viewpoint? Make sure to identify what a good outcome is before you get started and get everyone on the same page. All too often, marketers plan campaigns and commit their budgets without establishing a solid set of expectations about what impact their campaigns should have.

The best marketing campaigns have intentional measurement strategies planned in advance. It is very challenging to go back after the fact to measure, since you need to have the proper tracking in place — so consider what you want to look at in advance and ensure you have the right tools to do so."

"I realize my mistake now. I went full force into changes and updates but did not define my goals. This has given me so much information and a clear idea of how I need to plan a better reporting system."

"As you plan your campaigns, whether it is sending an email to your database or launching a new product, it is important to look at early-stage success metrics and then mid- to late-stage metrics as your campaigns mature. For example, when an email campaign first launches, you can look at it and open the click-through rates and conversions. Further down the line, when the information is available, you can measure how much pipeline each email helped generate. The metrics build into a focused reporting method stage by stage."

"That makes sense, so my reports can be gauged that way with more accuracy?"

"Exactly, but we need to know when to measure too."

Know When to Measure

"Some marketers only measure their campaigns immediately after deployment. In doing so, they miss out on some critical metrics. Other key metrics take time to mature, so you need to look at different sets of indicators throughout time. I would suggest looking at metrics in the following timeframes:

REPORT ON	PAST	FIRST WEEK	FIRST FEW WEEKS	3 MONTHS	6-9 MONTHS
	Previous Programs and Opportunities	Clicks and Opens	MQLs	Opportunities and Pipeline Created	Revenue Won

Measurement in Action

"This is real measurement in action. When you produce your largest asset — The Definitive Guides — you can look at metrics from past guides to help set benchmarks and goals. Then you can set goals that act as early indicators of success (shares and downloads) and those that may take longer, but help you get closer to understanding the ROI (pipeline and revenue won). Before you even launch the asset, define and agree on those metrics, as well as the intervals that you will reassess.

Measure Metrics that Matter

"Now we need to look at determining what to measure for each campaign, understand what is important for your marketing team to evaluate for campaign effectiveness and optimization as well what you need to report on to other stakeholders — your team, your manager, sales, the C-suite, etc.

We have early indicators of success:

- Lift in website traffic, new visitors, social shares, referring domains, form fill outs, comments, and site interactions.
- Subscription to email or RSS, new names, % new names per program
- Number of leads (right demographics, desired behavior), investment per lead
- Engagement score for set of programs per month

And of course, late indicators of success:

- Number of opportunities
- First-touch ratio
- Multi-touch ratio
- Pipeline

"Can you break down these early- and late-stage metrics down further for me?"

Early-Stage Analysis

"Certainly, I can, let's look at them separately. Firstly, there is early-stage analysis. This is a great place to start when you're launching a new campaign. Opportunities take a while to develop, but there are other important metrics you can track during this stage. In the top-of-the-funnel stage (TOFU), your main objective is to fill your pipeline with as many good leads as possible to generate more customer opportunities. To create early stage reports that keep track of metrics answer these questions:

• Which campaigns and channels are bringing in targets or leads most cost-effectively?

• Which campaigns and channels are bringing in the most highly qualified leads?

"Some metrics you should be tracking in your early stage analysis are.

Investment: This is the total amount spent on each campaign. This amount could be zero, such as for organic social media and blog posts.

Investment per New Name: You calculate this number by dividing the total investment by the total new names. This measures how much you're spending to acquire each new lead. An ideal cost is less than $30."

"So, if I remember right a new name is a buyer who has entered our database but has not engaged with your company yet. Right?"

"Yes, it is you catch on fast, Connie."

% New Names: This figure reveals how many leads are new to your database out of all the leads a campaign is generating. If you are looking to build the size of your database, a high percentage of new names are a positive indicator.

Investment per Lead: This number is derived by dividing the total investment by the total leads. It measures how much you're spending to acquire each new qualified lead and reveals which campaigns are the most efficient at attracting your specific buyer. Again, the ideal cost is less than $30."

"Can you define what a lead is as well, Connie?"

"Yes, it is someone who could potentially be a qualified buyer based on our buyer profile and is opted-in to our marketing communications through engagement with our brand."

"That's right, now we have."

Successes: The number of people, who take the desired action of your campaign. While successes often go untracked, measuring them reveals how truly effective your campaign is since the desired action can differ across channels. For example, if someone registers for an event or webinar, but they don't attend or watch the on-demand recording, then they may not be considered a success depending on your goals. On the other hand, for an email offering a whitepaper download, someone may need to download the whitepaper to be considered a success. Creating success criteria per channel gives you an apples-to-apples comparison of campaigns where the desired outcome is something different. But the main point, and the metric for making comparisons, is having taken that desired action. Remember to have strong alignment across teams on what your definition of success is for each channel. What determines a success can vary across teams and organizations, so it's important that you define this early on."

"I can see it is a great method to quantify not only what I am doing but also give proven and traceable results."

"Yes, but while it's not necessarily considered a metric, it's important for you to break down the costs of running each of your campaigns to determine how much you are investing in every campaign and channel. I'm sure this particular metric will be well received by Miriam. It will come in handy down the line as you evaluate whether your campaign was worth the investment and which channels are the most cost-effective. And if your cost increased as the campaign ran, be sure to document the changes and the factors that contributed to it. This will help you forecast the budget for your future campaigns of that nature, which in turn will give you leverage with your C-suite."

"I'm sure you are right, the more information I can give the better."

Middle-to Late-Stage Analysis

"Next, we need to look at middle-to late-stage analysis. Once your leads start to convert into opportunities, you can begin to determine whether your campaigns are worth the continued investment by analyzing the MOFU and BOFU stage in your revenue model. Creating mid- and late-stage reports helps you keep track of metrics that can answer questions such as."

• How fast are leads moving through the funnel? Are they converting at a good rate?

• Which campaigns and channels are positively impacting revenue?

• What is the return on marketing investment (ROMI) for each campaign?

Calculate Your Return on Marketing Investment (ROMI)

"Ultimately, the impact of your campaigns should translate into return on marketing investment (ROI), the main focal point of your nemesis I feel, Connie." Mr. G smiled as Connie nodded her agreement.

"There are two approaches to calculating ROI. One method looks at the investment on the campaign versus the return, which helps marketers make comparisons across all of their campaigns. The other method looks at total marketing costs, including the cost of staff. This is a more comprehensive approach that is not as commonly used because it includes several factors that are not campaign-specific, such as the costs of marketing staff, office expenses, technology, agency fees, and printing. I think in your case this method might be worth using. Remember not every campaign will have a complete ROMI calculation. Some campaigns will have softer goals, such as number of attendees at an event, but as always, the closer you can measure ROMI, the better you will be able to justify your investments. However, even the simplest ROI goals should include (as compared to cost) these points."

- Pipeline
- Opportunities
- Revenue

"With ROI goals in place, executives will see not only the program spend that goes out the door, but also exactly what benefits are expected as a result, which makes them much more likely to support your investment."

"That's exactly what I need to convince Miriam and also Dan that I am worth their investment and time."

"So modeling your ROI goals will also help you to do that."

- Identify the key profit drivers that will affect the revenue model and ultimately your profits
- Create "What if?" scenarios to see how changing parameters may vary the results and impact profitability
- Establish the metrics on how you will measure success

Allocate Value with Attribution Models

"Now keep in mind that it may take some time for your leads to move through the funnel, convert, and translate into ROI. To become more strategic about measuring the impact of your campaigns, start by recognizing that your buyer rarely makes a purchase as a result of a single touch. Conventional marketing wisdom, known as The Rule of Seven, proposes that at least seven successful cross-channel touches (forms of engagement) are needed in order to convert a cold prospect into a buyer. In fact, on average, 50% of leads are not yet ready to buy, according to Gleanster Research, so it's important to measure your campaign's impact across every touch point your lead encounters with your company. Attribution models offer marketers a set of guidelines that help determine which activities get credit for downstream activities, like sales opportunities created or pipeline/revenue generated. However, to accurately attribute these business results, first you need to know two things about each campaign."

Lead Source

"Firstly, lead source, which indicates the channel through which a new lead enters your database (PPC, social, sponsored content, website, etc.). The lead source will help you track which channels bring in the most leads, the most qualified leads, and the ones for which marketing is directly responsible."

Acquisition Campaign

"And secondly, acquisition campaign, which is a specific campaign that has brought a new lead into your database and indicates which of your campaigns bring in the most new names. Keep in mind that just because a campaign doesn't acquire many new leads, doesn't mean it's not valuable. Some campaigns are designed to generate brand awareness and attract new leads, while others are designed to further engage them and convert them into customers.

But by understanding which campaigns are best at acquisition, and combining that with revenue attribution, you'll know which campaigns bring you the best new names that eventually become paying customers."

"I know that if there is no proven income, Miriam feels our efforts are not cost effective. I can use this tactic to explain the process better."

First-Touch and Multi-Touch Attribution

"All of these methods will help you, I believe Connie, in proving your marketing campaigns are making a difference. A different attribution model will impact the valuation of your marketing activities and channels so let's go through first-touch and multi-touch attribution. Marketers have traditionally only measured first-touch (FT) attribution for their campaigns, meaning the original acquisition campaign gets 100% of the revenue credit. If someone comes in through a campaign, then continues to engage with your brand throughout different campaigns and touch points and finally turns into an opportunity, only the initial campaign will get credit for bringing in that customer. This model works best if your top goal is to grow your lead database with the right leads. What if you have a long sales cycle and your challenge is not just growing your lead database, but nurturing those leads until they're ready to buy?"

"This is one of my pain points, Mr. G, the long sales cycle and one Mike has mentioned more than once. He wants to lessen the cycle as much as possible."

"Then you will need multi-touch (MT) attribution, which credits the revenue to every successful marketing interaction with a lead. Buyers engage with your brand across channels throughout the different stages of the buyer journey. And with MT attribution, any campaigns that successfully touch a lead before the creation of an opportunity split the value of that opportunity evenly. This model works best if your campaigns are designed to maintain interest and engage leads throughout the sales cycle — which are most B2B marketing campaigns as you know."

"Do you have examples I can go through?"

"Sure, let's look at first-touch and multi-touch attribution in action. Imagine a lead arrives on your website and fills out a form to download your eBook on analytics, officially entering your lead database. Now that you have his contact information and know he's interested in the topic of analytics, you send him an email about an upcoming analytics webinar you're hosting. You target him with the right message at the right time — as he's currently looking for an analytics solution to evaluate his marketing data — so he registers for your upcoming webinar. In the meantime, he continues engaging with your company, downloading some survey statistics on marketing analytics from a third party report hosted on your site.

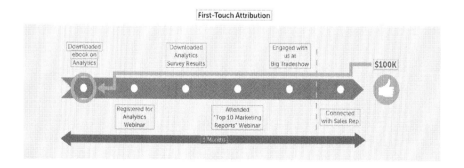

On the day of the webinar, he visits the link that you sent him to attend. As a follow-up to webinar attendees, you send out a recording and discount code to register for the next tradeshow you're attending. This lead, being interested and fully engaged with your company, registers and attends and is eventually connected with a sales rep leading to a closed deal. With first-touch attribution, this is his first engagement with your company. Take a look at this diagram, Connie."

"Now let's say that for this same scenario, your company decides to allocate the revenue credit by multi-touch attribution. In this case, all successful touch points would get equal credit for the acquisition, except for the analytics webinar registration. This is because, sometimes, webinar registration is not considered a success for this channel, only attending a webinar or watching the on-demand recording is a campaign success. In this case, the deal credit gets distributed across the eBook download; analytics survey download, "Top 10 Marketing Reports" webinar attendance, and tradeshow attendance. As you can see, multi-touch attribution paints a more complete picture and shows you how all of your campaigns work in conjunction throughout each stage of the buyer's journey to result in a new customer. Remember that getting the most accurate multi-touch attribution requires looking at campaign successes, not just conversions. This is the second diagram.

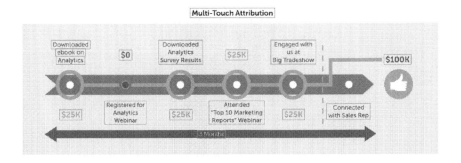

"I think you should list some first-touch (FT) and multi-touch (MT) metrics that you should be tracking in your mid- to late-stage analysis."

FT Opportunities
This is the number of opportunities created by the sales team (interested, have budget, have authority, have the need, have the time, etc.) calculated using FT attribution.

FT Pipeline
The amount of FT opportunity the pipeline generated. This reveals which campaigns are the most efficient at acquiring the right leads.

FT Ratio
The amount of FT pipeline a campaign generated divided by the total investment on that campaign. The golden metric for a good campaign is one that generates pipeline at least five times the investment.

MT Opportunities
The number of opportunities created by the sales team calculated using MT attribution.

MT Pipeline
Amount of MT opportunity pipeline generated. This reveals which campaigns are the most efficient at pushing leads through the sales funnel.

MT Ratio
The amount of MT pipeline a campaign generated divided by the total investment on that campaign. Again the golden metric for a good campaign is one that generates pipeline at least five times the investment.

Revenue Won
The amount of money your company won from this deal. This will vary depending on the deal size and may increase over time as you cross-sell and upsell to your existing customers.

"These are great points. Do I keep these reports on FT and MT separate?"

"Not at all you can customize your reports to combine FT and MT attribution for a comprehensive view of how all your campaigns bring in new leads and help push leads along in the sales funnel, or you can split them by FT and MT metrics for a more focused comparison of how effective each campaign is at each of these objectives. Now, let's dive into these metrics. Ask yourself what is the marketing team's specific impact on each of these deals? Leads get assigned to the sales team and turn into opportunities to ultimately be closed by them, but with Marketo's Opportunity Influence Analyzer, you can track how each of your marketing campaigns influenced an opportunity or closed deal throughout a customer's entire lifecycle. You can follow each individual lead's journey throughout their engagement with your company – from their first interaction to all the different interactions that ultimately led to a closed deal."

Comprehensive Analysis
"Aside from just measuring your campaigns from start to finish, it's important to look at ROMI in terms of overall channel performance. While the success of each of your campaigns may differ, a comprehensive view of your marketing channels can reveal some very valuable insights for both existing and future campaigns. Within your marketing automation system, you can view your channel performance in a variety of ways. Take a look at this Marketo Advanced Report Builder, you can see four different visual reports that reveal the amount of pipeline created, investment per new name, ROI, and revenue won for each channel.

Campaign Name	Next-Gen Analytics Campaign	
Campaign Objectives	Introduce a new breed of analytics and generate interested prospects	
Campaign Duration	Feb-Apr (90 Days)	
Campaign Components	2-part Webinar Series, Exec Brief, Technical Whitepaper, Buyer's Guide, Display Ads, AdWords, Tech Summit	
Target Audience/ Segments	CDO, Data Scientists, VP IT Ops	
Key Messages	Prescribe next best action based on inline insights. Blow away competition with real-time graphs & dashboards	
Campaign Goals	1,500 responses, 15 opportunities, $3M pipeline, 4 deals, $1m closed bookings	
Early-Stage Metrics	Conversions, successes, new names, % new names	
Mid- to Late-Stage Metrics	MT opportunities created, MT pipeline created, MT revenue won	
Campaign Budget	$200,000	
Expected Campaign ROI ($$)	5x program spend to bookings ROI	

"Based on this data, you can see that your blog is your most cost-effective channel in terms of bringing in new names, while webinars bring in the most pipeline. However, in terms of the channel that brings in the most revenue, your online advertising efforts deliver the most results. Now do you have an understanding what metrics measure, how to allocate value, and when you should measure?"

"I certainly do and once again I am in your debt, Mr. G."

"My pleasure so now you can begin mapping out how you will measure the success of your campaigns to tie in ROI and give the fierce Miriam a reason to congratulate you instead of demean you."

"It would be nice to think that would happen, Mr. G, but maybe not yet. I will work on creating a metrics scheme and a reporting system that will give Dan, Miriam and Mike the 'numbers' and 'successes' they want. Now I must get back to the office, they might think I've left!"

Connie made her way back to the office and although she felt rather guilty for being out so long there was no reception committee asking her about her absence. Everyone seemed perfectly engaged in their tasks and only smiled when they noticed her. She returned to her work space determined to create the framework Mr. G had so kindly explained to her. Her confidence was back, and she would show Mike and the rest of the C-suite she was truly a MarTech Manager.

Chapter Five: Lessons learned

I know this chapter was all about Advance ROI measurement and very specific to B2B organizations but for some B2C this can also be applicable.

Your CFO/VC or money partners know that marketing is critical, but they will also need solid ways of measuring marketing.

Please remember, that if Inbound Marketing is your first phase to move to what we define as revenue driven marketing, then at some point in your ROI model you will need to reflect on how much of a top line revenue your marketing team or agency have been helping you with.

As we have been working now with 70+ B2B organizations, we have found that if you are a marketing manager or a CMO, you have to have your team focus on three high level buckets of revenue driven marketing.

A) Bucket #1 (NNN) Net new names (Company names, TDM/BDM (Technical/Business Decision makers). You should always be expecting the team by year 2 to bring in at least 33% of new revenue from this bucket.

B) Bucket #2 (reducing the Sales Cycle for small-mid size deals). You need to have a true alignment between Sales and Marketing. There needs to be a marketing manager attending your Sales forecast and they need to know exactly what deals are forecasted to close in the next two quarters. They also need to know what the road block is and if there are other decision makers, who need to be strategically added to a high touch campaign to help convince them to write the cheque or sign the contract.

C) Bucket #3 (Field Marketing). A roadmap of new products and services to your existing clients. Cross-selling and upselling to existing clients. This is what we define as the low hanging fruit and for companies, who are 5 years old or less, they always tend to forget to go back to their existing clients and help them know more about new products and services. Instead they rely on the sales teams to do so. However, the marketing team can easily streamline this process. We believe in this bucket specifically. We are now seeing the marketing funnel transforming into, what the CEO of HubSpot said (Flywheel), 'where it is a continuous process of serving and delighting existing customers.'

Customers

Chapter Six – Into the Darkness

With Mr. G's guidance and the implementation of several of his methods, Connie was beginning to see real results in her marketing strategy. And better yet her expenditure using the metrics showed actual results against costs in figure form, something Miriam had begrudging accepted. A call into Dan's office did not worry her one morning and she walked in smiling and confident. Mike was on one sofa and Dan the other.

"Good morning, Connie please have a seat." She sat on a chair, so she could face both men.

"Mike and I have been reviewing the inbound marketing you have been running. It has some good results and the figures are increasing gradually but we now want you to begin focusing on marketing specific organizations. As you know by now a B2B cloud device company like ours needs to be pro-active to compete."

"I have made specific targets for each marketing campaign, Dan. Is there another avenue of potential clients I need to focus on?"

"We have strong links with our client base and referrals, due to your website improvements, and they are making headway. Is there another option in your marketing compilation you could use to target a wider field?"

"I will certainly look into it, Dan."

"I will send you a group of potential companies, Connie that we want to approach."

"Thanks, Mike that would be helpful."

"Great, that's all good then? Sorry I have to rush off, meetings you know. I'm looking forward to seeing the results Connie."

Connie smiled as Dan left the office and faced Mike.

"So, is he or isn't he happy with my performance so far? He gives mixed messages."

"Oh, not to worry Connie, Dan is happy with your progress but as usual he always wants more. He has pressure from other sources that keep him hungry for more."

"Right, well I'd better get to it then."

Back in her work space, Connie scrolled through her tablet and then made several internet searches. She found ABM – account-based marketing and knew this method would enable her to focus her inbound marketing strategy to specific clients. Relaxing by the window in the space adjacent to the kitchen she read for an hour.

Account-based marketing (ABM)

ABM has recently seen a surge in popularity and practice among B2B businesses, a key reason for this resurgence is new digital ABM technologies make it easier to implement and less resource intensive to practice. This transition has removed the barrier that kept many small and medium-sized businesses, or SMBs, from implementing the strategy. Now, with the right technology, SMBs stand to make huge strides in business and revenue growth by implementing an ABM strategy.

The Benefits of an ABM Strategy

Today, B2B organizations of all sizes can benefit from thinking in account-centric terms — utilizing their resources more effectively and focusing their energy on target accounts. Specifically, implementing an ABM strategy in your SMB will help you:

1- **Improve marketing ROI**: Your marketing resources — people and budget — are precious and limited within a small company. With ABM, your resources are used more strategically, with the understanding that you are spending your time and money on the activities that drive the most results, for the accounts that matter most. Connie noted this item down she could use it for leverage for expenditure.

2-**Drive attributed revenue:** Because strategic ABM delivers a set of coordinated experiences to your target accounts across channels, you can understand the true impact each activity has on driving the sale. Therefore, you can focus your attention and resources on the activities that drive a real impact.

3-**Generate more conversions and qualified leads within Strategic accounts**: Instead of going after everyone, ABM's targeted approach offers a more focused field for marketers. Rather than having a steep attrition rate from new names to qualified leads as you would with more broad-based marketing strategies, you start with a pool of accounts that are already more likely to convert, fill the white space of contacts on those accounts that matter, and then give them personalized, focused attention. Connie hoped that the list, Mike was sending her would give her a good basis to start this ABM strategy.

4. **Drive business momentum**: Big wins make a proportionally bigger impact in smaller organizations. A big logo account wins in a SMB, versus in an enterprise, acts as a marker of momentum and business credibility. SMB's deploying an ABM strategy may have a smaller number of target account lists, but they ultimately result in more big-impact wins. Again, Connie made a note – percentage of successful gains.

5. **Align sales and marketing**: With ABM, account selection is a collaborative process between marketing and sales. Communication issues about what comprises a qualified lead disappear as your strategic account criteria are openly discussed. Account selection, targeting, engagement, and closing happens, while both teams have visibility into the progress and the ability to drive desired outcomes. Connie knew so far, the collaboration between the sales and marketing had been working well, she would need to reiterate the importance of team work.

After reading the whys and wherefores of ABM, Connie had some idea of the method but had to admit to herself she was still confused as to how it could be applied to Lancett ProCloud in particular and, more importantly, where she should start. Glancing at her watch she realized an early lunch could give her some time to think and hopefully discuss ABM with Mr. G.

Mr. G was at his usual table with earplugs in and talking into the screen of his laptop. *I'll have to be patient and wait until he is finished.* Connie ordered a sandwich and a drink and sat two tables down from Mr. G. He was focused on his conversation and did not acknowledge her. She finished her lunch and glanced at Mr. G, he was taking out the ear plugs and stretching his back. He smiled at her and beckoned her over.

"Good afternoon, Connie. How are you?"

"I'm good thanks. You seemed to be quite focused on your conference call."

"Yes, we had several conflicting views, which had to be discussed but I think we are now all on the same page."

"Well that is excellent." Connie bit her lip wondering if she should bring up the ABM or leave it for another day.

"So, what's your next exciting project?"

Glad he brought it up. Connie explained Dan's request and her research into ABM.

"Well, ABM marketing is a great tool to use and I think to implement it for a B2B company can be effective. Shall I explain?"

"As always, I am all ears, Mr. G."

Build an ABM Strategy That Works for You

"So, what does it look like to implement ABM? It certainly does not have to be an overly complex process. You can start small and then expand as you get more comfortable. There are three main steps. Firstly, identify and manage high value, target accounts. Target account selections vary for each organization because each one has its own unique targets and different reasons for going after specific companies or verticals. In some organizations, identifying target accounts may be as simple as the CEO or sales directors identifying accounts to pursue. In others, there may be several factors you use to determine your target accounts (including territory, industry vertical, lifetime value, and other considerations). You will need to collaborate with the sales on a list of target accounts, or the companies that are the best fit for your solution. It is crucial that you agree on your ideal customer profile or ICP.

"Actually, Mike is sending me a list of potential targets, so I will have a good starting point."

"Well, that's excellent. Then take your list of target accounts and expand the company profiles with the contact information of key stakeholders and decision-makers. This will assist in engaging them in every channel. Once that is done, you will have the systems in place to manage them. The next critical component is to engage those accounts with personalized content across different channels. Each piece of your target buyer's experience should be consistent and complementary—that means you have to think about the main channels, where your potential customer engages, have visibility into their actions, and the ability to orchestrate programs that drive desired outcomes (accelerate the buyer journey).

With expanded account information, you'll execute an omnichannel marketing plan and begin to engage those contacts in your target accounts. Your marketing automation platform and ABM technology will be instrumental in this stage, as you employ a variety of sales and marketing tactics, such as content marketing, events, personalized emails, and phone calls."

"This is where I need to work closely with sales and IT then, as they have the expert knowledge I can use to create the content."

"Indeed, a comprehensive program to engage is key, but remember that even after your sales team successfully closes a deal, your marketing team's job isn't over. After all, satisfied customers and brand advocates are one of the most valuable forms of marketing. Joseph Jaffe, author of Flip the Funnel, estimates that acquiring a new customer via an existing customer costs one-third as much as other methods of acquisition."

"Yes, I can see how we need to follow up and continue to engage."

"Last but not least, you'll need to measure the success of your ABM campaigns by focusing on account-level KPI's that reflect your marketing team's contribution to pipeline and revenue (ROI). This is where you analyze your results and optimize their engagement. How do you gauge the success of any strategy without understanding its revenue impact? Your ABM strategy needs to be measurable in order to demonstrate success with these targeted accounts and improve over time. Understanding your success at all levels — from account whitespace insights, to channel-by-channel account engagement, to account score and account-level rollup of lead data—not only will help you optimize the marketing activities and engagement you are driving for each account and person within the account, it ultimately provides sales with the information they need to close the deal. And for you in particular, Connie to have hands on figures for Dan, Mike and Miriam."

Drive Results with the Right Technology

"So, let's look at how to achieve the benefits ABM can offer your organization, it's critical that you choose and implement a digital technology that offers the three essential components that you need to be successful. You'll notice that the three essential components of an ABM solution mirror the steps to building an ABM strategy. Without these basic building blocks, your ABM strategy isn't adequately set up for continued, scalable success. Jot these points down, Connie so you can reference them later."

1.   Target and manage accounts and account lists
•   Easily identify and discover accounts
•   Prioritize and score accounts, including advanced predictive scoring capabilities
•   Organize target account into lists and show hierarchies
2.   Engage target accounts across channels
•   Listen and respond across channels such as web, email, and ads in real-time
•   Extension of a partner ecosystem to augment your ABM strategy
3.   Measure revenue impact on target accounts
•   Access data from a high level, program-wide view down to individual metrics for named accounts

"A platform that offers native ABM capabilities means that you can not only use it to practice your ABM strategy, but you can use it for your broad-reaching demand generation strategy. Not to mention, you'll only have to learn and buy one piece of technology instead of three—saving you time and money and more importantly you will be able to show Miriam your cost effectiveness."

"The more I can prove to her the better Mr. G. She needs figures in black and white to be swayed at all as to my requests for expenditure."

"So, let's refresh and make sure you understand the seven steps to start implementing your account-based marketing."

STEP 1: Assemble Your Account-Based Marketing Team

"In order for your account-based marketing strategy to be successful, it's crucial that both your sales and marketing teams are involved in setting expectations, defining your goals and KPI's, and determining the role ABM will play at your organization. Before you begin planning your first ABM campaign, you'll need to assemble a core ABM team. The members of this team will vary depending on your organizational needs, but at minimum, it should be made up of team leads from sales, sales development, and marketing."

"I already have key people that are engaged in my inbound marketing strategy, so I have this part figured out but can you remind me just in case I have forgotten something?"

"Okay let's list them out, shall we?"

Business/Sales Development Reps
Your sales development team will be responsible for working with marketing to execute inbound and outbound ABM efforts.

Sales Database Administrator
This data guru will keep the contact and account data in your CRM accurate and up-to-date.

Marketing Operations Manager

The administrator of your marketing automation platform will be responsible for aligning contacts and accounts with marketing activities based on their stages in the purchase decision.

Content Manager

This storyteller will work with marketing, sales, and customer success to supply collateral for every stage of the account's journey.

Graphic Designer

Your creative lead will collaborate with your content manager to develop all your ABM collateral.

Account Executives

These salespeople will get to know your target accounts inside and out and ultimately be the ones to close the deal.

Sales Leader

Your sales team manager or director will be instrumental in setting goals and developing account-based selling processes.

Customer Success Managers

Your customer success team knows your customers better than anyone else, and it's their job to help turn your accounts into advocates.

Executive Stakeholders

The leadership at your organization — including your CMO, VP of sales, and/or CEO — should also have a stake in your account-based marketing strategy.

"Now I know what you are thinking, Lancett ProCloud isn't that large a company, but smaller teams with fewer resources can still succeed with account-based marketing. The important thing is to make sure all key stakeholders are represented on your core ABM team and have a say in your goals and strategies."

"I was worried there for a minute, if I told Miriam we had to hire more personnel she might have exploded!"

"It is workable in any size company you just need to define everyone's role.

STEP 2: Define Your Goals And Strategy

"With your assembled core account-based marketing team, it's time to define your goals. What do you want to accomplish with ABM? Your goals will inform your strategy, so it's important that everyone on your core ABM team is on the same page.

Common goals of account-based marketing include:

A) Successfully launching a new product
B) Executing a competitive takeout
C) Building market share in an existing segment
D) Getting more value from existing customers
E) Entering new markets, verticals, or segments
F) Targeting strategic named accounts

"As you have told me, Mike wants more account-based marketing to accomplish a variety of goals, so as it will depend on your resources and the size of your team, you may initially want to focus on one goal and gradually expand, or you may want to immediately transition to an entirely account-based strategy. There are four ways to approach ABM; I will list them for you."

1:1 ABM
Targeting 1-10 high-value, strategic accounts with personalized messaging
ABM Lite
Targeting 10-100 accounts that share similar characteristics, challenges, and initiatives
Programmatic ABM
Targeting 100-1000 identified accounts using ABM-inspired tactics
Bolt-On ABM
Supplementing lead-based nurturing with account-based advertising to expand reach to include an entire account

"As you can gather from these descriptions, 1:1 ABM is by far the most resource-intensive way to do account-based marketing, so my advice is to reserve it for extremely high-value logos. Which approach or approaches your team takes is highly dependent on the goals you've been set by Mike and the resources he has given you."

"With this information I am sure I will be able to tailor-make goals to suit Lancett ProCloud, thanks Mr. G."

STEP 3: Select Your Technology

"The next thing to remember is without technology we would not have the ABM revolution, because without the growing landscape of ABM software, it would be impossible to do account-based marketing at scale. That's because of three main factors.

• ABM technology helps you engage your customers on their terms via digital channels rather than just emails and phone calls.

• ABM technology makes it possible to engage not only an individual lead but also the entire account — even if you don't have their contact information in your database.

• ABM technology is versatile. It allows you to personalize your marketing based on personas, sales stages, campaigns, or activity in your CRM.

This will give you, I know Connie, a variety of account-based marketing tools, which are available on the market. Let's look at how you can pick the ones that work best for you. I believe the best resources for discovering and comparing ABM technology include.

• Technology review sites such as G2 Crowd, Capterra, and TrustRadius

• The Terminus Cloud for Account-Based Marketing

"Make a note of this link, you can find a collection of 40+ ABM tools that align with all the stages of the flipped funnel: Identify, Expand, Engage, Advocate, and Measure

- The Account-Based Marketing Stack Grader

"With this interactive tool, you can grade your marketing technology stack, allowing you to identify gaps and overlap in your ABM software."

"I can see how it will give me options, I can put into practice."

STEP 4: Identify And Prioritize Target Accounts

"Exactly, so once you have team agreement on your primary reasons for doing ABM and selected the best technology for your goals, you'll need to identify the accounts you want to target. These accounts should fit your ideal customer profile, or ICP. If you don't have a documented ideal customer profile, use the Defining Your ICP Worksheet to help you and your sales team, have a productive conversation about the accounts you should focus on. It is important to engage everyone, Connie. This is the time for marketing and sales to determine precisely which accounts to go after. To assist in the identification process, you can use any number of ABM technologies — such as predictive tools like Mintigo, Infer, EverString, and 6Sense and data tools like Data.com, Oceanos, LeadGenius, and Node — to help pinpoint companies that fit your ICP.

STEP 5: Select Your Channels And Craft Your Messaging

"Now remember, Connie account-based marketing is this effective because it allows you to proactively engage best-fit accounts, rather than waiting for qualified leads to come to you. You need to choose which channels to use to reach those accounts. You can deploy your account-based marketing campaigns using channels and activities such as email, direct mail, social media, video, website, blogs, display ads, SEO ads, in-person events, infographics, webinars and virtual events, E-books and whitepapers. Don't try to use each and every one decides on what works best for your specific industry and target client."

STEP 6: Execute Campaigns And Begin Sales Outreach

"When I was jotting all those down, I was becoming rather anxious, glad I can pick and choose."

"Yes you need to focus on the avenues that you know will reach your targets the best. Once that is done, it's finally time to put your messaging into the market. Use your new ABM technology to deploy digital ads and engage your target accounts across the web, at events, and via direct mail. When your message has been in the market long enough to make an impression on your target accounts, it's time for your sales reps to begin outreach using more traditional channels like phone calls and emails. At this point, your marketing team will have already used ABM to generate brand awareness and engaged decision-makers at your target accounts, setting the stage for more effective sales conversations. But, please note your job as a marketer isn't over just because sales have started outreach. If you're running display ads using Terminus, make sure you refresh your creative approximately every 45 days to prevent ad fatigue and ensure your audience is getting the most relevant, effective messaging that will move your accounts through the buyer's journey. If an ad is seen too many times it loses its effectiveness."

"Much like a TV ad that is played over and over, you stop seeing it in essence."

"Yes, that's right. It becomes visual white noise."

STEP 7: Evaluate And Optimize

"Now as with any business strategy, you'll need to accurately measure your ABM campaigns and optimize them when necessary. Mike, Dan and Miriam will expect hard figures and that can be achieved now you have the seven steps to planning and implementing account-based marketing, put into effect. You need to put that knowledge into action by using these worksheets,

Perosna Worksheet, ICP Worksheet, and the Content Mapping worksheet. Let's explore which business challenges can be solved using account-based marketing campaigns. ABM Strategies Framework will help you select account-based marketing strategies based on your business goals and the level of sophistication of your ABM program.

Use the ABM Strategies Framework to identify must-try campaigns you can execute using account-based marketing and ensure you're nurturing your target accounts from the time you identify them to the time they become customers — and beyond.

***Visit www.flawlessinbound.ca to download the tools that will help you to build your ABM foundations. ***

"Let me ask you Connie, what are the three primary use cases of account-based marketing?"

"There are demand generation, sales pipeline, and customer marketing."

"You are obviously listening and learning very well, Connie. Yes, that's right and within these categories; marketers can apply seven essential ABM strategies."

Demand Generation Strategies

"You need to remember account-based marketing is not about generating net-new leads however, ABM is an important part of any demand generation strategy. There are three types of demand gen strategies that can be accomplished with ABM. Jot these down before I explain them."

- Pretargeting
- Account nurture
- Lead-to-account nurture

STRATEGY ONE - Pretargeting

"Pretargeting is marketing at its finest. It's a demand generation strategy designed to complement your outbound efforts. To generate demand and warm up net-new accounts for sales, you can deploy relevant digital ads across social, video, mobile, and display. By serving targeted ads to stakeholders at your best-fit accounts, you can drive greater engagement — and not just with a single lead, but with all key decision-makers at each company. The biggest benefit of a pretargeting strategy is the ROI. When you place your ads in front of only the people who you want to see them, you avoid wasting money on unqualified accounts. If you're employing a 1:1 ABM strategy, your ads and marketing offers can even be highly personalized to each individual."

"This will enable me to prove to Miriam that I am contributing to the ROI, something she continually reminds me."

"Again, you will have the ability to measure the success of the strategy in black and white. That should keep her happy."

STRATEGY TWO - Account Nurture

This strategy focuses on account nurture campaigns aimed to engage key stakeholders at target accounts that you already have in your database and convert them to the sales pipeline. Because the B2B sales cycle is long and often complicated, many of the accounts you're marketing to won't immediately be ready to make a purchasing decision. Don't make the mistake of letting these accounts go to waste just because they're not going to turn into immediate sales."

"Mike has asked me to reduce the sales cycle and this method will assist me with that."

"Yes, it will, because by using the account-based nurturing it will continue to present your messaging and content to those accounts over time and keep your company top-of-mind until they are ready to convert into a sales opportunity.

STRATEGY THREE - Lead-to-Account Nurture

"With this strategy the lead-to-account nurture strategy is unique because it only applies to bolt-on ABM. If your goal is to generate demand, while dipping your toes in the ABM water, then I believe this maybe the strategy for you, Connie. As you use inbound marketing strategies to generate leads, you can "bolt on" account-based marketing by expanding your reach at those leads' companies. You can do this by using digital ads to nurture the entire buying committees. Lead-to-account nurturing and bolt-on ABM solve one of the basic challenges of lead-based marketing: being unable to reach the entire buying committee within a company. Bolt-on ABM is the fastest way to extend marketing's reach to all of the influencers and decision-makers in an account, while nurturing an individual lead. This type of ABM is easily automated and can be added to existing marketing automation flows."

"I'm sure I can enlist Roger's help, he's our IT guru."

"Good idea, Connie, but note that bolt-on ABM, don't provide the same efficiency gains or personalization as the other types of account-based marketing. One of the key benefits of the other types of ABM is that marketing dollars are not wasted on a "spray and pray" approach. Instead, the entire budget is spent on marketing to targeted accounts, so my advice is to identify if you have a successful, high-converting lead generation program already, as this may be a good place to start with ABM. Or if you're not generating lots of high-quality leads, begin with a pretargeting strategy to target net-new accounts."

"I can take a look, but I think we are the latter case at the moment."

"Make the strategy work to your benefit, Connie."

PIPELINE VELOCITY - STRATEGIES
"Pipeline velocity strategies are an important part of account-based marketing because they help move your best-fit accounts through the sales cycle more quickly. Something Mike will appreciate I'm sure. There are two major pipeline velocity strategies that can be executed using ABM.
- Pipeline acceleration
- Wake the dead
    Connie laughed at the second point.
    "Oh my goodness, that is funny."
    "There is a reason, but I'll get to it in a minute."

STRATEGY FOUR - Pipeline Acceleration
"Firstly, pipeline acceleration campaigns support sales efforts to engage more influencers and decision-makers at target accounts and move them to the next positive stage in the buying cycle quicker. You can do this by using digital advertisements, sales rep engagement, field marketing activities, and events to educate and build a relationship with your potential customers through each stage of the buying process. At many companies, pipeline acceleration is a vastly underutilized strategy. That's because traditional marketing methods — emails in particular — can feel intrusive during the sales process. Not only that, but they're limited to the same contacts that your sales team is working. With an account-based pipeline acceleration strategy, however, you can use tactics like digital ads to reach additional stakeholders, helping to build consensus at your target accounts and move them through the pipeline promptly."
"So, Mr. G, if I understand this right, we are announcing ourselves to all levels of our target accounts employee structure."
"Yes, that is it in a nutshell."

STRATEGY FIVE- Wake the Dead

"At any given time, your database is full of "dead" accounts that aren't actively participating in the sales cycle. But don't be fooled; these accounts aren't actually dead! To bring these inactive accounts back to life, you can target them with ABM campaigns to revive their interest. Not only does this remind your target accounts about your solution, it also allows you to reach additional contacts at each account — contacts that may be more receptive to your messaging and more likely to engage with your brand."

"So unlike traditional methods, when a contact leaves the company or is promoted to another position and the lead goes quiet, we still have the ability to engage additional ones?"

"A perfect way of stating it, Connie."

CUSTOMER MARKETING - STRATEGIES

With this in mind remember that account-based marketing isn't just for winning new business. It's also incredibly effective for retaining your current customers, helping them be successful with your solution, and generating more revenue from your customer base. The two key customer marketing strategies that benefit from an account-based approach are.

- Land and expand
- Renewal and upsell

STRATEGY SIX - Land and Expand

"Selling to enterprise accounts can be tricky, especially when they're divided into smaller divisions or subsidiaries that operate independently and often have different points of contact. This is where you'll want to "land and expand." If you've done business with one division of a complex enterprise company and are hoping to expand into others, you can use ABM technology to present ads to those target divisions' key decision-makers. These ads are especially effective when they're hyper-personalized, highlighting case studies and testimonials from your target buyers' coworkers."

STRATEGY SEVEN - Renewal and Upsell

"The goal of renewal and upsell campaigns is to increase renewal rates and contract values of your current customer base. This campaign strategy requires close collaboration between your marketing, sales, and customer success teams. In order for an account-based renewal and upsell campaign to be successful, you need to combine marketing initiatives like direct mail, email nurtures, and advertising campaigns with personal outreach from your customer success team and/or sales reps."

"I will need to employ all the sales team in this strategy to ensure it functions at its best. More homework for me Mr. G, but I am not complaining. Far from it, your help is immeasurable to me."

"Thank you once again, Connie. Now you need to ask yourself, how do I measure and optimize my ABM campaigns?"

OPTIMIZATION

"While many traditional marketing strategies don't allow you to optimize your campaign until it's already run its course, account-based marketing is an agile strategy that's designed to be tweaked and modified throughout any campaign."

"Oh, now this I like. I can give Miriam and Mike real time figures."

"Yes advertising at the account level allows for real-time optimization. You can use ABM technology to see if your advertising creative and marketing messages are falling flat with your target audience and swap them out on the fly. Terminus makes it easy to automate A/B testing to create the most effective ads. You can also optimize your ads manually. Compare them side-by-side to determine which colors, copy, images, and calls-to-action are generating the most clicks among your target audience."

"Again, I can enlist Roger's expertise with this part of the marketing campaign."

"And another important part of the optimization process is gathering feedback from your sales team, which should happen continuously as you run your ABM campaigns. Connie make sure you ask your sales team the following questions.

• Have we been successful in penetrating the key accounts we wanted to target?
• Which messages in the market are getting the best feedback from our target accounts?
• Has the quality of your sales calls improved?
• What can the marketing team do better to support our goals?

"The combination of quantitative data and your sales team's responses can guide you as you update and optimize your campaigns."

"I will be able to track everything using this method and with such great adaptability changes can be made easily and quickly. I like it more and more."

Account-Based Marketing KPIs (Key Performance Indicators)

"Yes, it gives you great flexibility. Measuring the success of your account-based marketing campaigns is a lot like measuring the success of any other marketing program, except this time, you're restricting your measurements to key accounts. Your KPIs will depend on your business goals and the type of campaign you're running. These are the eight most common account-based marketing metrics. So I will list them off for you."

1- Marketing Qualified Accounts

With account-based marketing, you'll shift from marketing qualified leads (MQLs) to marketing qualified accounts (MQAs), which provide a much more comprehensive picture of your prospective customers. For an account to be labeled as an MQA, it must fit your ICP and meet a predetermined level of engagement among multiple contacts at that account. Accounts that don't fit each parameter of your ICP shouldn't be disqualified, but they should require a higher level of engagement to be considered MQAs.

2- Engagement Rate

Ask yourself are your target accounts engaging with you? Look at whether accounts are clicking on ads, have a high velocity score, or are visiting your website. With ABM, you should focus on increasing engagement with the entire account — not just a single lead. You can also look at the account's score within your marketing automation platform to determine engagement levels.

3- Reach Within an Account

Track how many net-new contacts you reach with your ABM campaign. This metric is a great indicator of brand awareness. At a macro level, it will also give you an insight into the size of your typical customer's buying committee and help you target your marketing more effectively.

4- Pipeline Velocity

Keep track to see if your account-based marketing campaign moves accounts through your sales process faster and ultimately closes deals faster. Ask what is the timeline of stage progression from first touch to opportunity? And also look at from opportunity to closed-won deal?

5- Conversion Rates Throughout the Funnel

Did your ABM campaign increase the number of target accounts that progressed to the next positive stage in your sales cycle? This metric can be measured by many different parameters depending on the stage of the sales process and your business goals, but some common goals to track include meetings set, opportunities created, and target accounts converted to customers.

6- ROI

What is the return on your investment for each account-based marketing campaign? It's important to note that the ROI will not be immediate because ABM is a long-term business strategy and not a quick fix.

7- Marketing Influence

Since B2B sales are typically complex with multiple touchpoints and long sales cycles, there is rarely one tactic or touchpoint that is responsible for an opportunity being created or a deal being closed. Because of this, it's important to understand which deals marketing influenced and where in the sales process the influence occurred. By comparing that data to deals that were not influenced by marketing touches, you'll be able to measure marketing's influence on pipeline, ROI, and the sales process overall.

8- Churn Rate

Ask what percentage of customers are being targeted by an ABM campaign churn. Is this number lower than your overall churn rate?

"Do I utilize metrics here then?"

"Actually no, Connie metrics don't matter. Let me explain."

Metrics That Don't Matter

"Traditional lead-based goals and metrics do not directly apply to ABM. Remember, your goal is to speak the same language as your sales team — and that language does not include the word lead because it's all about the account! That's not to say these metrics don't matter at all. While these numbers are still indicators of engagement and shouldn't be disregarded completely, they should not be considered success metrics in most ABM campaigns. By using account-focused KPI's to track success — and optimizing based on your results —you will build the most impactful ABM campaigns and demonstrate ROI for your organization. Note these down."

1. Net-new leads
2. Marketing qualified leads (MQLs)
3. Form fills/web conversions
4. Click-through rate
5. Cost per click

"In conclusion account-based marketing is a modern take on classic B2B strategies, bolstered by new technology and a commitment to sales and marketing alignment. It starts with flipping the B2B funnel as we know it, then identifying and targeting best-fit accounts to turn them into customers and advocates."

"So, I will need to work closely with sales to identify the target accounts and formulate a system of tracking the success rate using these methods. I feel Miriam and Dan will be more inclined to agree on my Inbound Marketing Strategy as Phase 1, since we will be working on ABM as Phase 2 for our full Marketing implementation."

"What I am trying to convey is that you cannot start (Account-based marketing) without the foundation, which is (Inbound Marketing)."

"So, it is best to have concrete figures to show them prior to announcing my plan. Thank you so much for this advice, it is invaluable to me. Once again I am in your debt."

"Not in my debt at all, Connie. I find it has a benefit to me as well. It gives me a chance to refresh my Inbound marketing knowledge but also link it to account based marketing strategy since now you want to go deeper into account or vertical marketing. If you have time later this week I could go through the changes in B2B buying processes."

"I will certainly make the time Mr. G, how about next Thursday at 5 'clock?"

"Let me check my schedule."

"Mr. G scrolled through his reader device. Connie could see a plethora of appointments and notes on his calendar."

"You certainly have a full schedule by the looks of it. If it is not convenient we can meet the following week."

"No, I have a conference call at 3 o'clock on Thursday but it should be finished by 5. If it runs over a little can you stay?"

"Yes, Bruce is away on a training seminar, so I am perfectly free all of Thursday evening after work."

"Excellent then Thursday it is. Take care and put those strategies into action. You will succeed Connie, I'm confident of that."

Connie thanked Mr. G once again and left the coffee shop, her mind buzzing with new information and a newly acquired confidence that with Mr. G's help she would make her position of Mar-Tech Manager a success at Lancett ProCloud.

Her excitement showed on her face as she relayed Mr. G's advice to Bruce over supper.

"He sounds like a perfect mentor, Connie and one who is extremely generous with his expertise. How old did you say he was? Do I have competition?"

"Oh, Bruce not all, you know I love you. I was fortunate to bump into Mr. G that first day and he did say these sessions are aiding him as well."

"Well, I love you too and am glad you have such a fantastic mentor. Now, no more work talk let's find a movie to watch and relax."

"What a great idea, it will do me good to just unwind. What type of movie shall we watch?"

"I'll see what's available while you put some popcorn in the microwave and fill up these glasses. I promise not to pick all war movies."

"Oh, I hope not, they are really not my thing but no soppy love stories either, I'm not in the mood for sickly sweet."

The next morning, Roger hailed her to his workspace, looking side to side making her nervous.

"Just to warn you the agency you hired for the website content isn't performing well. I heard Mike speaking to Dan earlier."

"Oh no, I was so convinced they had the right credentials. I'll take a look. What do you think of their content?"

"To be honest it is rather basic blog writing and reiterating the same content over and over."

"Why didn't someone say something earlier? I've been so focused on other marketing strategies I dropped the ball on this one. I'm going to have to work on this right away. Thanks for the warning, Roger."

Connie sat at her work station and scrolled through the website, it became apparent quite quickly that the agency was just regurgitating the same content over and over. *Well I'll have to tell Mike we need to drop them and find another agency.* She went back to her notes on hiring agencies and reviewed them again.

Make sure the agency has experience in your industry in your area.

Don't go with the lowest price – outsourcing to a third party or ordinary templates could be used.

Ensure you are in direct contact with the web designers and have the ability to update content yourself.

Look over their portfolio and read testimonials.

As she read the list, Connie realised she had adhered to the list in part but also knew she had not monitored the website for several months. The initial content had been good but now without her input the content writers had become lazy. She picked up the phone and made a call. Afterwards she went to find Mike and report on her discussions.

"Mike, do you have a moment?"

"Sure, what's up?"

"Actually, I have to come clean and say I dropped the ball on the website agency. It's no excuse but with the trade show organization and the inbound marketing strategy, I admit to having left the website agency to its own devices."

"Well you and me both, Connie. I haven't looked at the site for a while myself."

"Unfortunately, the content has been repetitive and uninspiring, so I made a call and told the agency we no longer needed their services."

"I see and what do we do now about the content?"

"If you can bear with me for a week or so I will find another company but will make sure I keep a close eye on the content from now on. I'm sorry."

"Well, as you say, you have had quite a number of tasks on your plate. Can we make use of any of the content in the meantime?"

"Yes, it can be revitalized jointly by Roger and me until such time as another agency is approved."

"Great, well keep me in the loop."

Grateful Mike understood, Connie went back to her workstation and began researching content agencies in their area. She also browsed through several competitor websites to see if a web content company logo was stated at the bottom of the pages. It might be a good place to start her investigations. She also made out a new list of requirements for the website, one she wanted to discuss with each agency.

- Creative (from copywriting to video/multimedia production)

- Search engine optimization/marketing

- Social media management/marketing

- Search engine marketing

- Email marketing

- Analytics

- Online advertising in all its forms -- Instagram promoted posts, Facebook sponsored posts, Google AdSense, etc.

- Content marketing

- Website development/coding/strategy

- Marketing automation

- Inbound marketing

- Public relations

- Blogging and content creation

- Branding awareness

- Traffic

- Leads

- Sales

- App downloads

Then a second list of what she needed to consider.

Clearly define our needs and expectations.

Consider time we are willing to dedicate to the partnership.

What money are we willing to invest?

Define the skills our team possess and lacks and create a program to complement and improve.

Decide on agency type:

> General vs Specialized Services
> Creative vs Industry Niche
> Global Reach vs Local Reach
> Large Agency vs Boutique Agency

Monitor accountability – deliverables, metrics, reporting and goals.

Timeframe for campaign progress reviews.

On-going evaluation for course changes or re-prioritizing for events or performance.

Feedback – report to the agency on their efforts.

With a set of requirements and the list to hand, Connie got to work. The sooner she found a more competent agency the better and, if she could keep the costs the same or lower that would be a bonus. After a few searches she found a great article, which gave her more information on handling websites.

Creating a Digital Experience that Engages. High performing Websites that last - Seven Core components to make it all happen.

Ever wondered what the expiration date is on your website? Unfortunately, there's no windshield sticker reminding you that it's approaching, or label suggesting you should take a whiff before using. Most website designers and developers have advised a redesign every year or two. Just 730 days (or less) before brands should take another long hard look at their online selves and question, does this site still accurately reflect my brand?

Does it support my users and stand out from my competitors?
Especially when you think back to the plight of your last launch, this doesn't seem like much time at all. But there's a reason why your website requires an upgrade annually or every other year. The web environment is changing — and fast. So are the behaviors and preferences of your users. And this rate of change isn't slowing up any time soon. It's actually getting more intense.

Here's what we know about today's website users:
They have a limited attention span
They browse more often via mobile devices than desktop
They are increasingly drawn to visual content
They are looking for clear, concise answers
They love an exceptional user experience (UX)
They value convenience, speed and intuitiveness
Does your Website Cater to these behaviors and preferences?

If not, it's stale and we'd bet it's not performing as it should. The good news - website designers and developers have been chasing change since the advent of the internet and getting quite good at it. Instead of focusing on what users want today, the new course is to create websites that are scalable and capable of constantly adapting based on actual user engagement to provide a continuously optimized UX. For brands, this means a much longer shelf life. These websites are high performing. Designers and developers carefully calculate and construct them from the ground up using a core blend of approaches and strategies, such as Growth-Driven Design, Mobile First, and Progressive Enhancement. They also incorporate advanced styles and features, including strong content, eye-catching visuals, new scroll techniques and unique navigation to better engage and delight visitors. Each of these components contributes to the UX in a specific way, and collectively empowers websites to deliver a top-notch performance. But before we dig into these components and what they mean for your website and user, let's take a look at the problems these components address.

The Problems with Traditional Website Redesign?
1. Marketing gets pulled from its focus on business goals to assist with branding and messaging, which stifles any momentum they've gained in the market.
2. Organizations place significant cost, resources and energy into the website upfront without any guarantee that the finished product will perform to their standard. And the entire process is largely based on assumptions about what the brand thinks they know about their audience.
3. Redesigns have a way of running over budget, drifting out of scope and surpassing their intended due dates.
4. Websites are launched and left to linger in cyberspace without the necessary care to help them succeed. That care means implementing an inbound strategy to help

users find the website, observing how visitors interact with it, and applying what's learned to improve the form, function and overall UX.

Before brands know it, two years fly by, and it's time for a complete redesign again. And once more, they have little information to go on for improving the site's performance. Enter, core component No. 1

Core Component 1 - Growth-Driven Design (GDD)

With traditional website construction, the site is built, polished and launched with fingers crossed. The hope is that assumptions made about audience wants and needs are correct. The reality is that there is no warranty. And too often, assumptions miss the mark. With Growth-Driven Design, website developers take a more adaptable approach. Instead of launching finished product, they launch a more pliable website that represents their best assumptions about what brand audiences want and need. Then, they observe audience impact closely to validate assumptions and adjust the website according to these validations until all website features truly align with audience wants and needs (not just a guesstimate of what those wants and needs are).

This strategy for website redesign implements a systematic process that extends throughout the course of a year and beyond. Simultaneously, it supports marketing momentum. Here's how it works:

Phase 1: GDD
Discovery & Launch
Pad Development
Approximate time frame: 3-6 months

This phase must be done from the user's perspective, and involves setting goals, creating a strategy, and of course – plenty of persona research.

First, interviews and keyword research should be performed on the current website and its users to gain user feedback regarding how users arrive at a site, how they interact with it once there, and the cause for any drop-offs or bounce rates.

This information validates assumptions about why users visit a site, what value they receive once there, and how/when they prefer to access it (desktop, mobile, at home, at work, on the go, etc.).

Next, brands and redesign teams brainstorm a master "wish list" that embodies every possible feature and function that could serve these validated assumptions improve the UX and increase the site's overall performance.

Apply the 80/20 Rule
The 80/20 rule states that 80 percent of results can be attributed to 20 percent of efforts.

Once the wish list is complete, the 80/20 rule is applied, and the list is whittled down to what the brand and redesign team believe are the top most impactful elements. In other words, the list is segregated into "must have" and "would like to have" lists. The "must have" list becomes the core features that define the true purpose of a website.

From here, traditional redesign takes back the wheel. Content and messaging are crafted, information architecture is performed, wireframes are made, design, programming and development takes place, and light UX testing is performed before the site is launched.

This entire phase is done relatively quickly, after which point, the redesign team and brand stands by for audience impact.

PHASE2: GDD - Optimization and Ongoing Development
Approximate time frame: Ongoing
This is where things get interesting. Phase 2 will involve creating and assessing monthly sprint cycles and will require a fundamental shift in thinking. All focus will now be placed on the site visitor and how they interact with the new website. A four-step process guides this phase:

1) PLAN
Here, redesign teams and brands decide what will be accomplished during each monthly sprint cycle.

The current website's performance is also compared with goals to get a baseline understanding of where things are.

2) DEVELOP
Next, the brand must create traffic flow by experimenting with different tasks and deliverables. Content should be created based on user feedback and input from relevant departments (marketing, sales, etc.). Validation tracking codes should be embedded within content campaigns, and target marketing and content distribution channels should be utilized to drive traffic to the new website.

3) LEARN
As content generates data, redesign teams and brands must analyze results to even further validate or eliminate assumptions about what target audiences truly want and need. Content on the website (both text-based and visual) must be adapted to better resonate with audiences based on these newly discovered facts, and new findings should be documented for future use.

4) SHARE

Finally, new findings should be shared with marketing and sales teams so inbound marketing and sales approaches can be even further refined to better reach target audiences. As you can see — growth-driven design alleviates the pain points of traditional website redesign.

Marketing Goals Are Supported During And After The Redesign Process.

The number of assumptions brands use to guide decisions are significantly reduced, and websites receive the ongoing care they require to reach top performance. The entire idea of rebuilding your website every two years is challenged by growth-driven design, which enables your website to continuously evolve as the wants, needs and expectations of your target audiences do. But the real unsung hero is the data generated throughout the GDD process, which will be fed back into other parts of your business (marketing, sales, product design, etc.) to improve the overall operation.

Core Component 2 - Mobile First Strategy

Mobiles have already taken over Internet browsing with about 52.7 percent of people worldwide using their smartphones, wearable's and tablets instead of their desktops to surf. This percentage is expected to continue climbing, which means every website needs to be optimized for a variety of screen sizes. Mobile optimization makes websites look great and function well for users on mobile devices. But that's not what we're talking about. Truly high performing websites dig deeper with a mobile first approach. As the name suggests, mobile first means designing and developing for mobile before considering display and function on larger screens. This forces designers and developers to solve the challenges of mobile before thinking about more manageable large-screen displays. This isn't just making things fit on a variety of screen sizes. Mobile users may not have a stable Internet connection, and they operate on less electric and computing power. They frequently browse on-the-go, too, which means changes in lighting (especially sunlight) must be considered when creating the viewing experience.

Core Component 3 - A Progressive Enhancement Approach

There are two general approaches by which a website can be designed. Complex to minimalistic, which we call graceful degradation, and minimalistic to complex, which we call progressive enhancement.

Graceful degradation

Graceful degradation builds for the most sophisticated browsers first, and "gracefully" strips away features and ornamentation to enable the same site to work on older, less capable browsers. Poor quality may get a passing grade by this approach because the focus isn't on the user, it's on the browser. It's not uncommon for users with old browsers to receive a subpar UX on a site built, using the graceful degradation approach, and many website development professionals don't agree with it. After all, everyone deserves a great UX.

Progressive enhancement takes the opposite approach, building a core foundation first, and gradually "enhancing" complexity from that solid infrastructure. Sounds a lot like mobile first, right? Except the focus isn't on screen size, device or browser, it's on the content (HTML) and ultimately, the UX.

Progressive Enhancement

Progressive enhancement places greater value on accessibility and layers technologies in a way that allows all user types to access basic Webpage content and functionality, outdated or not.

You'll see this "layering" compared to a cake, an avocado — basically any food with distinct strata.

- At the core is content or semantic HTML markups that reinforce the meaning of the Webpage information by enabling text-based, speech-based, robotic and outdated user agents to properly navigate it.

- Wrapped around this core is a website's presentation — the external style sheet (CSS) that dictates how a Webpage will look, both in layout and style and allows visual-based user-agents to display or alter the display accordingly.

- Lastly, the outermost layer is the client-side scripting (JavaScript), which allows for interactivity (if available) to enhance usability.

The Case for Progressive Enhancement

Progressive enhancement is considered "the right way" to build a website for several reasons. First, the style and script is wrapped around the content, which means no matter which of the thousands of user-agents is being used, visitors can still interact with content however their agent allows. Progressive enhancement also improves SEO by serving actual page content as HTML, which is the easiest way to get search engines to crawl your pages. Like growth-driven design and mobile first approach, PE focuses on building a solid foundation using only the components most critical to function, before it builds up the bells and whistles. This ensures an outstanding UX for all user types.

Core Component 4 -Powerful Content

If your entire website is built in layers around (and in support of) content, its content better be on point. This isn't something that just haphazardly falls into place over time, either. Powerful content requires serious user research (including deep audience insights and demographics to flesh out buyer personas) and optimization. Despite its gravity, content is often the last detail brands consider during a website redesign. They assume it will be written along the way (you know, during all that free time), or they devise a shortcut to plug the old content into the new site, and this creates a dangerous pitfall for the UX.

Think about how much information you encounter each day via email, social media, online resources and applications. As this sea of information swells and rages on, it's becoming increasingly more difficult to connect with target audiences. Putting useful information out there isn't enough anymore.

Content must be specifically optimized for the individual user in terms of quality, tone, style, and messaging and action ability. It must speak directly to individuals in a way that personalizes the experience for them. It must engage them, delight them, and clearly guide them to a next step. Remember, users today have limited attention spans, which means long, arduous blocks of content should be replaced with concise value propositions with solution-focused messaging.

Recycling old content or writing new content as an afterthought, will reduce the power of all the other steps you've taken to create a high-performance website (including extensive consideration for the UX). So if you don't have the time, manpower or talent in-house, hire a professional writer or talk to your inbound marketing agency for research and writing support.

Core Component 5 - Strong Visuals

Just how short are attention spans today? According to a study by Microsoft Corp. — officially less than that of a goldfish. Seriously — we're talking about 8 seconds before our minds wander on to the next thought, which gives brands little time to more deeply engage website visitors. This got designers, developers and brand experts thinking: How can we get our messages across in less time?

It's well documented that about 65 percent of the total population are visual learners. When ideas, concepts, stories and data are associated with imagery, they become more appealing to the masses and, more importantly, the information resonates deeper than text or audio alone.

"Content accompanied by a relevant image gets 94 % more views"

According to HubSpot, content accompanied by a relevant image gets 94 percent more views and 59 percent of top-level executives admit that if they have the choice to read text or watch a video, they would opt for the video. But remember, simply incorporating images and video isn't enough. These strong visuals must align with the brand and messaging and must also be responsive to cater to all user types.

Core Component 6 - Smooth Scrolling

If your website's architecture chops up the flow of your brand story into layers upon layers of different subpages, you're doing yourself a serious disservice. Not only does this make a chore of navigating your website on mobile devices, it also interrupts the narrative, and hampers your ability to effectively communicate how your product or service meets the user's wants or needs.

Instead of clicking to access segmented information, single-page design and parallax scrolling will guide visitors through information in a single, or few fluidly scrolling pages to empower your website's storytelling ability.

Parallax scrolling is a graphics technique, wherein the background images move more slowly than the foreground. This creates an illusion of depth. Visitors scroll text on one plane while the imagery on the underlying plane moves at a different pace. Not only does this style of design help mask the length of content, it also visually engages your visitors and encourages them to keep scrolling through your story.

Core Component 7 - Clean Navigation

Naturally, a single-page parallax scrolling website is going to influence navigational changes. Instead of extensive drop-down navigation lists that take up valuable screen real estate, navigation is becoming subtler. Take, for example, the "hamburger menu": three horizontal lines stacked atop one another, indicating more navigation options for users. We're also seeing more large icons or "cards" indicating a pathway for users to follow. These navigation alternatives are less distracting and allow content to take center stage while at the same time, providing an obvious path for the user.

Core Components COMBINED

The one thing that will never change is change itself, which means the highest performing websites go beyond meeting the immediate behaviors and preferences of today's user. They do more than create a personalized experience for specific audiences. High performing websites learn, adapt and grow in accordance with the world around them. They are lifelike in their response to engagement, and they constantly evolve to deliver an optimal UX. By incorporating these approaches, strategies and features into your next website redesign, you will maximize your investment and meet your audiences in motion.

The grand takeaway — website redesigns need to stop focusing on just the now and start focusing on both the now and later. Is your website designed and developed for adaptability, scalability and on-going optimization?

Connie realized there was a lot more to the website than she had first thought. The article gave her an informative and unique insight and one she would certainly utilize.

Chapter Six: Lessons learned

A) Account-Based Marketing is not for everyone.
B) While ABM is a proven strategy for enterprise deals — *your Fortune 500 deals* — Inbound is a proven strategy for small and medium-sized business (SMB) deals
C) You can also think of inbound marketing as feeding into your ABM funnel. Because if an inbound lead ends up being part of a target account, ABM can pick up right where inbound leaves off.
D) The Differences Between Account-Based Marketing and Inbound Marketing

1. **ABM is highly targeted**. Instead of relying on broad-reaching campaigns that aim to draw a larger number of prospects to you, ABM focuses on just those prospects that are most likely to buy and uses personalized campaigns to engage them specifically. To source these high-quality prospects, account-based marketing professionals build ideal customer profiles (ICPs) using firmographic and technographic data (and sometimes predictive analytics).

2. **ABM focuses on accounts, not markets or industries.**
   Account-Based Marketing pros gain a deep
   understanding of their target accounts to create content
   and campaigns **optimized** for them. This is different
   from your typical approach to content marketing where
   you're addressing a broader market or industry.
3. **ABM targets both prospects and customers.** ABM's
   goal is to "land and expand" using optimized
   campaigns to bring in new customers and act on
   opportunities to grow current accounts (i.e. cross-sell,
   upsell).
A. Choosing your partner in the journey is as critical as
   choosing your journey. Deciding on who is the correct
   Inbound Marketing Agency to work with is critical to
   the success of the marketing program as the strategy
   itself. You need to choose an agency that has worked
   with at least 20-30 accounts before your account. You
   do not want them to be learning on your dime.
B. GDD, Growth Driven design is the more agile model of
   building a website, based on the Inbound Marketing
   methodology. Gone are the days where you spend 20 to
   30K on a website and then in two years the website is
   fully absolute. Deal with your website as your sales rep
   that needs product knowledge, update every couple of
   weeks. Also, you may need to replace your sales reps, if
   they are not performing well, it is the same thing. with
   your website. However, you cannot be doing that every
   two years so GDD fixes this.

Chapter Seven – Re-birth of the B2B Buyer's Journey

Connie utilized the reporting strategies Mr. G had outlined at their last meeting, during the week and engaged the sales team in identifying target accounts, which she relayed to Mike. As well as listing the marketing team and their roles and interaction, she also laid out the reporting method for KPI's and MQL's and ultimately ROI.

"This report is very concise, and the information is well set out Connie, a job well done. So, you are confident you have this inbound marketing working for us?"

"Yes, Mike, the system allows for tracking and reporting at every level and I'm sure Miriam will be happy about that."

"The more figures we can give her the better, and I think Dan will be impressed with this goal focused program too. If you need anything more, please let me know. Good work, Connie."

Bolstered by Mike's praise and the confidence she felt, Connie worked closely with each member of the teams, so everyone understood the system and how it worked. She looked forward to her next meeting with Mr. G. His help had made such a difference to her success at Lancett ProCloud and her knowledge of inbound marketing strategies.

On Thursday evening, Connie walked over to the coffee shop to find Mr. G in full discussion on his laptop, with ear phones in and a total focus on the discussion. She ordered a coffee and sat to one side waiting for his conference call to finish.

"Sorry, Connie I kept you waiting, it was supposed to be a straight forward discussion but as you know not everything goes to plan. Anyway, I'm all yours now. Shall we dive straight into the changes of the B2B buying process?"

"Sounds great. I did pay for a coffee for you so I'll grab that first."

Once they were sitting at Mr. G's preferred table he began.

How has the B2B Buyer Changed?

"The B2B buying process has changed, and so has the B2B buyer. Gone are the days when salespeople actively "sold" to prospects and marketers would participate in "interruption marketing" – doing their best to get in front of prospective customers regardless of their level of interest or qualification. Thanks to the Internet, social media and other major online influences, prospects are spending more time on the web doing independent research, obtaining information from their peers and other third parties. Companies are meeting prospective buyers earlier than ever, and they must avoid having sales engage with every early-stage lead that is not truly sales ready."

"So we need to identify if an account is sales ready prior to engaging the sales team to communicate with them?"

"Yes exactly. Let's look at the risk factor."

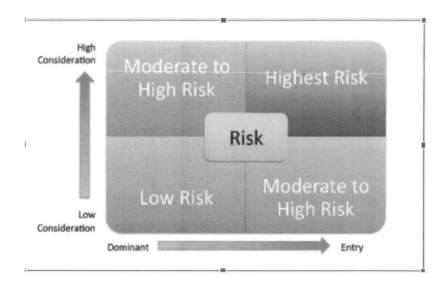

Why Marketers Must Reduce Risk in the B2B Buying Process

"Research shows that the B2B buying process is a highly emotional one, one that lends itself to irrational behaviors and heuristics, or quick methods of coming to a solution that are, at best, educated guesses. The emotion that most impacts the B2B buyer is fear (e.g. job security, loss of professional credibility, monetary loss, etc.) B2B marketers must do their best to minimize this fear by eliminating risk, which can be done only through building trust with prospects. While there is organizational risk involved in the process (often stated in the procurement or RFP process), personal risk is what marketers must seek to understand best. This type of personal risk is often unstated, but different for each person in the buying committee and a potential source of internal tensions and ineffective buying processes. Many qualified leads disappear because of personal risk, and when sales and marketing don't acknowledge and tackle this fear, revenue suffers."

"We need to identify the risk factor for an account prior to engaging them in the buying process, while lessening their personal risk. I can see how this method would eliminate wasted effort on the part of the sales team. Something I can report to Dan and Miriam as a cost effective strategy."

The Changing B2B Buyer - Analyst Facts

"Yes, Connie it is important to remember that business buyers are people, not faceless companies. Rational decisions get clouded by emotions, motivations and desires. I can quote a few articles here on the subject. Laura Ramos - Will B2B Marketing Become Obsolete? (Part II), The Forrester Blog for Interactive Marketing Professionals, 2008. 'B2B marketers must stop pushing out communications and start listening to what buyers need.

Customer research, segmentation, under-standing the buying process and creating relevant information that engages prospects in conversations – and ultimately long-lasting relationships – all require marketers to understand their customers deeply.' And Marketing Needed for Sales 2.1, Sirius Decisions, 2009 – 'Buying 2.0 is a better metaphor for the buying/selling interactions of today's selling environment as the hunter has become the hunted. Buyers are more informed and seek information independent of sales. Buyers have access to overwhelming amounts of information but seek intelligence they can trust to support their decision making process. How sales people want to sell has little impact on how buyers are choosing to buy. The knowledge-driven buyer has raised the bar for sales people to be more informed and better prepared to bring value to the interaction.' And Sales Enablement 3.0: A Transformation of Sales Enabled by a Transformation of Marketing, IDC, 2009 'The shift from product-led selling to relationship-led selling calls for a significant transformation of sales — enabled by a transformation of marketing.' So we need to review the ways we engage buyers in this new era of inbound marketing. Let me list them out for you."

Engaging the Changing B2B Buyer – Basic Techniques
• Pay attention to the emotional needs and cues of B2B buyers and have sales engage with only sales-ready leads.

• Provide prospects with sufficient amounts of relevant information to help guide and educate them during the buying process.
• Encourage sales to approach every meeting armed with as much knowledge about the prospects and their organization as possible.

• Leverage face-to-face sales meetings to help build trust and ongoing relationships with prospects.
• Be where the prospect wants to be – participate in social media.
• Make best use of marketing tools like marketing automation and CRM.

Engaging the Changing B2B Buyer – Adv. Techniques
• Eliminate risk by developing thought leadership through relevant marketing assets, blog postings and more. By becoming a leader in your category, you build trust with prospective customers.
• Consider the various feelings of risk felt by every individual in the buying committee and how personal agendas and internal tension can affect decision-making.
• Create marketing personas for key decision makers to promote more relevant and consistent marketing and sales interactions with prospects.
• Strive to establish yourself as a "preferred vendor" in your industry by differentiating your product or service and building brand awareness.

Buyer Stages – Different Perspectives
        "With the changing B2B buyer comes new ways of looking at the different buying stages involved in the B2B decision-making process. By evaluating these different approaches and perspectives, you'll be able to formulate the stages that make the most sense for your own organization. These stages are key to your success, Connie."
•   Traditional Buying Stages
•   Stage 1: Awareness – Identify a business need
•   Stage 2: Consideration – Determine possible solutions
•   Stage 3: Research – Evaluate different solutions

- Stage 4: Purchase – Select a solution and negotiate the purchase
- Buying Stage Framework (according to analyst firm, Sirius Decisions)
- Stage 1: Loosening of the Status Quo
- Stage 2: Committing to Change
- Stage 3: Exploring Possible Solutions
- Stage 4: Committing to a Solution
- Stage 5: Justifying the Decision
- Stage 6: Making the Selection
- The Buyer Sphere (according to research firm, Enquiro)

"According to B2B research firm Enquiro, the buying process is not a simple logical, rational and linear process where a prospect moves neatly from one stage to the next; rather, prospects move chaotically forward and backward through the process as they balance rational decision making with the emotional impacts of fear and risk."

"So we need to make their transition from potential customer to buying customer as smooth as possible using our knowledge of their risks and formulating a plan to furnish them with as much product knowledge as we can, to enable us to convert them to an account. This will be a learning curve for the team but I'm sure I can explain it well enough that they are on board."

"Yes, Connie once you have the sales and marketing teams aligned it becomes easier for them to approach clients."

Social Media and the Changing B2B Buyer

"Remember social media also plays a key role throughout the entire revenue cycle, beginning before prospects are even identified (while they research or follow though leadership on social media sites), to after they become customers, (as they remain loyal customers through retention and cross-and up-sell opportunities). Marketers can use social media to reduce feelings of risk and build trust with prospects, and ultimately drive revenue and new business. You will need Roger to monitor the following."

• Listen to what unidentified prospects are saying through social media, in which valuable relationships are built through blogs, Twitter and other non-traditional marketing vehicles.

• Engage prospects with greater relevancy by using what they say on social media sites to enhance profiles, trigger more targeted nurturing flows and provide deeper insight into their conversations with sales.

• Continue to build profitable relationships with new customers through more informed retention marketing and cross- and up-sell activities.

• Different Conversation point around Revenue attribution to the Marketing effort

How can we Measure Revenue attribution to our Marketing effort

"Now, this is also important for you, Connie. CMO's require that each new marketing dollar they invest drives organic revenue growth. As we now understand the buyer's journey does not follow a linear course. Without revenue attribution, you are exposed—unable to allocate time, money, and resources to the marketing efforts that produce top-line results. If you can't quantify the collective impact of marketing touch-points, you are left guessing. And that eventually gets you fired, when you guess wrong."

"I hope that is not an option, Mr. G. I want to make a success of this position and prove my worth."

"Yes, of course you do. Revenue attribution is a tough issue to scope out. But it's well worth the effort. Forrester research analyst Tina Moffett stated, "B2B companies are seeing an average of 15 to 18 percent lift in revenue as a result of implementing a closed-loop attribution system and then optimizing marketing programs based on the more sophisticated analysis." The size of the prize, a 15 to 18 percent lift, makes revenue attribution worth pursuing. That's a game changer and one you can show Miriam to align her to your inbound marketing improvements. And it's none too soon. CEOs and boards have put chief marketing officers under the gun to prove the ROI for marketing expenses. Unfortunately, as CMO's share more data to become more accountable, this has had the opposite effect. All too often, members of the C-suite find unexplainable discrepancies and gaps in marketing data. Worse yet is when marketing explains discrepancies in a way that shows the C-suite that marketing data is not as reliable as data from the other functions. One CMO candidly shared, "Every time I have what I think is bulletproof evidence of marketing ROI, I find myself exposed when someone on the executive team pulls on a thread that I can't explain. Each time this happens, it's more difficult to come back to a skeptical audience."

"This is exactly my problem, Mr. G. I have to supply my CFO with a provable correlation between expense and ROI."

"You are not alone, Connie. CEO's, COO's, CFO's, and boards rarely understand marketing and commonly view it as a drain on EBITDA. While executive teams accept marketing as a necessary function, they have little patience for the marketing budget discipline because they don't see a clear connection to revenue. Adopting revenue attribution enables marketing leaders to change the conversation, using language the C-suite understands. By tracking marketing contribution and revenue attribution in a way that proves marketing's impact on top-line growth, CMOs take a crucial step toward building confidence and trust."

Understanding Revenue Attribution

"Let's begin by establishing a common definition to bring clarity to the discussion. Revenue attribution is the methodology for assigning revenue dollars to marketing touch-points that occur during the buyer's journey. It involves connecting marketing and sales data to measure the impact of marketing efforts on revenue from closed/won deals. This practice allocates credit to all marketing touch-points, across all channels that ultimately produce the desired customer action. The foundation of the new terminology points to accountability. But thought leaders and vendors have inundated marketers with a barrage of attribution-like terms. To make matters more confusing, analyst firms are seeking to brand specific expressions rather than help establish a shared lexicon. I think it is important to go through some common misconceptions before we start fleshing out revenue attribution."

What's the difference between marketing contribution and revenue attribution?

"Marketing contribution is the methodology for tracking marketing-sourced and marketing-influenced leads through the funnel. The key to this measurement is that contribution is tracked as leads are delivered from marketing to sales and never from closed wins back to marketing. The best practice for determining your marketing contribution is to capture the primary source of each marketing-sourced or marketing-influenced lead. Then track qualified leads in the CRM all the way through the funnel as they convert to pipeline opportunities and closed/won revenue. By doing this, and you have a believable marketing contribution KPI. However, marketers lose credibility, when they take the list of closed/won deals and then gold-dig their way back to past email and trade show interactions, for example. That is sheer happenstance, not cause and effect. The CEO and sales leader are experts at sniffing out this shell game. Pipeline and closed/won revenue numbers are the bookends to a robust marketing ROI. Marketing contribution to the pipeline and revenue should be the top KPI's of a B2B marketing team."

"How do I correlate the marketing and revenue figures then?"

How does marketing contribution interlock with revenue attribution?

"Marketing contribution and revenue attribution are two different types of measurements, and you need both, Connie. The value of the contribution KPI is that it quantifies the impact of marketing. The value of revenue attribution is that it tells you the "why" behind marketing contribution: what's working, what's not working, and where to allocate budget. Without revenue attribution, marketing contribution metrics can become unwieldy at the pace of growth expected by management. As the marketing function shifts from activity metrics to hard-hitting revenue and pipeline contribution metrics, marketers struggle to scale their efforts in proportion to incremental budget investments."

"This is something I need to focus on, the figures are all that counts as far as Miriam is concerned and with her influence over Dan, when it comes to expenditure over income without quantifiable figures, she could potentially push for Mike and Dan to terminate my inbound marketing program all together."

"That is exactly why you need to put these strategies to work, Connie. First, when some marketing channels are proven to work, they cannot be scaled at the same rate of acquisition cost. The reason is inventory limitations and increased costs per activity as you go deeper. Examples include search keywords, social ads, and vertical industry email blasts. Second, marketers can't legitimately pinpoint with precision what marketing actions caused the result. This causes marketers to overstate the impact of integrated campaigns since the orchestration of touch-points had an impact overall — and if you can't isolate the exact elements, you must give the whole campaign credit."

What's the difference between BI visualization tools and revenue attribution?

"So what's the difference between BI visualization and revenue attribution?"

"Well, business intelligence (BI) visualization tools such as Domo, Tableau, and GoodData help you see and understand your data better. These tools can be used to bring disparate data sources together and then displayed to tell a story. BI visualization tools help enable the assembly and display of revenue attribution data. But they require a guiding strategy."

"I will need to utilize these tools then to accumulate the data into one place?"

"Yes, they will allow you to assemble and display the revenue data from disparate data sources."

How do BI visualization tools relate to revenue attribution?

"Think of revenue attribution as the brain and BI tools as the arms that the brain controls. Vendors for BI tools will talk about revenue attribution because the attribution revenue reported by the BI tool has value to the buyer. When buying a BI visualization tool, you may see a promise of revenue attribution. I would advise you to make sure you read the instructions for whatever tool you decide to purchase, in order to uncover all the groundwork, you must do to perform the necessary inputs before the BI visualization tool can spit out a revenue attribution report."

"Is there a favoured tool you would recommend?"

"They are all similar, Connie, but by researching each one I'm sure it will become clear which one will align the best for your company and its industry."

"Then I have some homework to do here."

Planning Your Implementation

"Revenue attribution is an advanced form of tracking that must be built upon a solid foundation of basic tracking fundamentals and accurate CRM data. Technology vendors serving this space oversimplify the implementation. Conference presenters minimize the day-to-day trench warfare necessary to do revenue attribution right. This is a task that requires a lot of effort and discipline. But it's worth it. In an interview with B2B marketing leaders, who have successfully implemented revenue attribution, they reported their confidence rate in the data on a scale of 1 to 5, with 5 being "highly accurate." Surprisingly, even these capable marketing leaders rated the accuracy of their attribution models at only an average 3.6."

"That seems like a rather modest rating."

"Indeed, Connie, Leo Tucker, senior vice president of global marketing at PGi, focused his team on revenue attribution and implemented it successfully. But when asked about the top challenges, he stated, "The attribution data is only as valuable as the data in the CRM system that can be appended. A close second was getting tracking in place around the globe with my international marketing teams. I didn't want this to be a North American view. It was important to have a global view of revenue attribution." Tucker uses revenue attribution reports to allocate budget with confidence, knowing the precise marketing touchpoints that are moving customers through the buying process. When interviewing CMO's, I also dove deeper with the member of the team, who was involved in the implementation. When vendors say they integrate seamlessly with your CRM, realize that's only half the battle. Integration with your CRM and marketing automation is the price of entry for the technology provider. Companies fall into the trap of adopting an attractive technology and then letting the technology dictate the solution. The best practice for implementing revenue attribution takes careful planning to determine your requirements for the technology."

"In other words, I should not become blindsided with the technology."

"Yes, that's right. Make it a tool to use not a tool that determines your solutions or technique."

How do I provide visibility into touch-points?

"You may be ready to go, but chances are your initial steps will involve getting your house in order. So after the marketing leader establishes the project charter, have marketing operations map all the marketing touch-points, both digital and physical. You should indicate a status for each one like this."

- We currently track consistently world-wide

- We currently track consistently in some regions, but not world-wide

- We do not track, but can with the right tagging or reporting (physical sources)

- We do not track, and do not have the capability to track with existing systems

"In a working session with marketing operations, map each planned marketing touch-point to the corresponding status. You'll identify many gaps such as content syndication, field marketing, international campaigns, and so on. Closing these gaps requires training, process, and discipline. The result of this exercise is readiness for implementation. If you're thinking this is too hard, remember — if you don't close the gaps, you'll have reduced visibility into the series of touch-points that drives leads through the funnel."

"I can see this will be an intensive exercise, but I'm sure with your direction I can make it happen Mr. G."

"You have implemented other strategies we have discussed successfully, Connie. I have no doubt you can succeed with this one."

How do I establish a marketing-to-sales handshake?

"So now, it's gut check time. Is there a solid service-level agreement between sales and marketing on how to manage marketing-sourced leads? Has it been adopted? Every sales force has a few lone wolves. But as a whole, do sales and marketing cooperate enough to make this work? If the foundation is weak, stop any effort to pursue revenue attribution right now. Your peer in sales must require his or her sales team to work from the marketing-sourced contact records in the CRM."

"I have the backing of both teams and they are open to cooperation, so I feel we can move forward with the SLA."

"That's good news. Many sales and marketing teams do not initially want to work together so you are one step ahead."

Connie smiled her thanks.

"I can give you an example, Connie. Marketing-sourced qualified leads should be provided to sales. Then that lead record should be converted to an opportunity record, and later a closed/won deal. Through the duration of the prospect's life cycle, sales and marketing should work in concert from the same CRM record. All bets are off when sales close a lead and open a net-new opportunity. The same principle is true for sales opportunities that marketing affects. Marketing's influence should be attributed to the sales opportunity record. Matching up sales wins after the fact is a recipe for corrupted cause and effect. The opportunity and sales history data in CRM systems doesn't lend itself to revenue attribution without some level of manual effort. Companies that do this really well have some level of manual validation. World-class companies have a regular cadence of meetings between sales operations and marketing operations to review opportunities and wins and validate proper revenue attribution. Without a firm sales and marketing handshake, the attribution model is sunk. For revenue attribution to be believable, it must be developed on the foundation of a common CRM record between marketing and sales. Break this cardinal rule and you'll be left with a sales team that doesn't believe the attribution numbers. Yes, it's unfair, but it's the reality. World-class marketing leaders embrace it and so should you."

"I can see this may be a potential minefield, Mr. G., but I will encourage cooperation and once we have numbers to report it will be proof the method works."

How do I select the right revenue attribution model?

"The more you can involve each team member the better, Connie. If someone believes their contribution is making a difference you will have a strong cohesive team. Let me go through the five main attribution models for assigning revenue dollars to marketing touch-points that occur during the buyer's journey."

Revenue Attribution Models: One Size Does Not Fit All

"Different revenue attribution models suit different business needs, depending on the length and complexity of the buyer's journey. Note this list down."

1) First Touch Attribution
All revenue credit for the conversion goes to the first touch-point, when a lead or contact interacts with your marketing message

2) Last Touch Attribution
All revenue credit for the conversion goes to the last touch-point, when a lead or contact interacts with your marketing message.

3) Linear attribution
Equal revenue credit is distributed across all marketing touch-points with a lead or contact.

4) Time Decay attribution
A sliding scale assigns the most revenue credit to the last marketing touch-point closest to the conversion; the remaining touch-points get less credit the earlier they were in the path. This sliding scale can also be reversed.

5) Algorithm attribution

Customized algorithms analyze the relative value of each marketing touch-point, and constantly refine themselves to optimize revenue credit allocation.

"After reviewing these models, your first thought must be, "What dunce wouldn't pick multi-touch?" With a great foundation of tracking and data, that may be the case. However, the right model depends on the fit to your particular business needs. There are five variables to evaluate when selecting a model: buying process dynamics, market influences, capability, capacity, and data integrity. So, you will need to define the following."

Buying Process Dynamics.

"The complexity, length, and number of decision-makers involved in your buying process influence will determine whether you adopt a simple model or a more complex, multi-touch approach that provides visibility into the entire series of interactions. Companies with a single decision-maker and a fast-moving buying process may focus on simpler models, knowing that what's most important is getting a first-time visitor right to sales. In contrast, a complex ERP software company, for example, will benefit from a more complex multi-touch attribution model that captures the entire series of touch-points. There are four determining factors."

Market influences. The attribution model should fit to match the largest challenges you face in filling the top of the funnel and converting eyeballs through the mid-stages of the funnel. If your company is in a fast-paced market and you have a known brand, then your challenges aren't first touch at the top of the funnel. You are going to focus your attribution model on the difficult work of converting mid-funnel, or maybe even focus on the last touch.

Capability. Match the model selection to your ability to execute. Do you have the foundational systems and the capabilities on your team for a more complex model? I would suggest Connie not to bite off more than you can chew by having the attribution model extract more value than it provides. Attribution modelling is an advanced capability that should not take precedence over foundational efforts to get the marketing team on track.

Capacity. Even if the marketing team has the capability, it must have the bandwidth to execute. Running a lean team requires you to consider the value of the insights offered by each model in the context of the resources you can deploy. It's a tough call.

Data integrity. The condition of your data must be solid before you even think about overlaying a revenue attribution model on top. Your foundation of tracking, reporting, and contact record management must be at a sufficient level to consider complex models. If data integrity is weak or in question, then start with a simple approach.

Fitting Business Needs

"**What would your advice be then, Mr. G on selecting a model?**"

"I prefer simplicity, even if you have the capability to implement a more sophisticated model. For your case I would either go for one - chose first-touch revenue attribution and with last touch. Take these examples for instance. Nicholas Miller, head of marketing operations at Phillips 66, selected first-touch revenue attribution for his B2B marketing effort. "First touch is the more valued method for our organization," says Miller. "In my experience, understanding when a prospect first raises their hand is critical as it allows us to truly optimize our spending around filling the funnel. While last touch does show the conversion point, it does not reflect what created that initial interest.

In a world that is flooded with marketing propaganda, a prospect's journey is typically not decided by one source, but multiple. Once on the radar, we focus on moving the prospect through the funnel via solid nurturing campaigns." Mark Goloboy, vice president of demand generation at Brainshark, selected last-touch revenue attribution. "We chose last touch because it's easier to tell the story from a business perspective — makes sense to everyone. First touch doesn't inspire confidence and requires a leap of faith for the business to see the tie to revenue." He also decided to start with a last-touch attribution model to minimize implementation risk. Brainshark recently implemented a multi-touch approach and has started to transition its measurement from last-touch to multi-touch attribution, for the planning value those insights will bring marketing. So, you see defining your model and method can make all the difference Connie to the results."

Proving How Marketing Investments Generate Revenue

"As you are aware the C-suite looks sceptically at the meaty marketing budget, and it's largely a mystery to them. CEOs, COOs, CFOs, and boards know that marketing has a role to play; they just need a better tie-in to the revenue. They want to believe, but without revenue attribution it requires a leap of faith. Marketing leaders are met with scepticism when they present the executive team with a waterfall report of marketing-contributed pipeline and wins. This view doesn't show what marketing and sales teams are doing along the buyer's journey, and it does not account for the totality of effort. Worse yet, the contribution approach is undermined when someone identifies one win in the list of contributions that had nothing to do with marketing. Revenue attribution provides the executive team with a complete view of how marketing and sales work together. This results in a greater appreciation for the value of marketing's total effort to generate revenue."

"With this model I am sure to convince Miriam that a collaboration tactic results in proven results."

"Yes, you will have a clear view of how the revenue was generated. For example, Clint Poole, senior vice president of marketing at Lionbridge, used revenue attribution to make marketing tangible to the executive team. "Revenue attribution started a whole new conversation," Poole says. "They [executive team and board] wanted a customer-centric understanding of the marketing and sales interaction. Non-sales and marketing execs started to have deep dialogue about the whole journey." Revenue attribution gives you the ability to have a very different dialogue with the CEO and board. Take the time to review specific examples of buyers who came through the funnel. Break down all the marketing and sales touch-points along a time line to illustrate the buyer's journey. These examples show the totality of effort. Seeing real examples helps the executive team understand the whole buyer's journey, and makes a sceptical audience believe. In the past, you may have cited buyer research indicating that over half the customer's purchasing journey occurs before a prospect reaches sales. Revenue attribution enables you to prove that point and connect it to revenue. Now you can demonstrate how each marketing dollar spent generates revenue. This results in the board, and the CEO, giving you more marketing budget to invest. And with each new dollar invested, organic revenue growth accelerates."

"Oh my, I am looking forward to showing my CFO how each step of the Inbound Marketing Strategy as Phase1 and Account-based Marketing as Phase 2 of the implementation works and the results in revenue with figures to back it up."

"Talking a C-suite's language enables them to not only understand how the marketing is working, but also gives you clear data on results and revenue. Now, you will need to excuse me because I have a family function to attend in an hour. Again, it has been a pleasure, Connie and I look forward to hearing how you have implemented these methods at our next meeting."

"I have some homework to do to define which tools I should use, but again you have given me a great starting point and a guide on how to implement these inbound marketing strategies. Enjoy your evening."

Connie shook Mr. G's hand and put her notepad in her bag. With so much information she knew she needed to revise it while it was fresh in her memory. Back at home she did not delay in going over the bullet points she had made and began planning how she would identify the tools best aligned to Lancett ProCloud's products.

Within a month, Connie had increased the marketing profile of the company and impressed not only Mike and Dan but also, all be it grudgingly, Miriam. Results backed up with solid figures and a good ROI, Connie felt not only confident but in charge of the marketing at Lancett ProCloud.

Bruce could see the difference in her demeanour and she oozed success. A new purposeful stride, her head held high but most of all she was happy, which made him glad.

"To get a compliment from Miriam on my figures was the highlight of my day, Bruce. I never thought it would happen but with Mr. G's incredible help and some concentrated research, homework and determination I'm where I wanted to be. You helped me as well and I'm so grateful you kept me positive. I love you."

"It was the worth the cajoling, late nights and the tears, I was more than happy to wipe away. I have to say I especially enjoyed the role playing. I had every confidence you would succeed. I love you too."

Chapter Seven – Lessons Learned

1. To evolve from a marketer or MarTech to a marketing manager would require you to change your language and the way you look at things. How to present your ROI and what you should be focused on.

2. Moving up from a marketing manager to a director of marketing or a CMO is a completely different game all together. Please remember a CMO evolving to a CEO has a higher probability than a CIO evolving to a CEO. The reason is very clear. CMOs are closer to business, revenue and clients. They are also in the middle section between sales/branding/new of expanding and scaling. They are also the first department to be deployed to open new markets or speak to a different market segment.

3. Please reflect on how Connie evolved in her approach during the journey so far. Be open minded, sometimes you must unlearn to re-learn. Mentors are critical to any success you have. Choose your mentor and advisors very carefully but the minute you decide to learn make sure you listen and become coachable. Or you will be wasting everyone's time and money including yours.

Chapter Eight – Return with the Elixir

With her marketing strategy gaining momentum and the C-suite impressed with the ROI, Connie turned her focus to finding an inbound marketing agency. After several discussions with Mr. G, she knew the more traditional creative agencies, social media agencies or even PR agencies were not going to enhance the marketing plan she had put in place. What she required was an inbound marketing agency that would act as a business partner and not deal with her as if it is another retainer revenue for them. She'd learnt that she needed to be looking for, not just a traditional Inbound Marketing Agency, but a professional service organization that would help her unlock a true business potential for her organization and success in helping B2B tech organizations in three different aspects - Marketing, Sales and Services. With time pressing she had arranged to meet Mr. G. with the main focus on his expertise for finding such a company. Much to her surprise Mr. G had agreed to meet with her on Saturday and she spent Friday evening compiling a list of questions to ask, as well as refreshing her memory on key points she had already learned concerning inbound marketing.

Connie gave Bruce a peck on the cheek as he left for a day of golf. The sun was shining, and it was a beautiful day.

"I don't see why you have to waste this beautiful day and a Saturday, working on this inbound marketing, Hun. Couldn't you see Mr. G. after work?"

"Well, I could but there is a great deal to go through and I don't want to be rushed. We will be enjoying the day too; we're meeting at the conservatory gardens. So I'll have beautiful surroundings while I discuss everything."

"I'm not convinced you will enjoy the day, seems to be more work than play for Connie these days. You have to switch off sometimes you know?"

"Bruce, I do switch off. I am so close to my goal it would be stupid to lose impetuous now. I promise I will walk around the gardens and lake after my meeting and take lots of photos."

"Okay, but I expect you to keep that promise."

"Now, go and have fun on the golf course and not too many drinks on the 18th!"

Once Bruce had driven off, Connie doubled checked she had her notebook and her tablet was in her bag. The drive to the conservatory gardens was pleasant enough although busy as early morning shoppers drove to the malls. She found a parking spot and then texted Mr. G.

'Hi. I'm parked on the west side. See you at the central foyer in a few.'

As she walked into the building her cell beeped.

'I'm just inside the bistro with a window seat.'

Connie walked through the plant filled foyer enjoying the aroma of flowers and foliage, she looked left and right and easily spotted Mr. G., his hand raised in welcome.

"Good morning, Connie. This is a wonderful venue for a meeting."

"Good thanks Mr. G. I don't think I've ever seen you so relaxed, what's going on?"

"I closed a deal today that has been a trial from start to finish but now both parties are happy with the compromises I came up with, I can sit and relax in my triumph. Well, until the next time that is. Ensuring both sides of an agreement are satisfied is a balancing act and this one, in particular, took all my capabilities to keep the deal from falling through. Now, enough of my tales of woe, we are here to discuss inbound marketing agencies, right?"

"Yes, that's right. I want to make sure I employ a company that will supplement the marketing I have put in place and enhance our company profile in the market place."

Choosing An Inbound Marketing Agency

"You are quite right, Connie choosing an agency that will complement your current strategy but also add enhancement is key to building a solid marketing platform. So let's see. While a specialty or two like social media or email is to be expected, any firm that asserts themselves as an inbound agency must offer four core services. These services are each comprised of several tactical components. But to execute in a way that delivers real value and maximum impact, all these tactics need to be performed together. Seeing that an agency can fold all these tactics together into one cohesive strategy is a good sign they know how to execute and get results."

"So, I will need to research them carefully and make sure they have these core services as my primary focus."

"Yes, that's right. The first core service of inbound marketing is an agency's ability to generate traffic to a website through SEO, blogging and social media sharing. Second, agencies should be able to tell their clients they can develop the premium content needed to capitalize on that traffic by building landing pages and managing online lead generation efforts. Third, agencies need to be able to construct targeted lead-nurturing campaigns aimed at converting those leads into customers. Finally, in order to iterate and improve, analysis and measurement need to be present at every step in the process. As you now know, being able to dig into the results of your online efforts is critical. Doing so on a regular basis will allow agencies to repeat successes and tune underachieving campaigns to get better results."

"You taught me well, Mr. G and I will make sure reporting and analysis is second nature to any prospective agency I think about working with."

"Excellent, remember they must offer the right services and deliver the inbound services that matter most. Now to assist you with that research there are key questions to ask. Make notes of these.

1. Do they offer Traffic Generation, Lead Generation, Leads-to-Customers and Analytical-Focused service packages?

2. What tactic or tactics does their firm use to deliver each of these service packages?

3. What past or current client example(s) best illustrate success they have delivered for each of these services?

"An inbound marketing company must know you and your business, so be specific in your discussions and I must stress attention to detail is vital. They should know their capabilities and what is required for inbound marketing success. Therefore, any agency worth considering should be able to plot out the specifics and details for the campaigns and strategy they propose for your business. Building on the goals and challenges identified in the sales process your potential partner agency should be able to outline their approach in terms of the four core services and explain all the tactics they plan to employ in their execution. Expect a timeline for each chunk and a description of the resources they're likely to need along the way. Make sure each component of the strategy they are proposing to you, as well as what comes before and after each piece, make logical sense. Take these examples as a guide.

Does your business have no web presence? Then traffic generation services like SEO, blogging and social media need to come first.

Is your website underperforming from a lead generation perspective? If so, your agency partner will need to ensure that your site has decent traffic and then begin crafting premium offers and landing pages.

Are too few sales being attributed back to the website? An agency brought on to help with that challenge will (again) need to look at the traffic and lead numbers to ensure quality is present, and then begin crafting targeted lead nurturing and email follow-up sequences. Obviously, the ability to measure and interpret data is a baseline skill for each of the core services, and each agency you consider should be able to set benchmarks, identify trends and take action."

"I can identify where we need assistance easily with the tracking I have in place, so that will help them pinpoint problem areas."

"Next they should present a clearly-defined delivery process. An agency with a solid, proven and logical plan of attack is the one you should strongly consider. Again, key questions to ask are."

1. Given their understanding of your situation, goals and challenges, what do they recommend you do first, second, third, etc.?

2. How does that situation, and the plan they are recommending, match that of other customers they worked with?

3. What do they see as the most critical piece of inbound marketing for your business and goals?

Goal-Orientated Sales Process

"You need to ensure the agency of your choice conducts a goal-orientated sales process. In essence a marketing agency's pitch should be tailored to your business specific challenges and goals. The sales process of a good inbound agency will start with your goals and challenges, and dovetail into how they can help you. You're sure to see slides about who they are and what they do, but they should understand that their services are most compelling when they can be seen as potential answers to the business challenges you are facing. They should begin by asking about your goals, and the timing and urgency around meeting those goals. Also, how are you being measured? What metrics and benchmarks are most important to you? Also, what does the size and makeup of your internal team look like?

If this marketing agency has a department, who focus on sales enablement that would be a good indicator. You do need them to be technical in their marketing tactics but if they can also show you that they can help in understanding your sales process, that is also a great indictor. The reason is, as you evolve in your Inbound and account based marketing implementation, your sales process needs to change so if the same organization, that helped you build the marketing phases (Phase 1 Inbound Marketing and Phase 2 ABM), can then go back and review your sales process and insure that both marketing and sales are truly aligned, they will be a great fit for your organization.

"That's a useful piece of information to consider, Mr. G."

"Getting answers to these critical questions at the outset will allow them to prescribe a plan unique to your business. Your goals and challenges should be natural segues into discussions around their capabilities and case studies. So, the key questions to ask here are.

1. Have they worked with clients who have faced challenges like yours?
2. How does each piece of what they are proposing take aim at your challenges and goals?
3. What is the timeframe for achieving those goals, based on the strategy you have in mind/outlined for my business?
4. What have been the results of their own firm's inbound efforts?
2. Does what they are outlining for you match what your own firm does online?
3. What are some key lessons they have learnt from using inbound marketing for their own business?

"These are quite in-depth questions and several I would not have thought to ask."

"The more information and data you can gather the better to ensure you employ the best agency for your particular company requirements, Connie. The agency should maintain a website optimized for inbound and can cite itself as a case study. Obviously, they will most likely talk the talk, but does the agency you are considering walk the walk? Meaning: do they do inbound for themselves? Digging into their site for a solid YES or NO answer to this question will give you interesting insight into just how good they really are at what they do. Because you're in "hiring mode," your trips to their site have likely been dominated by scouring their services and client testimonial pages. But take a step back from these self-promotion-heavy pages and ask yourself, do they do the things they're proposing for me? Do they blog with the frequency they say I will have to? Are they active on social media? Can Call-to-Actions buttons and premium content offers that convey thought leadership be found throughout their site? A truly effective inbound marketing agency should be its own best-case study. Think twice about engaging with a firm that doesn't make the services they sell a priority for their own business."

"A good point, Mr. G., if they can demonstrate their own inbound marketing strategies is in place for their own needs and it is successful then they should be proficient in making our inbound marketing system work as well if not better."

"Take this as an example. You're sitting at a conference table. A prospective agency partner is projecting some flowchart-heavy PowerPoint slides and outlining the inbound marketing strategy they've designed for you. While you're following the arrows and considering their capabilities, you should be asking yourself two key questions: "have they done this before, and if yes, can they replicate that success for me?" Any inbound agency truly hell-bent on delivering ROI for you will be eager to show you how they've done it for others. Ask for these client success stories early on. These testimonials should include not only glowing remarks from their clients, but also numbers and campaign strategies that summarize the impact of their work. Make sure you consider the four core services of inbound marketing when looking at these numbers and testimonials. Do these case studies cite proof that these guys were able to increase their customer's website traffic? Did leads increase? Did they help turn those leads into customers? Make sure the accomplishments that they are boasting match up with the outcomes you want for your business. Ask prospective agencies for references. As long as there isn't a conflict of interest or a non-compete in place, they should gladly hand names over. Award them bonus points if the client they refer you to is still actively working with them. Retainer work means that an agency has delivered and earned an ongoing commitment. Again, note these key questions to ask.

1. Can they provide case study materials and references from other clients they have worked with?
2. What lessons do they plan on applying to your business from inbound success they have achieved for other clients?
3. What are the critical success factors for inbound marketing?

As Connie noted down more key questions, Mr. G. continued.

"A good inbound marketing company should present compelling case studies and examples of their inbound marketing prowess. These should showcase their specific areas of focus – an agency should specialize not generalize. To help you gauge this ask these questions.
1. Have they worked in your industry before?
2. Which piece of inbound marketing is their strongest capability, and how does the strategy they plan to lay out capitalize on that in particular?
3. If they have worked in your industry before, how familiar are they with your thought leaders and key blogs? If not, how do they plan to go about finding these?

Mr. G. smiled as he watched Connie typed on her tablet with fierce concentration.

"I would recommend you also ask - does the prospective agency you are talking with have a sweet spot? If yes, is that sweet spot service or tactic-specific? For example, maybe they've done SEO for years and gotten phenomenal results. Or is their sweet spot industry specific? Meaning they have crushed numerous client engagements in your industry (or a close relative to your industry) before. If they do have one of these sweet spots, look to see if they align with your challenges and goals. They should. Use the sales process to get a solid handle on your prospective agencies' areas of focus. If they have a service sweet spot, like social media for example, they should know the fastest and most sure-fire ways to leverage social media for traffic and leads. Or, if they've worked in your industry before, it's likely that they know lots of key industry terms and thought leaders – which will make content easier to create at the outset. Specialties like these examples can shine extra bright when incorporated into a comprehensive strategy spanning the four core services. Just make sure your agencies' biggest strengths make you stronger."

"I like that – their strengths make us stronger. I will keep a note on my computer screen."

"You need to ask these key questions as well.
1. To what extent do they plan on using members of your team for content creation, etc.?
2. How do they plan on setting those folks up for success and ensure the pieces they work on with you is a good use of their time?
3. How has involving client team members in your efforts worked in the past?

"I had not thought that there might be cooperation between the two companies, but I like the idea of it. With our team's knowledge and their expertise, we could certainly reach the targets Dan has been asking for."

"Yes exactly, the agency needs to teach and train your internal team and knows how to and also wants to, leverage your team's industry expertise. In essence, inbound marketing hinges on effort. Effort to create content. Effort to Tweet. Effort to research keywords for SEO. Effort to blog. Effort to think about conversion events on your site and how lead nurturing campaigns could be tuned to better perform. It requires lots of effort. Any agency you hire will need to spearhead and facilitate all these efforts but should also be able and eager to train members of your internal team on how to do things like blog and use social media. Consider all the different sides to your business. There are no doubt sales and marketing departments – but what about operations? Manufacturing? Research and development? Packaging? Think about the remarkable content folks from these different departments could contribute to your businesses inbound marketing efforts. Consider how much more visibility a tweet will get if it's tweeted out by 15 or 20 members of an organization, rather than just the company account. An agency truly worth its weight will be eager to talk with all of your employees, train them on inbound marketing best practices and harness their brain power. The more hands on deck, so to speak, the quicker things take root and begin yielding results."

"With that kind of cooperation, I can see the right agency will make serious improvements and advances."

"Yes, the more collaboration the better, Connie to make your inbound marketing strategy a success. Now, we should look at the capabilities of an agency that either resides in-house or with a trusted partner. In reality they should be able to explain how it does what it does. We know that a complete inbound marketing strategy is comprised of many different tactics. It's like a puzzle – but not because it's confusing. It's a puzzle in the sense that it's got a lot of pieces. Pieces that should not stand on their own, but when put together, make total sense. And to truly succeed online, business will need to execute a comprehensive strategy that is inclusive of all the right pieces. Assembling the pieces together into one, cohesive strategy is the job of your agency. Each piece is crucial, and it is important that you understand a potential partner firm's capability at the outset of your relationship. Make your prospective agency provide details of how each step of the strategy is going to get done. Because there is a possibility that they might not have the talent in-house to deliver a service entirely on their own, ask who is responsible for creating/building each piece. They might outsource. Agencies that use partners for technical pieces of the work, like website design and integrations, will be relying on the schedule of another when they make the handoff. Probe them about who their partners are, how long they have been working with them, general timetables and what pieces of the work will get shifted to them. Let's list the question you should ask here.

1. Do they do all their inbound marketing work in-house?
2. If yes, who on their team specializes in what?
3. If no, to whom do they outsource what? And how long have they worked with them?

"In your opinion Mr. G., should I dismiss an agency that outsources?"

"Not necessarily Connie, if the two companies have had a successful and long-standing collaboration there is no reason to reject them. It is all a matter of asking the right questions and research. One point you should consider carefully is if they possess strong project management skills. Inbound marketing is a serious production and the marketing agency you hire should want to run the whole show. As you know, Connie inbound marketing is an organic process. It requires time, elbow grease and coordination. Any inbound marketing agency you choose to partner with is going to need to make requests of your time. They'll do it at the beginning of your relationship to get up and running fast, and on an ongoing basis, to ensure their methods stay sharp and in-line with your business. They will need to understand who your customer is and get a sense of the types of content that will be most effective in attracting them to your site. They'll also need to add forms and other inbound elements to your site. To accomplish these tasks, an agency will need to get inside your head, and inside the heads of others on your team. They will also need to get on the calendar of your website admin! So ask yourself does the agency you're considering have the process and communication skills to make you think they will make reasonable and realistic requests of other employees on your team? Also, have they set clear expectations around what each inbound component will require in terms of time and resources? Do you get the impression that they can manage campaigns with lots of moving parts? They should. A good agency will make your life easier - not the opposite. So the questions you need to ask here, Connie are.

1. What types of requests, technical or otherwise, do they anticipate making of yourself and your team as the engagement kicks off?

2. What types of requests do they anticipate making of yourself or other members of your team on an ongoing basis?

3. What project management software, spreadsheets or other orientation materials should you expect to receive and when?

"The right agency that places emphasis on measurement will succeed faster. The Internet is an infinitely measurable place. This makes each piece of the inbound methodology track-able and interpretable. This should be a fact leveraged heavily by any inbound agency you are considering working with. Your prospective agencies should have presentations littered with the words "metrics," "benchmarks," and "analytics." Words you are now familiar with, Connie."

"Indeed, I am and they have made such a difference to how I maintain my marketing plan and report my figures."

"Yes, you have goals and you are trying to meet those goals by hiring this agency. Therefore, your agency should be as focused on charting success in a data driven way as you are. Progress made toward your goals should to be measured at every step of the way, and an inbound marketing agency worth its weight will be able to track all campaigns and report on performance regularly. So you need to ensure you have the answers to these questions.

1. How will they measure the success of the campaigns they are proposing?

2. How often will they report back to you on these campaigns and progress being made towards other key metrics?
3. What adjustments can be made if certain metrics are over or underperforming?

"I can see the benefit of knowing these points, Mr. G. now I have my own metrics in line I will require a similar report structure for the agency I choose."

"Another aspect of the agency you should consider is their transparency. They should value transparency and want you to see everything that they see. I would suggest asking the following."

1. What online software packages does their firm use to execute and manage inbound marketing?
2. Will your team be trained on this software?
3. How often will they share wins and progress with you?

"I must stress that you make sure the agency you are considering embraces transparency as a core value. While you're not likely to see this word next to a bullet on a PowerPoint slide, an agency can infer and prove they are transparent with their clients by citing and discussing the three main business practices. Firstly, they should outline a regular meeting schedule in their sales process. These meetings allow the agencies a regular venue to raise questions and/or concerns as an engagement is ramping and progressing. Second, agencies should jump at the chance to train your people. The more you understand what is being done and why, the more you can partner with your agency and set their efforts up for success. Third, truly transparent inbound agencies will insist that you have login credentials to the online marketing software they use to run your campaigns. These accounts are loaded with data, and they should be open and comfortable with you walking around in their world. Transparent agencies make their end client part of the team and get better velocity for it. They solicit input and feedback often and couple their knowhow and judgment with their client's industry experience to craft killer inbound strategies and call audibles where needed."

"I can see the importance of transparency as both companies will have access to each other's systems and a certainly of trust is key, I'm sure."

"Yes, that's right Connie. There has to be trust and transparency on both sides to make the partnership work well and gain success. So, in conclusion, you're short on the time and manpower needed to implement and execute key inbound tactics like blogging and social media. Fortunately, there are marketing agencies out there that specialize in the inbound methodology to help. But like any other agency partner, make sure this agency is a good strategic match for the type of goals and challenges you have, as well as your internal teams and processes. Agencies whose personalities, leaders, skill sets and core values map to the attributes I have mentioned will be well-positioned to deliver."

"All these points are certainly going to make my decision making a lot easier Mr. G. and once again I am in your debt. I did wonder though if I might request a little more of your time to go over building an inbound marketing campaign. I have put in place a series of improvements and strategies but want to make sure I am making the right choices. Is that too much to ask? I can come back another time if you prefer."

"Not at all Connie, let's look at it as a refresher on what makes an effective inbound marketing campaign. As you know by now, the world of marketing has changed. Pushing out your message by buying, begging or bugging people for attention no longer works. People are not sat at home or in their office waiting for your direct mail, cold call or billboard ad to reach them. They no longer rely on brochures and trade magazines to decide the products and solutions they need. Instead, they are searching the web, using social media and looking for peer reviews. They are actively seeking out the answers to their frustrations and problems. To remain effective, marketers have to change their approach and adapt to the way people behave now. They have to recognised that traditional outbound techniques are broken and instead adopt inbound methods. So, let's look at the characteristics of an effective inbound marketing campaign."

Helpful

Inbound marketing is educational. It provides the answer to a question, need or concern that a prospective customer might have. Examples of helpful marketing materials include 'how-to' style blog posts and 'step-by-step' webinars.

Timely

Inbound marketing is available at the right time for your prospective customer. When they are facing a certain challenge and are actively searching for a solution, they are going to be won over by the company that provides them with the answer to their problem. This isn't about hoping your email blast hits the right target; it's about carefully crafting content so that it is ready when your prospects are looking for it.

Consistent

In order to make marketing people love, you need to consider the experience of the user across their different lifecycle stages: from the first time they encounter your brand, through their interaction with your website and content, to the point of converting into a customer, and their long-term success as one. By making this movement across different lifecycle stages consistent and fluid, you remove hurdles and encourage your audience to become evangelists for your brand.

"Now, we've covered the key characteristics of inbound marketing, let's look at how you can implement your inbound marketing campaign. For each campaign, there are some specific components that you need in place:

• Start with your compelling marketing offer
• Then get the offer on your website
• Create automated workflows around the offer
• Content marketing your offer through email, blog & social media channels
• Analyze the results

"I have these in place but need to ensure I have each component of the campaign correctly focused."

"Rightly so, Connie. You need to ensure you have created compelling content offers. It can be difficult to continually think up new content ideas for your inbound marketing campaigns. To overcome this hurdle, it is useful to stop thinking of yourself as just a marketer and start thinking of yourself as a publisher. But what does this mean? How can thinking like a publisher and a marketer help you to create compelling content offers? Publishers have a detailed picture of their target audience. So, inbound marketers need to do the same; they need to develop marketing personas. Knowing this information will give you a target audience for your content. So, instead of writing content for the sake of writing content, you will be creating content that is designed to be helpful, useful and interesting to the specific people you want to reach. So let me ask you this, what is a marketing persona?"

"I know this one Mr. G. A marketing persona is a detailed picture of our ideal customer. Developing our marketing personas will help us to know the main challenges, frustration and problems our persona is facing and how we can engage effectively with them. It is a complete picture of the person we are trying to reach, including likes, hobbies, digital hangouts."

"Well done, that is exactly right. You really do your homework! So what stages of the buying cycle do you need content for? Content plays a critical role in every stage of the buying cycle, from generating awareness about your company to helping convert leads into customers. But the types of content you should use to achieve each of these goals are often very different from each other.

Awareness
The prospect gets acquainted with your brand or realizes they have a need for your product/service.
Research/Education

The prospect identifies the problem and researches potential solutions, including your product/service.

Comparison/Validation
The prospect examines the options and begins narrowing the list of vendors,

Purchase
The prospect decides from whom to buy.

"Can we go through how we find the right content topics then?"

"Yes, of course. In order to find what content topics capture the attention of your target audience, you should look at past data that you have access to. For instance, what are the most popular blog articles you have published? What are some of the most viewed pages on your website? Your historical performance should dictate your direction for new marketing content. If you don't have access to marketing analytics that give you this type of intelligence, look in the public domain (Google news, Google trends, Twitter trending topics) for popular and newsworthy industry stories. Piggyback on this information by adding a personal spin, your expertise and comments. You need to find the right format. Obviously, you can create content in different formats, from text-based content like whitepapers, reports and eBooks to media content like webinars, videos and audio interviews. While you can host an internal brainstorm session and come up with creative ideas for different content formats that you can produce, it's important that this new content matches the needs and preferences of your target persona. If you have exiting landing page data, use this to find the content formats that are the most popular. For instance, if webinar offers usually out-perform eBook offers, then you should take this into consideration when creating your compelling content offer."

Compelling Content Offer

"How can I create these content offers?"

"A good question, Connie, as well as coming up with compelling content ideas, it can be a real challenge to get the actual content created. But, there are several techniques that you can use to help: Recruit a Team of Content Creators. You don't have to be the only one creating your company's inbound marketing content – by delegating you use different voices from inside your organization- technical, sales; customer service people, c-level executives, product managers, and others in your organization all have a unique take on important aspects of your business. Get your coworkers to contribute.

- Ask them to co-write a whitepaper or an eBook.
- Interview them and posting short videos that share their expertise.
- Invite them to give presentations or answer questions in webinars.

"You can also look outside your own company for help creating content. There are online content marketplaces, such as Zerys and Odesk that connect marketers with legions of freelance writers and editors who will take on blog posts, eBooks, and other writing jobs for you. You can specify the topic, your desired style and tone, and your intended audience, and you typically don't have to pay unless you accept the finished article. Another great way to create content is to repurpose. Almost every piece of content you create can be adapted, reused, modified and republished in another format. Make a habit of finding multiple ways to package and distribute the same information in different formats."

"Can you give me some idea on how to do that?"

"Certainly, you can combine text from an old whitepaper with new videos to create a multimedia eBook, or turn videos or webinars into blog posts and eBooks or vice versa and use commonly asked questions and comments from webinars to create a new eBook. By repurposing successful content, you already know that the topic area is one your prospects are interested in."

"There is a lot of content I know is viewed regularly so I can start with those and build from there. Repurposing is a great idea."

"It will aid your production of content in various areas of your website and attract more clients to it. Now, we need to look at offers. To start generating new leads from your offer, you need to place it on your website. You will do that by creating a landing page, a web page that features a description and an image of the offer and a form for visitors to fill out in order to receive the resource. This transaction is a type of information exchange, in which the visitor gets the offer they are interested in and you receive the contact information of your visitors. This is the basic process of lead generation. A good landing page will target a particular audience, such as traffic from an email campaign promoting a particular eBook, or visitors who click on a pay-per-click ad promoting your webinar. Therefore, it's important to build a unique landing page for each of the offers that you create. You can build landing pages that allow visitors to download your content offers (eBooks, whitepapers, webinars, etc.), or sign up for offers like free trials or demos of your product. Creating landing pages enables you to target your audience, offer them something of value, and convert a higher percentage of your visitors into leads."

"I have discussed landing pages with Roger and I would like to refresh myself on how to make effective landing pages. Although, Roger is quite capable, I feel he uses the same format and it may not be driving the leads as I would wish."

Effective Landing Pages

"Okay, well traditional formats are commonplace but what you need to do is make effective landing pages. There are several key components that make a landing page effective for converting a higher percentage of visitors into leads. The key areas of importance are the headline, the content of the page, and the form. Let's look at each of these, explain why they're important, and discuss how to optimize them then you can check to see if Roger's pages adhere to these components or not. I would think it would be easy enough to guide him to make subtle changes if required without upsetting him. So there are several key components that make a landing page effective for converting a higher percentage of visitors into leads. The key areas of importance are the headline, the content of the page, and the form. Let's look at each of these, and explain why they're important, and then discuss how to optimise them."

Headline

People's attention spans are short, especially online. This means you need to make sure your offer is as clear as possible. A good rule of thumb is to make sure your landing page passes the "blink test" – can the viewer understand the offer and what you're asking them to do in less than five seconds? Make sure your title makes your offer immediately clear so that the viewer understands what the offer is right away.

Body

The body of your landing page should provide a description of what your offer is and why your visitors should download it or sign up for it. Make the specific benefits of the offer clear. Format the body of your page in a way that quickly conveys the value of the offer and the action visitors need to take. For instance, use bullet points and numbering to simplify the visual layout of the text, and use bold or italicized text to highlight the main points.

The Image

Your landing page needs to feature an image of the offer you are presenting. Visuals have the power to instantly capture the attention of visitors and should be leveraged to the fullest in your marketing. For instance, depending on what your offer is, you could feature an image of the cover page of a whitepaper or eBook, or headshots of webinar presenters.

The Form

Remember that the ultimate goal of your landing page is to get people to fill out your form. Make sure that your form appears above the fold so that the viewer does not have to scroll down on the page to see it.

"Given these points I'm sure I can steer Roger in the right direction."

"The other critical factor you need to consider is the effect of the length of the form on the prospect's willingness to fill it out. If the form is too long, prospects are going to stop and evaluate whether it is worth their time to complete all those fields. So, you need to find a good balance between collecting enough information and not asking for too much information that prospects are not willing to give it. The length of your form inevitably leads to a tradeoff between the quantity and quality of the leads you generate. A shorter form usually means more people will be willing to fill it out. But the quality of the leads will be higher when visitors are willing to fill out more forms fields and provide you with more information about themselves and what they're looking for. Therefore, shorter forms usually result in more leads, but longer forms will result in fewer, but higher quality leads. It is a fine balance and one you should take care to compile."

"I'm sure I can investigate industry websites and see which forms are used currently by other firms. It will be a good starting point anyway."

"We should look at calls to action as well, which will get people to your landing pages. As you know the goal of a call-to-action is to drive traffic to a landing page. In order to increase visitor-to-lead conversion opportunities, you need to create a lot of calls-to-action, distribute them across your website. Placement is one of the most critical elements of leveraging the power of calls-to-action. So how do you decide which call-to-action belongs where? Simple - calls-to-action should be spread across your web pages. Your homepage should have a call-to-action. As your most frequently visited page, your homepage presents a huge opportunity to drive traffic to a specific campaign. Your product/service pages, About Us page and Contact Us page all need to include calls-to-action or the visitor will be deciding on their own what to do next. You need to help them decide what to do next."

"We drive the traffic with the calls to action to areas of the website that will attract our personas."

"You catch on quickly, Connie, yes that's correct. While calls-to-action are usually thought of as images and text placed on a website, the concept of a call-to-action can be found across all types of marketing. In all your marketing assets, you should be trying to drive people to get further engaged with your company. If the goal of a call-to-action is to drive traffic to your landing page, think about the different ways in which you can achieve that. For instance, you can use marketing emails and social media updates to drive traffic to your landing page."

Connie rolled her shoulders and smiled. Mr. G. raised his hand and ordered two more coffees. Once the hot beverages were placed on their table he continued.

"Once you have designed a stellar marketing offer and placed it on your website, but before you start driving traffic to it, you need to consider how you are going to nurture the new leads that you create. How are you going to further educate them about your company and product or service? You will need to use workflows."

Nurturing New Leads
What is a workflow?
Workflows are an automated series of emails or other communications that pre-qualify early-stage leads before handing them over to sales. Workflows are also known as advanced lead nurturing, marketing automation, drip marketing, and auto-responders. Their goal is to make your new leads more sales-ready.

By using workflows and nurturing your leads, you save sales time because you educate and qualify the lead to the point that they are sales-ready.

Getting the timing right
Study after study shows that email response rates decline over the age of the lead. In his Science of Timing research, Dan Zarrella, HubSpot's social media scientist, discovered that there is a positive correlation between subscriber recent visits and click through rate, one of the key metrics of engagement. Once you set up workflows, emails are sent out automatically according to your schedule as new leads come in. You might launch the campaigns and forget about them, but the emails will be doing the work for you, helping you qualify leads and push them down the sales funnel faster.

Targeting
Studies show that targeted and segmented emails perform better than mass email communications. Lead nurturing enables you to tie a series of emails to a specific activity or conversion event. It also means that your follow up communications can be relevant to the original conversion event. If you know your new lead is interested in social media marketing, you can use this information to send them further content that is Relevant to this interest.

Segmentation
Your contacts are not all the same. In order to do effective, targeted marketing, you need to break your contact database up into smaller groups or segments.
Creating smaller segments allows you to group your contacts by their interests, industries, geographies, etc., and then create experiences and messages specifically for each segment. This will increase engagement and help move your contacts farther down the funnel. For instance, you can automatically segment your leads based on any criteria, such as."
A Contact Property: A contact property is based on company name, state, size, industry, lead grade or lifecycle stage, etc.
A Form Submission: Segment based on eBook download, a webinar registration, a demo request, etc.
An Existing List: Segment based on presence in an existing marketing list.

"This is furthering our targeting to the personas then, right?"

"Yes, it is. Once you've created your segments, you need to figure out how you can help move them through your sales and marketing process in a way that caters to their needs. Create nurturing campaigns that will resonate with each segment and make sure that your lists of leads are updating in real-time to include new leads that need to be nurtured."

"And how do we market to existing contacts?"

"Now you have ensured all new prospects, who grab your marketing offer, will receive the appropriate follow-up communication, you can start thinking about sending traffic to your landing page. First, think about ways to notify your existing contacts about the new marketing offer you have released. Your email list should be one of the most powerful contact databases that you have access to. (Your social following represents another growing database of evangelists.) So how would you go about making this announcement to your email list?"

"Well, rather than the traditional method of mass emails that we all know do not work, I'm assuming it is by dedicated emails."

Tips For Your Email Sends

'That's exactly right, Connie. Dedicated email sends are generally easy to set up and measure. Still, there are some best practices that you should keep in mind when you craft your email.

Feature one call-to-action

Dedicated sends focus on driving results for one call-to-action. A case study of Kodak's successful list growth tactic explains, "these calls-to-action were not stuffed at the end of a newsletter or tacked onto another message. They were the focus of a dedicated email, which gave them much more impact."

Personalize Emails

Show your prospects that you know them. Personalized emails not only increase your open and click-through rates, but also demonstrate a deeper relationship with your audience. Make sure to use a consistent voice across your marketing communication.

"This was one of my few successes at my previous company; getting personalized emails out instead of hundreds of mailed envelopes that we were sure were put directly into the trash."

"I remember you telling me about that. The more personal a communication is the better it is for success."

Design mobile experiences

Make sure your email layout displays well on mobile devices. As more people start checking email on their smartphones, you need to optimize for that viewing experience.

Make your emails social and SEO-friendly

Make sure that your recipients can share your email content on social media. Integrate social media sharing buttons in your marketing emails to facilitate that activity. Also, make sure that your emails create a web-only version which will ensure you are leveraging your email for SEO.

Clone & reuse

Once you have your email template in place, building dedicated sends should be easy. You will generally grab some of the information already on the landing page, make a few tweaks to it and spend most time on nailing down the subject line.

Measure performance fast

Naturally, if you have one main message and call-to-action in your dedicated send, it will be easy for you to track progress. You can quickly check the email CTR, landing page views and conversions, and follow the long-term ROI.

"The next avenue to utilize is blogging and social media to promote your offer. Once you have announced the release of your new marketing offer to existing contacts in your email database, you can start looking for other opportunities to drive traffic to your landing page. This is where you can leverage your blog and social media channels. Blog and social media can increase the reach of your content and support your lead generation efforts. Just remember to always a call-to-action: a link to your landing pages with the marketing offer."

"How can we use our blog in this kind of campaign?"

"When putting your blog post together, optimize your writing to grab people's attention and to rank well in search engines. Don't forget to introduce a call-to-action to the marketing offer you want to promote! I can give you a few more tips for a blog post."

- Feature a compelling image: include an image that conveys what the blog post is about. This is appealing to readers and helps to break up the text on the page. A blog post that has some type of visual that's a photograph, a graphic or some type of infographic typically plays a little better than merely text.
- Write an eye-catching title: Headlines are the most important element of your blog posts. While there are quite a few elements that make up a successful blog post, one of the best things you can do to capture readers' attention and entice them to view your post is to write an awesome blog title.
- Format: In blogging, it is important to make the text visually appealing. Online reading is not like reading a physical book. Online reader will often scan a blog article first before reading it in more detail. They need to be able to immediately get a feel for what the article is about based on the sub-headings and anchor text. The added advantage of doing this is that you make the text much easier to read, which means more people are likely to read the full article

Social Media Sharing

"Next, give your blog content extended reach by including social sharing buttons on every post. This will encourage readers to share your content with their personal networks and expand its reach beyond your own connections."

How to Use Social Media in Your Campaigns

"Remember while Twitter, Facebook, LinkedIn, Google+ and Pinterest are all different social media platforms, they have something fundamental in common: the element of information exchange.

With the creation of a good marketing offer to promote, you make your job on social media much easier because now you have content to share! Why not list these other best practices, Connie, when it comes to promoting your marketing offer through social media channels?"

Plan The Timing Of Your Promotion
Control how often you share your offers to ensure your account doesn't turn into a spam-bot. This will be dependent upon your business. For example, a recruiter will be more likely to repeatedly share offers to job openings because users will naturally be vested in that opportunity. However, users may not be as willing to download the same whitepaper about, for instance, improving heating systems.

Decide On Your Networks
There are a lot of available social networks out there. Which one are you going to use to promote your offer? You probably don't have bandwidth to spend equal time on all of them. Look at your marketing analytics and your historical performance with different social channels. Identify the three networks that bring you the best results and focus on using them for supporting your campaign.

"In other words, don't spread our message too thin."

"Yes, it will lose momentum and it will be difficult to track the success across too many social channels. Focus on the ones that you know have the best traffic."

Map Different Content Based On The Network
Different social networks are effective at promoting different types of content. While visual content performs well on Pinterest and Facebook, simple copy works well for Twitter and LinkedIn. YouTube, on the other hand, is a strictly video sharing platform. Find out which social network makes the most sense for the type of marketing offer you have created and then promote your content offer more heavily through these mediums.

"Now that you have created a marketing campaign from start to finish, you need to revisit each element of the campaign and how it performed individually and as a part of a whole. There are a wide range of metrics that you need to look at to evaluate whether your campaign was successful or not. And I feel you have managed to create metrics of your own that assist you with this Connie."

"I do have metrics in place, but it is always good to refresh and review."

"Let us ask the questions, shall we?
- What if the campaign performance was poor? Different metrics tell different stories. So, if your performance was poor, you need to spend time and find out exactly which metric needs to be improved.
- If the number of views the landing page got is low, you need to work harder at promoting the offer and sending more traffic to it.
- If the conversion rate of the landing page is low, you need to focus on creating a more compelling offer or optimizing your landing page.
- If the number of new leads this offer brought you is low, it could mean that your existing contacts are not sharing your offer with new people. You need to either incentivise them or find venues of promotion to a new audience.

- If the number of customers the offer brought you isn't very high, that could mean your workflows aren't successful at qualifying leads to convert them into customers. You might need to revise the workflows and make them more powerful.

What if the Calls-to-Action don't perform?

"When it comes to calls-to-action, for instance, there are two key metrics that you can monitor in order to improve the effectiveness of this marketing asset."

- If the view-to-click rate of your calls-to-action is low, make your offer more compelling so that more of the people who see the CTA will click through.
- Sometimes the Call to Action is not just the colour, text or message. It can be the Chatbot that will quickly convert the lead or traffic into conversational marketing. Make sure to review your conversation marketing models.

Chapter Eight: Lessons Learned

In summary.

Choose a marketing agency or choose a professional service organization that has the capability of Inbound Marketing, ABM and sales enablement, as this will be paramount in the successful improvement of your Phase 1 (Inbound Marketing) & Phase 2 (Account based marketing).

You need a partner organization that can help you truly unlock the business potential of your company. And remember if they truly get the idea that eventually the traditional marketing funnel might eventually evolve onto a Flywheel, this would make the strategic in their monthly consultation with you even more important.

Chapter Nine – Preparing for the Future

Connie walked to space number one, where Dan, Mike and Miriam were sitting. There was a freshly brewed pot of coffee and hors d'oeuvres on a couple of plates. Her heart had leapt in her chest when she saw the email this morning.

Special meeting after the working day – need to know basis only. Attendees: Dan, Mike, Miriam and Connie. Space 1 at 5:30pm

A quick text to Bruce with her concerns had resulted in a twenty-minute cell phone conversation in the washroom as Bruce calmed her nerves.

"There is no way after the incredible impact you have made to their marketing success and the proven ROI you have reported, that they are going to fire you. Now stop worrying. If anything, they should be giving you a big fat rise or a huge bonus. Now breathe. I love you."

"Do you really think so? What if Miriam is unimpressed? What should I do if they let me go?"

"Again, stop worrying. With the figures you showed me, Miriam could only be impressed, in fact any CFO would be. You've made a huge difference to the company profile and its turnover. There is no reason whatsoever for them to let you go. You are letting your imagination get the better of you. Go and sit somewhere quiet for a while, listen to one of your meditation podcasts and calm down."

Connie thanked her husband for his calm reasoning and support and took a deep cleansing breath. She heard the outer door open so flushed and walked out of the stall.

"Heh, Connie how's it going?"

"Good thanks, Mia. I hear you are going to a big concert this weekend."

"Yeh, we fly out tonight at 7 pm and will be in New York overnight, have a day of sightseeing and then the concert in the evening. I requested Monday off because there is no way I will be fit for work."

"Sounds great – have a super time."

Taking Bruce's advice, she left the building and sat in her car and listened to a mediation podcast. With her breathing slowed, her mind cleared and the adrenalin not coursing through her body with anxiety anymore, she returned to her workstation refreshed. Ethan waved her over to his space shortly afterwards and the day's tasks overtook her thoughts. Now she walked to the work space overlooking the river valley breathing slowly and mentally chanting a mantra.

"Hi, Connie do come and sit down. Would you like coffee?"

"Maybe a small one thanks, Mike."

"I'll come straight to the point Connie; as I'm quite sure you have been apprehensive about this meeting. I can say with no contradiction, we have been impressed by your marketing strategy over the last twelve months, even though it was a rocky start in some ways. You have managed to increase our ROI in real terms and projected figures are good based on your progress so far."

Connie did not miss the look Dan gave Miriam as he spoke. If anyone had a problem with her it would be the CFO.

"Thank you, Dan, I have learned a great deal since starting here and you are right, I did have an inner conflict about traditional versus inbound marketing to begin with. I wanted to dismiss all 'old' methods but soon realized change cannot be done overnight. Mike, you were super patient with me and a great voice of reason at times, when I was running away with ideas."

"I admit I was out of my depth for a while there, Connie but you steered us as a team into inbound marketing. I was also impressed by how you involved everyone regardless of department and gave a real cohesiveness to the strategy."

"It is one of the main benefits of this kind of marketing, Mike. Departments do not work in isolation but utilize each other's strengths and expertise to formulate a brand across the company's profile."

Dan looked at Miriam, who was sitting quietly listening to the conversation. She looked over at Connie and said.

"As you know Connie, I was not in favor of hiring you from the start and made it clear that without solid metrics and a proven ROI that I expected Dan and Mike to concede and let you go. However, as Dan has stated you have improved our ROI considerably, so it is I who concedes."

"Miriam, I understood your concerns and it was that added pressure to succeed that made me more determined to make the targets Dan had given me."

"It wasn't just the added expenses I was worried about, Connie but how someone so young – forgive me but it was how I viewed you at the time, could even make such a difference. With such a large expectation from the venture capital company hanging over our heads, I was more concerned with streamlining and lowering costs than increasing them. I am not too proud to say that I pleasantly surprised at your figures. And may I say I appreciated your reporting methods, which have been clear, concise and ever-increasing."

The compliment from Miriam meant so much to Connie, that she had to resist hugging the older woman. There was still a barrier of age and seniority.

"Miriam, thank you so much for your candor and your approval, it means a lot to me."

"Well, I believe in giving praise where praise is due."

"You have given Lancett ProCloud your best efforts tirelessly this year and we all feel you have earned a place at the Summit."

Connie gasped. The Summit was the ultimate in accolade for top performers.

"Dan, I am honored you think highly enough of my work to afford me a place at the Summit. Thank you so much. I promise to continue making a significant difference to Lancett's profile and ROI in the years ahead. If you want me, that is?"

"I will fight anyone that tries to head hunt you away from us, Connie, you have my word on that. You are one of our best assets and I will ensure you stay with us for the long haul."

Feeling relaxed and appreciated, Connie thanked Dan, Mike and Miriam again for their kind words and settled back as they picked at the hors d'oeuvres.

"No more shop talk for tonight Connie. I will get all the details of the Summit to you next week. For now, go and enjoy your weekend."

"Thanks Dan, I will. I have an anxious husband waiting for my call so if you will forgive I will leave now."

"Of course, see you Monday."

Connie grabbed her jacket and purse then exited the building before stopping on the corner to call Bruce.

"Oh Bruce, you were so right they were so full of praise and even Miriam was complimentary."

"There now didn't I tell you? I couldn't see any reason they would want you gone."

"And the best part...I've been invited as a top performer to the Summit. I'm so excited."

"Wow, that is amazing, congratulations, Hun. You deserve it after all that hard work and obsessive studying and planning."

"It's not obsessive just diligent preparation and scheduling."

"I know I'm only teasing. So what time are you home? Should I put a bottle of champagne on ice?"

"Oh, what a lovely idea, I will be home in thirty minutes. Love you."

A week later Connie met up with Mr. G to share her news, he was at his usual table in Froth or Not?

"Good afternoon, Mr. G., how are you?"

"Well, hello stranger, I thought you'd abandoned me."

"It's only been a week and what a week. My CEO, VP of Sales and the fearful CFO all sang my praises at a special meeting last Friday. With your expertise and guidance and hard work on my part, they are extremely pleased with my performance and more importantly the success of the inbound marketing strategy I created and maintained this last year."

"Well, that is excellent news and for my part, I can only say it was your attention to detail and diligent listening that made it possible. I can offer advice and information but it's what you do with it that makes all the difference. Congratulations."

"I have been walking on air all week to be honest. Although, now I have to think about the future, so I can maintain the impetuous."

"Of course, there is no sitting back and reflecting when it comes to marketing and especially if you want to sustain your present in the marketplace."

"So what would your thoughts be on my going forward for next year and the one after that?"

"It is quite a coincidence, but I have been researching this very subject for several weeks. Do you have time to chat now?"

"Always Mr. G., I'll grab a couple of drinks and then I'm all too keen to hear."

With their hot beverages on the table, Mr. G opened his tablet and scrolled through to show Connie a link.

"You will find this interesting, Connie, I will summarize the article as it is too long to read through now but I suggest you do read it at some point."

Connie made a note of the link and sipped her drink as Mr. G. explained.

"The article is based on a global survey of 499 CMO's and senior marketing executives, plus in-depth interviews with leading CMO's. The research explores which technologies and customer trends are likely to change marketing organizations the most over the next five years. Marketers have spent much of the past decade working on perfecting their ability to understand the customer through personalization. What is different about 2016 through 2020 is how CMO's are matching that understanding with direct action that drives engagement—and doing so at scale. The survey data and interviews reveal that leading CMO's are pioneering a new model that blends a deep understanding of a customer's contextual situation with timely, tailored delivery of relevant content and marketing assets. To illustrate this process at work, the EIU developed a framework— "The layers of engagement"—that classifies the elements that contribute to a personalized customer experience, and how it creates value for a customer and for a marketing organization."

"This is certainly interesting, what insights did it give?"

"As you know CMO's own the customer experience full stop. This is reflected in eighty-six percent of CMO's and marketing executives believing they will own the end-to-end customer experience by 2020. This year's research analyzed the customer experience in terms of its role as a direct interface of a brand with its customer—everywhere, anytime and across platforms. However, as we both know marketing complexity is growing sharply, as customer experience overtakes mass advertising as a preferred channel to the customer."

"Yes, with your guidance, I understand the CMO's must learn to manage staggering amounts of complexity."

"Exactly, Connie. More than half of respondents to this survey believe the accelerating pace of technology change, mobile lifestyles and an explosion of potential marketing channels via connected objects and locations, will change marketing the most by 2020, driven by billions of possible interactions they create between a company and its customers. The top channels to the customer in 2020, will be social media (63% of respondents), the World Wide Web (53%), mobile apps (47%) and mobile web (46%). This will, of course affect publishing on centric channels like television; radio and print to score far lower."

"So, customer experience will drive brand equity more than ever?"

"Yes, it will. I would say CMO's are betting that a personalized, efficient and consistent customer experience will translate into customer loyalty and brand value. I believe future innovation will focus on small screens and no screens. Mobile devices and networks (59%), personalization technologies (45%) and the Internet of Things (39%) are the three technology specific trends that will have the biggest impact on marketing organizations by 2020.

"From my own research, Mr. G., I have realized that people conduct referendums on brands on a daily basis. They vote with their online searches, with their transactions, their social networking, and a host of other interactions that either enhance or degrade the value of brands."

"You are correct, Connie and this is how the consumer rapidly compares products and services but more importantly, they share the results with one another through ratings, reviews and other means. With all of this available choice, brands have never been more important — or more easily tuned out by customers.

While the primary value of firms in the industrial age was derived from how well they managed hard assets such as factories, product lines and distribution channels, the information age rewards and punishes firms based on how well they manage brands. Consequently, the increased pressures on chief marketing officers to raise the value of brands for this new competitive environment is transforming how CMO's must engage their customers, by understanding their buying behaviour and intent. In short, be able to predict what they're most likely primed to do next; and be ready to influence them at the right moment."

"Do you really think we can predict what a customer will do, Mr. G?"

"I think if you utilize the data correctly, it is indeed possible. If you think about it logically a single, best version of customer truth is derived from inputs such as demographics, psychographics, clickstream or purchase behaviour, customers' devices or locations, the content they're viewing, along with myriad other data points. These data streams are harmonized to portray a composite picture of the customer that provides the word "single" to the definition. However, for an image of a customer to become the "best" version of truth, analytic capabilities constantly evaluate the data against the criteria such as these. Maybe jot these down Connie."

Uniqueness: Is the data specific to the user or common to a target segment?

Privacy: Does the data require a customer's permission and/or consent?

Applicability: Does the data apply across marketing and business processes?

Value: Does the data help a marketer meet key performance or business goals?

"As you know internally, CMO's use a single, best version of customer truth as a strategy for integrating marketing analysis, creative development and marketing automation capabilities with customer management and support. Externally, this resource helps marketers be where the customer is in his or her journey to a transaction, both literally and figuratively.

"CMO's need to reorganize their departments around personalized customer experiences as a core strategy for creating and growing the value of brands. This model for brand building is not based mainly on a "**Big Idea**" — a single, unifying creative concept around which all marketing collateral is created and distributed across well-defined media and technology platforms to millions of people. Instead, leading CMO's are focused on data and analytics fueled by "**Big Capabilities**", which allow them to understand the immediate context of a person and then personalize his or her end-to-end customer experience across platforms, locations and physical objects."

"I remember we discussed personalizing customer experiences before, but this is a whole new level."

"It certainly is, Connie. We are refining and developing all the time. In fact, eighty-six percent of CMO's and senior marketing executives believe they will own the end-to-end customer experience by 2020. Making the transition to a Big Capabilities model of owning the customer experience across any platform or context requires a comprehensive understanding of the customer. Increasingly, this understanding of a customer's context emerges from a synthesis of data, technology and human analysis---a "single, best version of customer truth." This combines information about an individual's history, preferences and desires, with information about an individual's present and potential value to a brand. Only then can it become a unified asset or resource to be used by multiple organizational units, not just the marketing department."

"Engaging all of the company departments to work together as a unit was one of the facts Dan and Mike praised me for with my strategy."

"And so they should, it is the accumulative expertise that enables you to identify and attract new leads. The EIU developed a descriptive framework called "The Layers of Engagement" to illustrate some of the linkages between competitive pressures and the response by CMO's. This schematic only attempts to classify the various layers that contribute to a personalized customer experience, then map how those components deliver value to a customer and an organisation as it is a complex process. "In other words, Connie be everywhere and be ready."

"That seems like a tall order, Mr. G. but I'm sure with your guidance I will accomplish it."

"I am flattered by your comment, Connie but I think you have more of an understanding now of inbound marketing and its future."

"Well, without your help I'm sure I would not have achieved as much as I have, so thank you."

"It is my pleasure. Now before we get sidetracked back to the framework strategy. As we know smartphones and social media are not just for accessing content or communicate with each other, but a tool through which a growing number of people participate and create modern life and culture. This potent combination of powerful technology and new behaviours will evolve even more rapidly as trillions of sensors, tags and beacons spread into physical objects and the outside world. A new type of personalized cloud of devices, information and applications will travel with the customer, evolving and changing as she moves through her day. In this new environment, the core challenge for brands is to be everywhere and to be ready for however the customer chooses to interact. Can you make an educated guess which business environment trends will change marketing practice?"

"I would say the accelerating pace of technology change, mobile lifestyles and the explosion of potential marketing channels."

"You have been studying! Yes, you are correct. The specific technology trends driving those business environment changes by 2020 are mobile devices and networks, personalization technologies and the Internet of Things. By providing direct utility to customers in lieu of broadcasting messages to them, it offers new opportunities for marketers like you, Connie. But it also requires you to balance short- and longer-term time horizons more than ever."

"I actually saw an interactive YouTube channel, which is an amazing idea."

"It certainly is and the more your customer uses it the more data you accumulate. Taken together, these technology trends suggest a fundamentally different competitive environment for marketing, one based more on data and systems than on media and screens. It is an environment that prizes marketers, who can generate insight about the customer's immediate context and use that knowledge to drive engagement and dialogue. It calls for a different kind of thinker because the skills are changing."

"So, it is not just about identifying our perfect customer anymore but defining their needs in as a personal way as possible."

"You catch on quickly, Connie. The data not only allows you to increase your customer's experience, but also gather specific information to make that experience individual. It is all about numerous touchpoints as personalization blends a deep understanding of a customer's wants, needs and desires with timely and tailored delivery of relevant content.

At the moment, interactive media channels like the World Wide Web, social media and e-mail take the top three slots. However, by 2020, social media will increase sharply for marketers, while the World Wide Web will decline. By 2020, mobile apps and mobile web will overtake e-mail as top channels to the customers. Remember, Connie, the ability to personalize channels also plays an important role in customer acquisition, a core marketing objective."

"I need to stretch for a bit Mr. G and absorb all this for a moment. Can I get you anything?"

"Sure, another coffee would be good, thanks but only if you want to continue."

"Oh, I certainly do but sitting still for too long isn't good for me. Coffee coming right up."

With fresh coffee steaming at their side, Mr. G. and Connie continued with his summary.

"As I see it, in the near future more CMO's will come from science backgrounds, whether computer science or statistics to enable them to combine analytical and creative smarts, without these skills it will be virtually impossible to be an effective CMO. They need to be pioneering new and emerging technologies to engage their audiences.

"It looks like I may have to invest some time in learning more about the technology in the near future."

"Indeed, it may be a wise choice, Connie. Achieving personalization at scale is the biggest and most important challenge for us to get right. We have to work hard to create the kind of infrastructure that supports personalized marketing but that doesn't feel like an ad or an invasion but presents as an available benefit at the right point of a purchase cycle. Personalization at every touch point is a prerequisite for CMO's, who expect to own the customer experience.

Engaging customers with compelling, contextually relevant experiences is the new competitive high ground. CMO's have become laser-focused on CX because it directly hits both the top and bottom lines of business. Customer experience leaders account for 41% of revenue growth leaders and 43% of customer acquisition leaders. Given the importance of customer experience to the business itself, CMO's are being held accountable for CX across the entire organization, not just the marketing."

"I can see my role as Mar-Tech Manager is going to change dramatically as we go forward, Mr. G. I need to focus on CX rather more than I have in the past."

"Your role will change year on year, Connie there is no doubt. As long as you keep yourself well informed and utilize new methods, I am sure you will accomplish your goals."

"Thanks for the vote of confidence. I'm trying not to feel anxious at the volume of work required."

"You have handled the changes you implemented this past year and I see no reason why you cannot continue in the future. Don't let your imagination get ahead of you."

Connie let out a deep breath and smiled at Mr. G.'s encouragement as he continued.

"I found some interesting information, which I feel you should note. According to a survey, 86% of CMO's and senior marketing executives believe they will own the end-to-end customer experience by 2020. Coupled with this, marketing departments will exercise significant influence over business strategy and marketers exercising the same influence over technology. The top priority is a personalized customer experience, which is enabled by creating a contextually relevant customer experience and engagement that culminates in the human touch."

"Personalization is key then, Mr. G.?"

"It certainly is, Connie. A relevant and responsive website will enable engagement and a meaningful long-term relationship with customers. It should also ensure you receive the right data and that it is exchanged at the right point. Elevating a personalized, efficient and consistent customer experience requires that CMO's integrate multiple departmental agendas under a single umbrella. Utilizing the amount of information about customers is easier in this digital sharing age and it is expanding rapidly as more of daily life is digitized with connected objects and locations. Analytics is where speed counts most, as capabilities are critical for reducing huge data sets about customers into decisions and actions. It was common to run customer analytics as batch computing jobs at the end of a business day, rather than moment-by-moment but this method only reflected past behaviour not future behaviour. Revenue impact and customer acquisition are the best marketing success measurements of brand awareness or budget efficiency. Again by 2020, revenue impact will remain the top metric, with every other measure playing a more or less equal role in a suite of measuring capabilities."

"For your future in marketing, Connie I would take note of this conclusion."

CONCLUSION
"As CMO's adopt new innovations in marketing technology and best practice, they speed up the adoption rate of other innovations, as if in a chemical reaction. Only in this case, the volatile compounds being mixed are mobile and broadband technology, social media, data, analytics and, soon, the Internet of Things (IoT) and Artificial Intelligence (AI). To stay relevant in the midst of such change, marketers are moving away from just porting the same creative idea across technology and media platforms.

Instead, leading CMO's are organizing their departments to stand ready to engage the customer with contextually relevant, personalised experiences — everywhere and anytime. Of course, the irony is that the more powerful technology becomes for tailoring and targeting content and messages, the more complex and variable the customer journey starts to be. It may be that customers are accessing similar content on similar websites, apps or platforms. But in their journey to a transaction, people are stringing together and/or mashing up these technical and social elements in combinations that often are unique to them. This complexity will swell because CMO's no longer live in a world where they only need to engage the mainstream and the counter culture. Today's audiences traverse multiple mainstreams and counter-cultures via mobile and socially connected devices and services. Audiences in 2020 will do that and a lot more as IoT, virtual and augmented reality, plus AI cause interactivity to spill out of screens and into the outside world. It raises the question: How will brands find, win, grow and retain customers across fragmented audience environments with unlimited digital shelf space? The research suggests that marketers should organize around a single, best understanding of the customer and her context to drive personalized customer experiences across platforms and at scale.

As data and analytics capabilities transform marketing organizations, CMO's must master a new model of value and exchange based on personalized customer experience. According to Unilever's Keith Weed, customer experience-based marketing offers a better model than advertising for a crowded, information-rich marketing environment. "Brands need to help people simplify life, so we all don't go mad as this world becomes more complex," says Mr. Weed. "I believe that people who focus on that will unlock the true power of data."

"Mr. G., I can see from this article that I will have to develop more creative revenue driven marketing strategy that will match the overall business objective of my organization as the vision for the CEO and the board of director/VC firm has to grow 3-7X or even more in the next few years."

Chapter Nine: Lessons Learned

A) CMO's adopt new innovations in marketing technology and best practice, or they can just stay still, speaking about storytelling and branding. Or spend in PPC and measure visits and leads. They have to evolve to a business partner to the CEO. We are forecasting some CMO's will evolve to be the CEO of the organization, if they have the correct Corporate experience and if they have been shadowing the COO/CFO as well in their role.

B) CMO will have a bigger IT budget than a traditional CIO. 70% of your IT infrastructure will be in the cloud and all your MarTech technology is running from the cloud -HUBSPOT/Marketing/Drift/Website/Landing pages/Social media tools/Video platforms. CMO needs to be ready to get exposed to technology and articulate to the CIO why they need those technologies. The Marketing Technology Stack decision should stay inside the marketing department not the IT department.

C) CMO must be revenue driven and learn to always look at the whole picture. Also learn who you should partner with (Technology partner- MarTech) and Implementation Partners (Inbound Marketing Agency (who will soon evolve to be a professional service organization that will help you unlock business potential with Marketing/Sales/Service enablement). There are very few agencies that have started exploring that route, but it will eventually be the trend in the next few years. Pick your partners carefully so you can sleep at night.

D) CMO must understand that the buyer's journey is in constant change. They must be close to the Clients/Prospects/Sales teams. This will enable them to adjust the marketing collaboration to match the buyer's journey needs. Do not just fall in love with the

Product/Service/ or platform of your organization. The days of build it and they will come are gone. The marketing and the sales department are much closer to the customer than the product development team. You will need to act as a conduit for the product development roadmap. Remember NPS (Netpromoter Scores) are key to ensure the product development team is going in the correct direction.

Chapter Ten – The Summit, Are You Ready?

As the evening of the Summit drew closer Connie grew more nervous, questioning if she should really be included? What if Mike or Dan or even Miriam changed their minds, or she had peaked and from now on would lose momentum, sales and the all-important ROI targets. She fidgeted beside Bruce on the sofa, unable to concentrate on the documentary they had both been looking forward to watching.

Bruce pressed the pause button and the show's images halted. He then turned toward Connie and took both of her hands in his and gently squeezed.

"All right let's have it, what's going on?"

"Oh, I'm sorry I'm worrying about the Summit."

"Why are you worried, you have been given a prestigious and very public pat on the back for months of hard work and dedication?"

"I know logically that seems the case, but what if I've come to the end, and I can't maintain or surpass what I've already done?"

"Hold on, Hun you are spiraling into self-doubt, I don't think I've ever seen you like this. Even when old Gibbons rejected you time and time again you always got back up and found another way to present your ideas to him. The fact that your bosses at Lancett ProCloud have awarded you this honor is the very reason you should have no doubts. The figures talk for themselves, as I'm sure Miriam has told you and everyone who will listen. You made a huge difference to their marketing using your inbound marketing system, and as you told me yourself Dan has made more than the quota laid down by the venture capital company for this year. You reached for their imposed target and exceeded it. So no more worrying or uncertainty of what you clearly achieved, do you hear me?"

"You always have such faith in me, Bruce, thank you. I know I have made a great impact at Lancett ProCloud this last year and I am proud of what I have achieved."

"I feel a 'but' coming after that sentence."

"Well, if I hadn't met Mr. G. would I have achieved such success?"

"Now, come on. I know you are in awe of the man and I admit he gave you incredible direction, information and support but as with any teacher or mentor they can only do so much. You have to take all that information and make it happen."

"Bruce, he was so generous and helpful I will always be in his debt. And I know without him I would have floundered. It is one thing reading about inbound marketing in a book but to have someone like him explain it in real terms made all the difference."

"All right, so I get it, he gave you tools to work with, but it came down to you putting them into practice. Give yourself some credit."

"I know you are right and thank you for all your support this last year, you had your own problems to face and resolve so I am grateful."

"We are a team and we support each other, Hun. Without your understanding when I had to stay away so much with conferences and meetings and the fact you were also happy to listen to me droll on about commodities for hours, I would not have been able to cope. Now top up those wine glasses and watch this documentary. I'll go back to the beginning. No more worrying or doubts, right?"

"You are right, I'm stressing over nothing."

Four days later it was the evening of the summit. Connie had spent weeks shopping for the perfect dress and eventually found one in a rich burgundy. It was figure hugging but comfortable with a scooped back that was not too low and a neckline decorated with appliqué. She found silver shoes and finished off her look with matching silver necklace and earrings. With her hair freshly cut and coloured she turned back and forth in front of the full-length mirror.

"Wow, you look amazing!"

"Thanks, Bruce. It is an evening to celebrate as you rightly said and I am going to make the best of it. You look very handsome yourself."

"Well, after seeing you I had to make an extra special effort. Shall we go the taxi will be here any minute?"

As they turned to exit the bedroom a vehicle horn sounded outside.

"Perfect timing; let me help you with your coat."

Connie squeezed Bruce's hand all the way to the venue. He soothed his thumb over her hand constantly, giving her a reassuring wink as the car drew up to the large hotel. The facade was lit with golden lights making it shine like a beacon.

"Here we are, Sir, Madam. Enjoy your evening."

Bruce paid the driver and before he could get out, a doorman had opened Connie's door for her. She thanked him and put her arm through Bruce's as they entered the impressive hotel foyer. Dan and Mike were standing beside large double doors to the left and waved at them to approach.

"Good evening, Connie, you look sensational."

"Thank you, Dan, you are equally smart and Mike you do look good in a suit. This is my husband, Bruce."

With the introductions made, Mike showed them the table seating list and let them enter a huge conference room, laid out with tables and a stage at the far end.

"If I read the table plan correctly we are at the front, Connie."

"Oh goodness I thought it was the other way around, are you sure?"

"Yep, obviously you are a dignitary this evening, I'm just an extra."

"Stop fooling about."

They found their table at the front close to the stage slightly to the left. A waiter stood beside them as they settled and then presented them with a flute of champagne.

"I could get used to this!"

"Me too, oh Bruce isn't this exciting?"

After a couple of sips, Connie nerves began to recede, and she glanced around the room. There were people she did not recognize but eventually found Mia and Ethan a few tables behind. She waved them over.

"Come and sit with us for a while. How are you both?"

"Great thanks, Connie. I have to say I'm envious of your dress."

"Thanks Mia, it took some finding, but it was worth it."

The four chatted for a while but as the room filled Mia and Ethan returned to their seats. A short time later the double doors closed and the chatter in the room died down as an MC took the stage.

"Good evening everyone. It is wonderful to see you all on this night of celebration. We will have our main presenter shortly, but I wanted to assure you that there will be an opportunity to ask questions after his presentation. So please enjoy the expertise and knowledge of the leading expert in his field before we have the presentations and speeches. Please put your hands together for the man, who has done more for his specific field than any other, I present to you the inbound marketing guru, Saher Ghattas."

Loud applause filled the room and several people stood up to welcome the speaker. Connie's clapping ceased, and her eyes grew wide with astonishment as Mr. G. walked onto the stage. Bruce nudged her with his elbow, a frown on his face.

"What's wrong?"

Connie whispered back.

"That's my Mr. G."

Bruce turned to face her.

"What? That's the Mr. G you have been meeting and learning from all year?'

"Yes, that's him, I had no idea."

"Wow, Connie you had the top most expert in the field mentoring you, that is incredibly cool."

"I feel so dumb, Bruce why didn't I know? I researched absolutely everything but never questioned him about his work or anything personal. I think I should go and hide in the back."

"You are certainly not, you stay right here. This evening is about your success, enjoy it, and relish it."

The audience's applause subsided, and everyone took their seats looking expectantly at the man on the stage.

"Good evening everyone, it is an honor to be here tonight. I know that many of you have implemented inbound marketing strategies within your organizations and I hope to give you a glimpse at the future development of this remarkable inclusive sales method."

As he glanced across the room Mr. G.'s eyes fell on Connie. She blushed and gave a weak smile. Mr. G. winked back at her, and then turned to click a remote that initialized a large screen behind him. Connie took Bruce's hand, inhaled a deep breath and then concentrated on her mentor.

The Growth Dilemma of a Well-Run Company

"Firstly, I want to talk about how we can predict company growth with management backgrounds. You may be having great success as you offer good products or services and use best practices for operations by creating logical, repeatable processes; consistently measuring results; and refining procedures until efficiencies are maximized, and costs are minimized. Even after all this, do you find yourself frustrated because your business' growth curve tends to mirror market growth? You expect and want more and are ready to move beyond the status quo - but how? I can tell you that you are not alone in your predicament. A 2016 study revealed you have plenty of companies with other smart, operationally-focused CEO's.

Their companies are well-run, but are running low on fuel for growth. The good news is that the study also discovered that by adding one core competency to their top management, a subset of these operationally-focused companies were able to change their growth trajectory exponentially. So let's ask what drives growth?"

What Drives Growth?

"You will be surprise by the answer. A study looked at how companies performed and discovered that running a company well and growing a company are two entirely different beasts."

Connie glanced around as a murmur filled the room.

"Let me clarify. This study was the first ever to report that mid-sized company's fall into two distinct buckets: operationally focused or marketing-focused. Key to classifying companies in one bucket or the other was looking at the functional experience of their top management team, the CEO, and their direct reports. A cluster analysis of top management teams resulted in two groupings. The first is the marketing-oriented group (45% of those surveyed), which included companies whose top management teams comprised executives with marketing experience. The operationally-oriented group (55%) contained companies whose top management teams did not have marketing experience and who invested their energies primarily on driving cost efficiencies. So, in essence, the CEO's background is a key determinant of how a company is run. If they are from manufacturing, engineering, or sales, the company likely concentrates on operations. If their background is in marketing or information technology (IT), they are focused on the market.

While analysts were initially surprised that information technology gurus clustered with marketing pros, it became evident they had developed their marketing orientation because their rapidly changing market highlighted the need to be responsive to customer needs. This diagram gives a clearer view."

The screen displayed a graph for the audience to see.

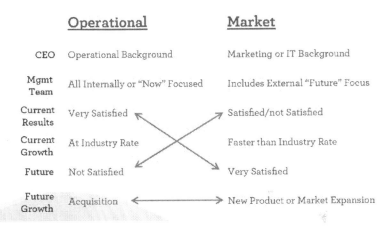

	Operational	Market
CEO	Operational Background	Marketing or IT Background
Mgmt Team	All Internally or "Now" Focused	Includes External "Future" Focus
Current Results	Very Satisfied	Satisfied/not Satisfied
Current Growth	At Industry Rate	Faster than Industry Rate
Future	Not Satisfied	Very Satisfied
Future Growth	Acquisition	New Product or Market Expansion

"The study discovered several key differences between running a company well and growing one. When managing a business, you optimize operations inside the four walls of the company. When growing a company, you're looking outside to the market and bringing that knowledge inside to transform the company's offerings to serve the market better. The skill sets needed to run day-to-day business operations like a well-oiled machine are very different from those required to grow a company. Now for the *'Breakthrough Insight'* - if the study had stopped there, it would have been interesting, but not particularly useful. However, it went a step further and revealed that when operationally-focused companies become more market focused, they grow faster than their peers."

This statement resulted in more murmuring from the audience. Mr. G. smiled at Connie, she returned the smile and had to remind herself that she should refer to him as Mr. Ghattas now, although it didn't feel right somehow.

Gearing Up for Growth

"Let me explain further working harder and harder to squeeze incremental savings out of your operational costs is like riding a bike harder and harder to increase your speed. You reach a point when your muscles are screaming, and incremental effort makes little impact. Once you are pushing the pedals as hard as you can, the only way to have a major impact on the speedometer reading is to add gears to the bike. Just as you can increase the speed of a bike by adding gears, you can grow your company's bottom line by integrating three marketing growth gears. I am sure that many of you have seen the rewards of inclusive marketing methods but other executives who have not steeped in years of strategic marketing, might consider marketing to be expensive, flaky, creative stuff. They view marketing as a black box that they put dollars into and hope for a little magic, but are often sadly disappointed with lackluster results. They might also think marketing is simply about spending money on communications, such as advertisements, website development, or brochures. As we know while these are marketing tactics, if you work on them without incorporating the three marketing growth gears into your strategic planning process, your fear of the black box will likely be realized. In contrast, when you add the three gears as an integrated set, you transform that black box into a growth engine. Does anyone know what these gears are?"

Connie lowered her head as Mr. G. looked directly at her. She realized he was asking her to answer the question.

"The three growth gears are perspective, purpose and precision."

"Exactly right, thank you."

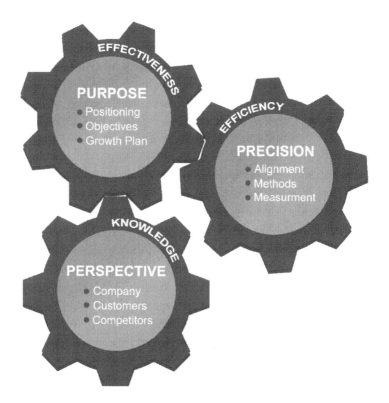

Perspective: Your Company and the Market it Serves

"I want to clarify each of these gears so you have an idea of how each one can assist you in your marketing. To ensure business decisions are market-based, your growth plan should start with an assessment of your company, the customers or consumers you serve, and the businesses that compete with you."

Company

"Firstly, know your business. Ask these questions to understand it better. From the market's perspective, what does your company do better than your competitors? Are you known for it and fully exploiting that strength? What are your business' passions? What drives your economic engine?"

Bruce leaned over to Connie and whispered."

"He's good, isn't he? I didn't realize your mysterious Mr. G. was this fireball."

"I think I'm still in shock. I lucked out meeting him on that day for sure."

They both turned back to listen.

"A natural extension of your strengths and passions is your products and services. Which are most profitable? Which are growing the most? Also, your customers are a reflection of your business, so look at your most profitable customers and figure out what they have in common. These commonalities could help you discover a market segment to exploit for future growth.
Equally important is examining the nature of customers that are weighing down your profit margins. Less profitable customers could be squandering resources that could be better deployed. Perhaps they are not a good fit for you, or you need to pursue an alternative approach to lift profitability levels. Using this self-analysis helps you to dig deeper, discover the true value your company offers, and which customers can benefit most from your services. The result is a sharp, high-definition picture of your company. The better you analyze and know your company the better."

Customers

"We all know what our customers mean to us, but have you ever examined what's important to them? What do you mean to your customers? Put yourselves in their shoes and think about their hopes, fears, and drivers. How can your product or service make their lives better? If you sell business-to-business, how can you help drive your customer's profitability? Armed with an understanding of your customer, you are empowered to become a more valuable partner."

Competition

"Since no company operates in a vacuum, success is not only about your business. It's also about the competition — where they are today and where they are going. If you can ascertain what drives their economic engines, it will help you plot their potential paths. Once you can project where they are going, you can make an educated decision on whether to travel in their wake, which can be challenging, or take a different track."

Purpose: A Clear and Compelling Focus

"By applying your market understanding to your company you develop a purpose. This includes positioning your company and determining its growth drivers, along with deciding how to change your products and services to meet the market's needs. The final piece of the puzzle is to create a marketing plan where all tactics build on each other and work in sync."

Connie did not realize she had spoken. Mr. G. glanced her way and gave a slight nod.

"As this young woman has just voiced, having a clear brand position is relevant to your prospects and customers. It also differentiates your company from your competition and provides a laser focus for your marketing efforts. For example, it's not enough to say your business is "innovative," your services are "world class," or you are "customer focused" because many other companies make the same claims. Find a hook that sets you apart from your competition and leverage it in the marketplace. Since you have already reviewed what your business is best at and well known for, use that knowledge to develop a positioning statement that enables people to understand the unique value your business offers.

When you differentiate your company in a way that is relevant to your consumers, customers, and prospects, you reap the rewards of:
- Stronger customer loyalty
- Reduced pricing pressures
- Attracting talent, capital, and strategic partnerships
- Increased support from existing business partners

In addition to communicating your brand position externally, immerse employees in brand knowledge so they better appreciate how they can help build the business. The more you engage and inform your tem the better."

Growth Drivers

"Now ask yourselves where will your growth come from? While it's tempting to remain in areas you know well — current products in markets you already serve — this reluctance may put handcuffs on your growth potential. You should explore opportunities for new products, services, markets, and distribution channels. To weigh opportunities for expansion against each other, think through the following issues."

Mr. G. turned to the screen once more and clicked to a new diagram.

Where Will Growth Come From?

Prime Your Products for Growth

"You need to assess your product or service offerings to assure they meet market needs. Make sure services with the greatest growth potential are receiving the required marketing support. Look at sales and research data to determine which of your services are best aligned with today's customer requirements. Most importantly, look into your crystal ball...

There was a stifled chuckle from his audience at this statement.

"Yes, I know crystal balls are hard to come by these days but in all seriousness, you need to establish how long profit streams of today's products and services will endure. Just like people, products age. Plan to replace mature products, whose profit streams will decline, with new alternatives that fit your company's positioning and promise growth based on market trends."

Dig into Distribution Options

"Your distribution choices can either set your company apart or restrict your business. Consider whether market conditions or your product offering have changed in a way that makes a new sales channel attractive. For example, over the past decade, many companies embraced the realities of the Internet and moved beyond brick and mortar distribution to e-commerce. I was reminded of this in conversations with an exceptionally smart young woman I met, who struggled to convince her former manager that e-commerce would improve the company's sales."

Connie acknowledged the reference to her problems with Mr. Gibbons and how she had voiced them to Mr. G. all those months ago.

"Even if your examination of distribution options does not lead to expansion into new channels, you may learn that business is being conducted differently in existing channels and requires modification of your sales cycle or pricing model. Making these adjustments to optimize your position in existing channels can be as important as expansion."

Open up New Markets

"If you offer a good product or service and your current market shows limited growth potential, it's worth exploring new markets. This exploration includes expanding geographically or reaching new market segments. There are several ways to do this."

A slide appeared on the screen with a list.

"As you can see here there are options to try but I would say embrace them all."

Reposition for new uses: An example of repositioning is what Arm & Hammer did when they let the world know you could do more with baking soda than bake cookies and cakes. It can be used for everything from odor elimination in refrigerators to brushing your teeth.

Expand geographically: Market to new user segments. Ask yourself if there are any other market segments that could benefit from your product. Growth in new user segments is a strategy Facebook has used. When it first launched in 2003, Facebook was targeted to college students. In 2005 its founder, Mark Zuckerberg, added the high school version. Then they expanded to Microsoft and Apple employees. Finally, in 2006, they expanded their reach to everyone 13 and older with an email address. By 2007, there were over 100,000 business pages. Over time, the social media site has morphed from simply meeting the social needs of college students to becoming a global communication platform.

Partnership possibilities: Developing new products and moving into new channels can involve a steep learning curve. Since navigating uncharted waters can be difficult, you may want to form strategic partnerships with companies that have strengths in these areas and can help you steer more safely to your destination. Also, if there are skill gaps in your organization consider whether you should fill those gaps and grow more quickly by aligning with trusted advisors.

The Reason to Grow

CEO's Vision Drives
New Opportunities

Easy finish

THERE – Why getting there is mandatory
-Future state
-Implications of achieving
-Real and intangible benefits

THE PLAN – How to get there
-What will be hardest
-Resource challenges
-Metrics/milestones

Easy start

Hard middle

HERE – Why staying here is unacceptable
-Current state
-Implications of staying
-Real and intangible problems

Creating a Marketing Plan

"When creating a marketing plan knowing your company's strengths and potential is key. With a well-defined picture of your company's positioning and growth drivers, you can establish some clear, measurable objectives. Establishing the "make or break" initiatives provides a focus for your marketing plan. The plan answers the question "how do you plan to get from where you are today to where you want to go?" The marketing plan must include tactics that are aligned with market needs and then you work together to achieve specific goals. Unlike the idea-of-the-day marketing approach that leads to that black box eating up your money, it is far more likely to deliver a healthy return on investment."

Connie nodded recognizing the advice Mr. G. had given her so generously and knowing her future strategies would be aligned with everything he was explaining to the audience now.

"Try to condense your strategic objectives, key initiatives, and core tactics onto a single page. Doing so shows, with great clarity, the critical things that need to be accomplished to succeed. This page is the top-of-mind Cliff Notes of your marketing operational plan."

With another click a new slide appeared behind Mr. G.

Precision: Measuring for Success

"Marketing tactics designed to deliver specific business results can be measured and refined in the same way as manufacturing processes. Each initiative is designed to support specific phases of your target customer's buying cycle such as the ones listed her."

- Awareness
- Consideration
- Decision
- Post-purchase support
- Referring your product or service to others
- Upgrades

"Since you know what you are trying to accomplish, you can gauge whether each tactic is producing the desired results. For example, is search engine optimization helping your website climb in Google's rankings? Is it attracting website visitors and increasing awareness? Are video demonstrations converting prospects into customers? My advice is to stick with what's working, but always test it to see if you can achieve even better results. If, on the other hand, some initiatives are not producing the planned outcomes, experiment with new or revised tactics. Before you try anything, however, set your objectives and decide how they will be measured. Always follow up to see if you achieved your goals."

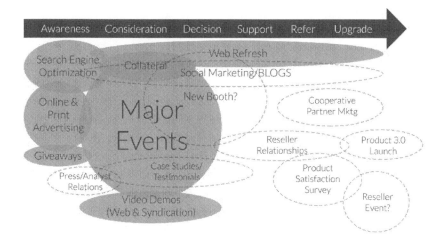

"I will also say it is also instructive to review marketing tactics to see which phase or phases of the buying cycle each supports and determine what percentage of your marketing budget is spent in each buying phase. If you find your marketing dollars are focused, for example, on the early phases of the buying cycle, and you are generating brand awareness or leads but not sales, you might consider redistributing the dollars to convert more leads to sales. They might be better invested in in-store promotions or sales efforts that turn interest into purchases."

Your Path to Growth

"In regard to the bottom line, research has shown that if you run an operationally-oriented company, you can substantially change your future growth path by developing marketing excellence within your operations. You do this by looking beyond the company walls to gain a market perspective on your company, customers, and competition. From that perspective, you develop purpose, which includes your brand position, future growth drivers, and an integrated marketing plan. Then you execute the marketing plan with precision and accountability, ensuring you maximize return on investment. The three gears of perspective, purpose, and precision have the power to turn the mysterious black box of marketing into your engine for growth."

This last statement was met by a resounding applause from the audience. Connie smiled up at Mr. G. – *he'll always be Mr. G to me* – he smiled back allowing the appreciation of his audience to be given for a few moments.

"Thank you all. If I may continue, I have covered how you can analyze and strategize the company but now let's take a look at this from the perspective of the VP of Sales. If you are a Marketing Manager reporting directly to the CEO, or to the VP of Sales and Marketing, you already know that you are under a huge pressure."

A wry smile crossed Mr. G.'s face as he glanced at Connie.

"First of all, you cannot succeed by trying to purchase media ads and then hoping that somehow the ROI will magically appear. We all know that this was true six to 12 months ago, but it really does not work anymore. Here are two reasons why:

1. Bigger competition will be giving you a run for your money.

2. You will not be able to accurately measure the leads that come from these ads. To an organization that wants to achieve their sales numbers this is just noise and expense.

"However, if you want to impress your VP of Sales and Marketing or your CEO, I believe you need a proper framework. If it is not measurable it is not accountable. If it is not accountable, then it is not affecting the top line revenue. If it is not affecting the top line revenue, then there is zero if not negative ROI for what you are doing."

Connie leaned towards Bruce.

"This is exactly what he helped me with."

"He is quite the motivator, Connie no wonder you wanted to spend time with him."

Looking back at the stage, they both became absorbed in the presentation again.

"Now, here is the real question that you need to ask yourself: Are you doing this just for brand awareness and not lead generation? If the answer is YES then go for it, but remember that very soon someone from the leadership team will come and ask you two questions:

1. How is this affecting my top line revenue?

2. Can you give me some meaningful measurements, and can you prove your ROI?

"Take it from me, you will not impress them that much, if you do not know the answer to those two questions."

"Can I ask what the six steps to revenue growth are?"

Once again Mr. G. looked directly at Connie, she answered knowing these were steps he had discussed with her. She answered.

1. Market Research

2. Corporate Strategy

3. Product Strategy

4. Talent Strategy

5. Marketing Strategy

6. Sales Strategy

"Thank you. You have a grip on this inbound marketing concept. To be able to make your number you have to make sure the six pillars are aligned properly. This is a concept called strategic alignment. What does that mean? It can more simply be described as planning the strategy for your company. I understand that you are not the CEO, but the Marketing Manager and you will be asked to work your magic.

Your company's marketing department needs direction, and this comes from the marketing strategy. It must build on the insights from the external marketplace and remain aligned with the corporate strategy, while also addressing how marketing will build demand for the company's products.

It requires choices on which market channels to invest in and which ones to forgo. One of the main goals of the marketing strategy is to set up the sales strategy for success. Best-in-class marketing leaders can produce a copy of their well-articulated marketing strategy."

After taking a sip of water, Mr. G. continued.

"Let us cover three questions:

1. What is a marketing strategy? A marketing strategy is an operating plan for a company's marketing department.

2. What does a marketing strategy do? A marketing strategy allocates resources efficiently to drive revenues.

3. What does it mean to use a marketing strategy? Using a marketing strategy means the marketing department builds buyer preference for the company's products.

"I hope you can see that buying media this, doing SEO that, web designing this, does not really cut it any more. Start designing marketing campaigns that attract buyers to your products/solutions, it will give you excellent results."

The Problem

"I know some of you are asking even when your campaign dollars are managed carefully, the campaigns often do not attract buyers. This can be due to either the audience not being well defined, the wrong programs were chosen, the wrong activities were executed, or the offers were not well developed. How can you know in advance which programs, activities, and offers will work?"

The Solution

"I am a great supporter of completing the campaign planning phase by answering the following:

1. What types of campaigns do we need to run (awareness, consideration, decision, competitive)? Or

(Replacement, up-sell, cross sell, migration, new logo, nurture, renewal, etc.)?

For each of the campaigns:

1. What are the objectives, budget, schedule and goals?

2. You need to have proper marketing automation software that can measure the full outcome.

"If you feel that you are using four or five different tools, this means only one thing: Whoever sold you the solution is making lots of money, and this is actually hurting your ROI story for when your VP of Sales confronts you."

1. For each of the campaigns, which personas are we targeting? What content assets and market messages will compel them to respond? Do you have a content strategy in place?

"One thing that you will see moving forward is that building your digital identity is long term and sustainable compared to buying your digital Identity. There is no quick fix solution but with a calculated and focused plan your campaign will be successful."

A spasmodic applause filled the room and Mr. G. nodded in recognition.

"As CMOs navigate the marketing talent gap, they are increasingly seeking performance-driven agency partners, such as Flawless Inbound, who are immersed in marketing technology and staffed with digital-savvy professionals. SMBs need partners that can deliver fully integrated solutions and in essence function as outsourced inbound marketing teams. Large enterprises commonly look for niche expertise in core digital disciplines such as content marketing development, paid search, SEO, social media monitoring, and analytics to complement internal marketing teams."

"The future belongs to dynamic agencies with more efficient management systems, integrated services, versatile talent, value-based pricing models, a love for data, and a commitment to producing measurable results. These tech-savvy modern marketing firms thrive on change and continually apply advances in technology. The right marketing agency can be a tremendous asset to your organization and play a critical role in propelling growth, but marketers must take a methodical approach to finding the right firms."

A new image appeared on the screen listing:

7 Rules To Keep In Mind When Evaluating And Selecting An Agency Partner.

1. *Partner with Performance Driven Firms:* Marketers are being held to higher ROI standards, and the same needs to be true of agency partners. Historically, marketing agencies have gotten away with reporting relatively meaningless metrics such as impressions, advertising equivalency, and PR value, or relying strictly on qualitative results. Leading marketing agencies build campaigns that consistently produce measurable outcomes, including web site traffic, subscribers, leads, and sales. Work with agency partners that care as much about performance and success as you do.

2. ASSESS THE ACCOUNT TEAM: The greatest value an agency can bring a client is staffing its account team with A players. Look for firms that have a history of recruiting and retaining top talent. Understand how your account team will be structured, including who is responsible for planning, production, account management, and day-to-day client communications. Also, consider if the firm you hire is outsourcing any services to freelancers

or partner agencies. This is a common practice, but it is important that you are aware of and have confidence in third parties that will be working on your account.

3. *Find Tech-Savvy Firms:* Agencies whose professionals are immersed in technology trends and innovations are able to more readily adapt their own business models, continually increase productivity, evolve client campaigns, and make strategic connections to seemingly unrelated information. Find out what marketing technologies the agency uses to run its own business, how it integrates technology into client campaigns, and how it ensures that it's staff remains current on technology trends.

4. DEMAND THAT DIGITAL IS INGRAINED IN THEIR DNA: Every agency that will be relevant in the future is a digital agency. Having a digital division or group within a traditional agency is not sufficient. Digital must be ingrained into the agency's culture and talent. Agencies structured in service-area silos — social, search, mobile, web, email, analytics — will face the same challenges as their corporate counterparts when trying to build digital marketing strategies and campaigns. Digital must be fully integrated, along with traditional activities, into every program and budget.

5. INVEST IN THE DOERS: The marketing services world is full of thinkers, talkers, and self-proclaimed gurus. Turn to agencies with demonstrated track records of success, starting with their own brands. Evaluate the strength of their website, the power of their staff's personal brands, the value and frequency of content on their blog, and their reach and engagement in social networks.

6. *Seek Systems for Success:* Prototype agencies are powered by systems that continually increase efficiencies and productivity, encourage creativity and innovation, and push professionals to realize and embrace their potential. All of this produces higher performance levels and more satisfied clients. Align your organization with agencies that take a systemic approach to professional development, project management, client services, monitoring, measurement, reporting, and communications.

7. *Find Partners, Not Providers:* Marketing agencies often look and sound the same. They offer similar services, tout impressive client lists, and flaunt industry awards lauding their creativity. But none of that really matters to your business. When selecting an agency partner, it is essential to move beyond the standard stuff and find partners who think and act differently and take a customized approach to your business. When all else is equal, it is an agency's culture and talent that determine its ability to positively impact your business. We have found that the most successful marketing programs are those built on strong client-agency partnerships with a foundation of trust, respect, and aligned expectations and goals. These are the relationships in which the client looks to the agency as an extension of its marketing team, not as just another vendor.

"These steps will ensure you partner with an agency team, that becomes indispensable through their hard work, insight, consultation, services, expertise, friendship, and professionalism. They must do the little things that build relationships and take the time to show you they care about your successes, both on individual and organizational levels.

Again, I suggest Flawless Inbound as the go-to agency for your inbound marketing needs."

Noticing a shift in concentration of his audience, Mr. G. rolled his shoulders and said.

"I think we can take a short break here, make sure to refill your glasses and I will be back shortly."

Connie began to raise her hand, but Mr. G. gave a slight shake of his head and walked off the stage and exited a door beside it.

"I wanted to say Hi. Do you think he will talk to me later?"

"I'm certain of it, Connie. Now let's take his advice and get some refills."

Bruce guided Connie to the long service table and ordered drinks for them both. They mingled with a few people including Mia and Ethan before returning to their seats. They were deep in conversation when applause once again filled the room. Mr. G. returned to the stage and nodded to his audience.

"If I may continue, I will make this as short as possible, so you will have time to enjoy your meals. I have a few thoughts I wish to share before I depart."

Perception is reality

"It's true. The way you interpret and understand the world directly affects your beliefs and the way you live your life. Perception creates bias as much as it creates understanding. It creates fear as much as it creates curiosity. I ask you. Do you want your reality to be narrow or vast? Will the bliss that ignorance provides be sufficient, or do you need more?"

"The truth is most people want more, even if it is on a subconscious level. Humans tend to trail blaze. From cradle to the grave, our society emphasizes the importance of education. Learning and discovering is what we do, but still it is increasingly hard to understand what you don't understand."

"So how do you learn to know what you don't know? Start by asking yourself: What don't I know? What do you want to learn more about? Most importantly, understand that it's OK to be wrong. In error there is growth."

Everything is Temporary

"Remember your good times are temporary and your bad times are temporary. So, when you're up, enjoy it, bask in it, and be grateful for it. And when you're down, know you will get through it. Know that it's not the end, and that it's just a rough patch. Life is full of twists and turns, ups and downs, and surprises."

We forget that it's about the journey not the destination.

"There is a lesson in everything. I think it's hard for a lot of people--especially young people -to appreciate life. Recognizing the full worth of your hardships and your blunders is key to appreciating the journey. It's just as important to stay humble and be grateful for the joy life brings you. So, my advice is this:

Everything is temporary, so make the most out of ALL of it.

The Importance of Being Present

"One of my favor quotes is by Lao Tzu, 'If you are depressed, you are living in the past. If you are anxious, you are living in the future. If you are at peace, you are living in the present. I would ask you all to take this to heart. More often than not, we tend to worry about what's to come, or dwell on something that's already happened. While it's crucial to care and consider your future, be careful not to let it hinder your present. Moments turn into memories. Enjoy the moment while you have it. It usually takes a lifetime of piled up worries for a person to realize: Worrying isn't productive."

Bruce squeezed Connie's hand and whispered.

"There you see I was right, worrying doesn't do any good."

She squeezed his hand and nodded.

"I know, but when you are in that moment of self-doubt it is difficult to not let it consume you. I will try to follow Mr. G.'s advice and yours. Love you."

"Living in the past is equally unproductive. There are benefits in being able to reflect on yourself and on your past. Remember paying attention to what you've been through and how that makes you feel matters. It takes a lot of emotional energy to grieve, process, and overcome. The balance of being able to take time to reflect, and to prioritize your future while spending most of your day in the present, is beyond valuable, its life changing."

Several cheers came from the room in agreement to this statement.

Do What You Love, Love What You Do.

"There was a huge mosaic near my university in London that said those words. I was grateful to walk past it almost every day and remind myself of the importance of loving your career and loving what you do. Your work is a considerably large aspect in your life that you dedicate yourself to. If you aren't happy in your career, that unhappiness will seep into other aspects of your life. And while nothing is perfect, it's important to work on yourself and position yourself to reach the goals and satisfactions you desire."

Most importantly: Invest in yourself.

"This goes for your non-work life, too. What habits and hobbies do you want to stop? Which ones do you want to develop? It's important to be conscious of the type of people and activities you surround yourself with. Information is like nutrients to your brain, be aware of what you are feeding yourself. Success isn't one triumphant moment. Success is a series of moments (and choices) leading up to bigger moments."

You are the only person, who can get in the way of living every day doing what you love.

"Bob Dylan said it best when he said, "What's money? A man is a success if he gets up in the morning and goes to bed at night and in between does what he wants to do."

Being Happy Takes Work

"The happiest people tend to be the ones who've worked the most on themselves. Being happy takes a lot of work. It's just as much work - if not more - to be unhappy. So, choose wisely. Being happy means at some point you decided to take control of your life. It means you decided to not be a victim and to put that energy back into yourself. Sometimes it's hard, but you have to pull yourself up and push yourself forward."

Your lifetime is a series of developments and personal growth.

"One of the worst things you can do for self-development is comparing yourself to other people. It's easy to get caught up in jealousy and wanting what other people have. Especially with the way we interact with social media. You have to remember that people tend to show only the best parts of their lives on those platforms. It's not fair to yourself when you see that and think, "I want to do that," or "I want to look like that". Not only does that distract you from being appreciative of what you have in our own life, it doesn't provide any productive input to yourself. Most often, your perception of someone's life is a fallacy. And even if it isn't, focus on yourself. It's your journey and your path that you should be concerned with. Being happy takes practice. Whether it's learning to let go of your ego or forming more self-loving habits, it takes practice. You only have one life, work as hard as you can to make it your best life. Before I leave I have supplied you all with a gift, they will be delivered to your tables after the meal. It's a book I've been working on for over a year and I have to acknowledge one person, whose enthusiasm, quest for knowledge and hard work, putting into practice what I relayed to her, gave me direction on how to set out the content and ensure the information was clear, precise and engaging."

Faces turned this way and that, while Connie's wide-eyed look met Mr. G.'s. She shook her head, but he motioned for her to stand up.

"I would like to introduce Connie Ryker, who's never-ending questions and thirst for inbound marketing knowledge ensured I covered topics and strategies from the viewpoint of someone coming into the method as opposed to mine with years of experience."

Connie stood slowly, her cheeks reddening. She turned around slightly embarrassed at the gazes of the people around her. As her Mr. G. joined in the applause, she gave a smile and shrugged. *I owe him this after all he has done for me.*

Mr. G. nodded and stood on the stage acknowledging comments and thanks. The applause filled the room and Connie and Bruce joined in as most of the audience stood in appreciation. The MC walked onto the stage to shake Mr. G.'s hand and turned to the audience.

"Thank you, Mr. G. for your insight and expertise and a compelling presentation, I am sure everyone here will be initiating inbound marketing for their future success. May I remind you that Mr. G.'s book will be presented to you all at the end of the evening, and he has graciously agreed to sign them if you so wish at that time. Again, put your hands together for Mr. G. the Founder and CEO of Flawless Inbound."

Biography: Saher Ghattas

Saher Ghattas is an exceptional, well-rounded leader, whose diverse experience as an executive and an entrepreneur, in both large and small businesses, has perfectly prepared him to understand and be the trusted advisor, with his team at Flawless Inbound, in helping in the full execution plan of revenue-driven marketing playbooks, especially when it comes to B2B organizations in the Technology/VAR/MSP and Engineering Space. He brings not only a strategic mind-set, but also leading-edge knowledge of sales and marketing that is seldom seen in someone who also has such a deep understanding of technology. Saher is passionate about leading a high-performance team to bring growth revenue into other organizations.

Saher's educational background in the computer engineering sector led to his early career as an award-winning sales team lead with tech giant Cisco Systems. His leadership talents led to management of P & L for the Western Canadian region and ultimate responsibility for large enterprise accounts.

A natural entrepreneur, Saher has been involved in multiple tech start-up companies in Canada and the US.

He has also been invited to be an advisor to a Board member of tech startups in the phase of VC Capital engagement and was brought in to focus on building an exponential sales and marketing plan to accelerate organizational growth and thus build a journey to higher ROI for the Founders/CEO and VCs.

Saher is currently Founder & Chief Revenue officer at Flawless Inbound, a professional service organization focused on helping B2B companies achieve their exponential growth through three pillars:

A) Marketing Enablement (Inbound Marketing and Account Based Marketing). Working closely with CMO/Marketing managers to build a solid revenue driven Marketing Department.

B) Sales Enablement (Bringing Sales and Marketing together, working closely with VP of Sales and building a full sales process that is Inbound Marketing Enabled.

C) Service Enablement (build a full service/customer support model)

Saher also have been invited as a public speaker in Marketing, Sales and Technology events in Canada and the US to educate, inspire and drive new exponential visions for Founders/CEOs/VPs of Sales and Marketing managers. Saher is a regular contributor to leading Marketing industry blogs and a frequent speaker on the topics of VAR/MSP/Technology, and Marketing and Sales best practices. He is also a member of the Forbes Agency council community.

Saher and his team at Flawless Inbound usually work with organizations that have very aggressive revenue growth in the next 18 to 24 months.

About Flawless Inbound

A professional service organization focused on helping B2B companies achieves exponential growth through three pillars:

A) Marketing Enablement (Inbound Marketing and Account Based Marketing), while working closely with CMO/Marketing managers to build a solid revenue driven Marketing Department.

B) Sales Enablement (Bridging the sales/marketing divide to enable collaboration. Working closely with VP of Sales and building a full sales process that is Inbound Marketing Enabled.

C) Service Enablement (build a full service, customer support model that helps in cross selling and upselling to existing clients.

Over the last four years Saher and his team at Flawless Inbound have worked with one hundred plus B2B organizations in Canada and the US utilizing the three pillars business potential and setting them on a path of exponential revenue growth.

Flawless Inbound has won the Top Digital Marketing Agencies Award from Clutch for the last two years, in the category of Marketing and Sales enablement for B2B organizations.

Flawless Inbound is an official member of Forbes Coaches Council.

The team at Flawless Inbound takes their Inbound Marketing Skills to the next level, helping implement Full Account Based Marketing (Vertical focused Marketing) for B2B organizations. They do so while remaining focused on three distinct and different departments found in any B2B organization: Marketing, Sales and Customer Service - ensuring that each department is focused on customer delight, while keeping an eye on exponential revenue growth.
Flawless Inbound can help.
Feel free to book a quick 30-minute discovery call with Flawless Inbound to start driving growth in your business.

Visit our website at www.flawlessinbound.ca

Feel free to connect with Saher on LinkedIn:
https://www.linkedin.com/in/saherghattas/

Citation of Resources

HUBSPOT
www.HUBSPOT.com

Emeritus Institute of Management
https://emeritus.org/

Digital Marketing and Customer Engagement program
Columbia Business School Executive Education

Cisco Systems
www.Cisco.com

Drift
www.Drift.com

Marketo (Currently being acquired by Adobe)
www.Makreto.com

CMO.com offers marketing insights, expertise, and strategies aimed at helping CMOs, senior marketers, and their teams deliver standout digital experiences.
www.CMO.com

The knowledge center offers a weekly strategic and a Tactical tip for CEO/Marketing/Sales leaders.
www.Flawlessinbound.ca

https://www.chiefmarketer.com/

35305871R00203

Made in the USA
Middletown, DE
04 February 2019